DR. BIZARRO'S
ECLECTIC COLLECTION OF
STRANGE
AND OBSCURE FACTS

STEPHEN SPIGNESI

PERMUTED
PRESS

A PERMUTED PRESS BOOK

ISBN: 978-1-68261-516-4
ISBN (eBook): 978-1-68261-517-1

Permuted Press, LLC
New York • Nashville
permutedpress.com

Published in the United States of America

DEDICATION

For my sister Janet, who will certainly like this book,
in memory of her Jerry,
a very fine gentleman who was taken much too soon.

TABLE OF CONTENTS

Introduction

THE UNLIKELY STORY OF DR. THALES BIZARRO

My dearie and I enjoy frequenting estate sales, tag sales, flea markets, and other repositories of the old, the forgotten, and, of course, the occasional treasure, and one of these excursions resulted in the eclectic selection of some of this collection.

We were at a front lawn tag sale at a Tudor-style house in the suburbs of Albuquerque, New Mexico. The house had gabled roofs, a beautifully embellished front doorway, and a giant bay window overlooking neatly manicured bushes. The mailbox had an elaborate "P" carved on it, which I would later learn stood for Pinkman.

As we browsed through an agglomeration of the both rarer and commonplace items at this particular sale, I spotted what I can best describe as a dossier...a collection of papers tied together by what seemed like a shoestring. Or perhaps a length of cooking twine?

On its cover was written in a calligraphy-like font, "Dr. Bizarro's Eclectic Collection of Strange and Obscure Facts."

This gave me pause, and just as I moved to flip over the top page, the homeowner, the lovely Mrs. Pinkman, walked up and said, "My sister Ginny found that in an old trunk that was in the attic when she and her husband bought the house. After she died, we discovered she had left it right where she found it! Imagine! We want to remodel the attic into a music room for our youngest son Jake, so we decided to sell as much of the stuff up there that we could."

"How much are you asking for it?" I said.

"Just the papers? There a chance you'd be interested in the trunk, too?"

I smiled and shook my head. "No room." I looked at my sweetie and said, "We're the ones who should be holding a tag sale, right, honey?"

Mrs. Pinkman nodded. "I understand. How's ten dollars sound?"

I flipped nonchalantly through the papers and my eye fell on words like "medieval," and "stigmatics," and "torture," and "miracles," and "fringe myths," and "Victorian asylum" and it took all my strength of will to not immediately pull out my money clip and hand over the Hamilton.

"Five sounds better," I responded with a smile.

"Yes, but ten sounds even *better*," said Mrs. Pinkman with a smile and a wink.

I paid the ten dollars.

Once we were home, I pulled off the string, and quickly learned who this "Dr. Bizarro" was and realized that I was likely holding his life's work.

Some of the accompanying biographical material suggested that Dr. Bizarro was a contemporary of Jules Verne and Baron

Munchausen—but unlike his peers, the writings of Dr. Bizarro were said to be not fanciful, but 100% true.

Pouring through his writings, I soon came to the realization that I had found a kindred spirit—a writer like me who found great pleasure in discovering strange facts and presenting them to a curious readership.

His manuscript, however, was by no means complete, so I took it upon myself to complete Dr. Bizarro's mission—to bring you, good reader, an intriguing and fascinating collection of arcana, facts, ephemera, history, and trivia.

So who was Dr. Thales Bizarro?

I learned that he was named for one of the Seven Sages of Greece, and it seems he spent a goodly portion of his life in the pursuit of unusual information. His surname "Bizarro," sometimes spelled "Bisarro," came from his Italian forefathers, even though he grew up in Santa Claus, Arizona, before moving to Unalaska, Alaska to attend school.

He was a cultural spelunker.

He collected information, but was quite particular regarding what he considered interesting enough to be added to his archive.

Dr. Bizarro was a student of the bizarre and was clearly wildly interested in history, and many of the chapters in this book appear to be based on research he had done over years of study.

However, you will find in this book chapters that nod to modernity, and those are my responsibility: In honor of Dr. Bizarro, I compiled some weird and unusual material myself and added it to his original collection. And as I was writing about the more contemporary topics, I would often ask myself,

"What would the good doctor say?" when selecting words and language to explain specific subjects. (At one point I realized that Dr. Bizarro would probably not call an abused execution subject a "poor bastid.")

My hope is that this will make for a genuinely eclectic collection of strange and obscure facts, in the tradition of Dr. Thales Bizarro's work and lifetime devotion to the peculiar.

Stephen Spignesi
New Haven, Connecticut
December 25, 2017

Chapter 1

ASTONISHING ABILITIES MANIFESTED BY SAVANTS

"I am still learning."
—Michelangelo's motto.

$\mathcal{S}$avant Syndrome, as it has come to be known, points up just how difficult it is to truly understand the functioning of the human brain.

In his groundbreaking 1989 study, *Extraordinary People*, Dr. Darold Treffert defined Savant Syndrome as follows:

> *Savant Syndrome is an exceedingly rare condition in which persons with serious mental handicaps, either from developmental disability (mental retardation) or major mental illness (Early Infantile Autism or schizophrenia), have spectacular islands of ability or brilliance which stand in stark, markedly incongruous contrast to the handicap...*
> *It occurs in males more frequently than in females in an approximate 6:1 ratio. The skills often appear suddenly, without explanation, and can disappear just as suddenly.*

Savants usually have extremely low IQs, some as low as in the 30s and 40s (compared to the genius IQ, of 140 and up), and yet possess the aforementioned "islands of ability" that are so extraordinary as to seem almost supernatural.

Savants who cannot see can draw like Old Masters; those who cannot speak can sing entire scores of Broadway musicals; people who appear almost catatonic in their daily lives can sit at a piano and flawlessly play complete classical concertos after hearing the piece only once.

"Odd" isn't the word for the talents and abilities these people manifest, and "awe-inspiring" doesn't even come close. Savants seem to possess brain functions that are, as of yet, beyond our complete understanding. Theories abound as to what role genetics and reinforcement play in these phenomenal abilities, but the truth is that much of what these people can do, and how they do it, is incredibly perplexing to the scientific and medical establishments.

One of the most notable cinematic portrayals of an autistic savant was in the 1988 movie *Rain Man*, which starred Tom Cruise and Dustin Hoffman. In that film, Hoffman played Raymond, a middle-aged autistic who manifested many of the abilities of the savant, including counting, memorization, and calculation. Filmgoers were astounded by what Raymond could do, and many challenged the veracity of the portrayal, but everything depicted in *Rain Man* was scientifically and medically accurate.

As you'll see from the following list of savant abilities, the most amazing thing about *Rain Man* is it seems that director Barry Levinson and company barely scratched the surface.

1. Musical Abilities

Many savants manifest incredible musical talents. Sixteen-year-old Blind Tom, a blind and severely mentally-challenged slave who died in 1908, toured after the Civil War and played the piano at virtuoso level for audiences all over the United States. Tom had a musical repertoire of over 5,000 pieces, and like many savants, could hear a piece of music once and play it perfectly, no matter how difficult or complex the piece. Tom was also somehow capable of assimilating a particular composer's "style." On command, Tom could improvise a musical piece in the manner of any composer he had ever heard, including Beethoven, Bach, Chopin, Verdi, and many others. Tom once performed for President Buchanan.

Other documented musical savants include the following:

- A twenty-three-year-old boy with an IQ of forty-seven who could play the piano by ear and could immediately sight-read sheet music.

- A girl named Harriet who had an IQ of seventy-three and who hummed perfectly the entire "Care Nome" aria from Verdi's opera *Rigoletto* at the age of seven months. (She was in her crib.) By the time she was four, she could play the piano, violin, trumpet, clarinet, and French horn, but she wasn't toilet trained until the age of nine. Harriet also manifested incredible memorization skills and could remember pages of the phone book and minute factual details about hundreds of symphonies. Like Blind Tom, she could also improvise in a composer's style and transpose between keys at will.

- A thirty-eight-year-old man with an IQ of sixty-seven who had perfect pitch, could sight-read music, and had an enormous knowledge of facts about composers.

- A twenty-three-year-old girl with an IQ of twenty-three who could play on the piano any song or melody sung or hummed to her.

- And most amazingly, a five-year-old boy who could identify the music that was on the *other* side of a record being played. If Side A was being played, he could also "hear" what was on side B.

2. Calendar Calculating

Calendar calculating is the ability to tell what days dates fall on and when holidays will fall centuries into the future. Probably the most famous savant calendar calculators are twins named Charles and George. Charles's and George's IQs tested between forty and seventy.

Some of their most amazing calendar abilities included the following:

- They could tell you on what day of the week any date fell in an 80,000 year span. (They were proficient 40,000 years into the past and 40,000 years into the future.) The twins were able to account for changes in the ways calendars were designed over the centuries when calculating the dates.

- They could tell you in what years during the next two centuries that Easter would fall on March 23.

- They could remember and recite the exact weather of every single day of their adult lives.

Although Charles and George could not even do simple math, doctors are convinced that math and complex calculating abilities somehow played a role in the twins's date determinations. Memorization of date tables and calendars also played a part, but scientists are sure that somewhere in the twins' brains, an "island of ability" existed that could do high math.

3. Mathematical Calculating

The math skills exhibited by savants include incredibly rapid counting abilities (Raymond in *Rain Man* could immediately count the number of toothpicks that fell on the floor out of their box), and the ability to do instantaneous complex mathematical calculations in their head.

Some of the things savants have been known to count include the following:

- The hairs in a cow's tail.
- The words spoken in a TV or radio broadcast.
- The number of cars on a highway over a period of time.

Some of the calculations savants have been known to make include the following:

- The number of seconds in a period of time.
- The number of seconds in a person's life.
- The multiplication of twenty-digit numbers.
- Square root calculations involving huge numbers.

Some of the calculations performed by savants have taken days, weeks, or even months to do. It seems as though some weird biological computer clicks on when the savant is given the problem and it doesn't turn off until the solution is arrived at. Many savants adept at calculating can usually add columns of numbers in seconds without paper and pencil (yet many can't even write), and they often exhibit the same level of problem-solving proficiency with division, multiplication, and subtraction problems as well.

4. Incredible Memories

Decades ago, a physician named Dr. Witzman attempted to describe the incredible memory capabilities of some savants. He said that they are often capable of "reproducing at will masses of figures, like railway tables, budget statistics, and entries in bankbooks." Eidetic (photographic) memories are one of the most amazing savant abilities. Anyone who has ever tried to memorize something knows just how amazing a photographic memory actually is. Medical students commonly grudgingly acknowledge that the only way to learn the necessary anatomical structures a course covers is by rote memorization. Med students have long turned to mnemonics to help them remember complex anatomical features of the human body.

Here is a look at some of the things individual savants have been reported as remembering:

- The exact configuration of the entire Milwaukee bus system.

- The complete music and lyrics of thousands of songs.

- Thousands of meticulous details about wars and historical events.

- Word-for-word recollections of complete short stories and in some cases, entire novels.

- The melodies, page numbers, and complete lyrics of every hymn in a specific hymnal.

- Thousands of addresses, often "industry-specific." For instance, some savants will memorize only the addresses of car dealerships, but they will remember every one in an entire city.

- Hundreds of foreign language phrases.

- Detailed and comprehensive biographical details about hundreds of historical personages.

- Decades of obituary records, including next of kin, addresses, and funeral homes.

- The contents of entire newspapers, both forwards and backwards.

- The exact number of bites of food taken during an entire month or longer.

- The precise number of steps walked during a certain period of time.

- The number of hotel rooms in every hotel in dozens of cities.

- The distances between hundreds of cities.

- The seating capacities of dozens of stadiums and arenas.

- Every number seen on every railroad car over an entire lifetime. (And in some cases, the savant has been known to not only recall the individual numbers on the trains, but to keep a running total of their sums as well.)

- Entire pages from phone directories. (Raymond in *Rain Man* could do this, but he only got to the Gs before his brother, played by Tom Cruise made him stop.)

- The times of the comings and goings of hospital staff members over a fifty-seven-year period.

- Voluminous stock market statistical data.

- The transcripts of entire radio and TV broadcasts.

5. Artistic Abilities

Savants with artistic abilities can produce impeccably artistic detailed renderings of something seen only once. Savants have been known to work with drawings and sculptures and they have created works depicting animals, insects, cats, and other forms of nature.

6. Mechanical Abilities

Savants occasionally are exceptionally good "with their hands." Some recorded mechanical abilities manifested by savants include the following:

- One savant once took apart a clock and rebuilt it as a fully-functioning windmill.

- Savants have been known to build detailed models of cars and boats after only seeing a picture of the vehicle.

- Some savants can draw accurately detailed blueprints.

- Some can instinctively repair appliances and other mechanical objects.

- Savants have been documented as being able to rebuild and modify multi-gear bicycles.

7. Extraordinary Sensory Perception

Some savants have extraordinarily developed senses of sight, smell, hearing, taste, and touch.

- One blind savant was able to pick out his own clothes and shoes by smell alone.

- There is documentation of a savant whose sense of touch was so highly developed that he could split a sheet of newspaper into two thin leaves, resulting in two sheets of newsprint one-half the thickness of the original.

8. ESP

Or Extra-Sensory Perception (which is different from Extraordinary Sensory Perception), appears to enter the realm of the almost impossible to explain. These abilities have often been considered paranormal and yet, there are savants who exhibit psychic and other "beyond nature" abilities. Some of the documented "powers" exhibited by savants include the following:

- A savant being able to hear (and repeat) conversations from outside of his hearing range.

- A savant apparently being able to read another person's thoughts.

- A savant able to perform "distant viewing"; seeing accurately something happening rooms, or sometimes miles, away.

- A savant who was capable of precognition, i.e., being able to accurately predict the future.

Evidence of these paranormal abilities further complicates our understanding of the Savant Syndrome. Or perhaps it clarifies it? Consider this: What if savants are using parts of their brains in bizarre ways that we still cannot understand and their manifestation of psychic abilities is something we might all be capable of, but savants are just tapping into them accidentally?

9. An Extraordinary Sense of Time

Some savants have an incredibly developed sense of the passage of time.

- One savant could tell to the minute the exact time at any time of the day or night, but could not read a clock.

- One savant knew exactly when commercials would begin and end, even when out of range of the TV.

- Savants can tell exactly how much time has passed during a specific period without looking at a watch or clock.

10. Extraordinary Directional Perception

Sometimes found in savants who have never been out of their house or have never traveled in their lives.

- Some savants can recall exact travel routes of individual trips taken, including every right and left turn made.

- Some savants can memorize maps and precisely reproduce them, to scale.

- Some savants can give detailed travel directions to a certain place even if they've never been there and often even if they're blind.

17 Incredible Savants Throughout History

1. **Jedediah Buxton** (1707-1772): mathematical genius. He once measured the Lordship of Elmton by walking across it and then providing the size in square inches. This was, of course, in the pre-calculator age. He measured by his paces and then did the calculations in his head.

2. **Gottfried Mind** (1768-1814): painting savant. Mind was known as the "Raphael of Cats" because he could paint cats vividly without any professional training. And he did so his entire life. He did, though, on occasion, draw other animals, like bears and rabbits.

3. **Daniel Tammet** (1979-) learned to speak Icelandic in a week and once recited pi to the 22,514th digit from memory. Most of us would consider learning Icelandic *at all* a major achievement. Tammet is an author and public speaker and can speak ten languages. He is one of the most-studied savants of all time. He also invented the language Manti.

4. **Stephen Wiltshire** (1974-) was flown over Tokyo for twenty minutes and then drew a thirty-three-foot long picture of the city in flawlessly accurate detail. Like Elaine on *Seinfeld*, most of us can draw the horsey and

the house with the smoke curling out of the chimney. But a thirty-three-foot drawing of a city is outside the reach of most.

5. The late **Kim Peek** (1951-2009)—the real-life inspiration for *Rain Man*—could read two pages of a book in three seconds. His left eye read the left page, his right eye read the right page. And he perfectly remembered everything he read. This reminds us of President James Garfield, who could write Latin with one hand while writing Greek with the other hand at the same time, doesn't it? Perhaps POTUS Garfield had a touch of the savant to him?

6. **Leslie Lemke** (1952-) can play 8,000 songs from memory after having heard them only once. He never had any musical training. Lemke is blind and has an IQ of fifty-eight.

7. **Orlando Serrell** (1968-): mental calculator. He became able to do incredibly complex mathematical calculations in his head after getting hit in the head by a baseball when he was ten. He is also able to recite the specific details of the weather on every day since his accident.

8. **Rüdiger Gamm** (1971-): mental calculator. He can do complex mathematical calculations on demand, can speak backwards, and can tell you what day of the week July 4, 1776 fell on. (It was a Thursday.)

9. **Jerry Newport** (1948-): mental calculator. Jerry is the inspiration for the movie *Mozart and the Whale*, which

is about him and his wife, Mary, both of whom have Asperger's Syndrome.

10. **Derek Paravicini** (1979-): musical prodigy. Derek is blind and has severe autism and learning disabilities, but has perfect pitch and can play the piano at professional performance level. He can also improvise in a multitude of styles. What makes his genius all the more impressive is that being blind, he's never learned to "read" music and has never seen a piece of sheet music. Everything he can do comes from his head.

11. **James Henry Pullen** (1835–1916): gifted wood sculptor. Pullen was developmentally disabled, mute (although he could say—badly—"mother") and socially aggressive and antagonistic. But he found his gift of working with wood and went on to sculpt incredible works, including ships and even a guillotine he rigged over the door of a man he disliked. (It misfired.) He was known as the Genius of Earlswood Asylum.

12. **Tony DeBlois** (1974-): musical savant. DeBlois can play twenty musical instruments, and has over 8,000 musical pieces memorized. He was born premature and is blind. He has a band called Goodnuf and the movie *Journey of the Heart* based on his life was made in 1997.

13. **Alonzo Clemens** (1958-): animal sculptor. Clemens has an IQ of between forty-five and fifty and cannot feed himself. Yet he can create meticulously detailed sculptures of animals. He is considered an extraordinary example of Savant syndrome, specifically the phe-

nomenon of acquiring skills following a head injury, which Clemens sustained as a toddler.

14. **Richard Wawro** (1952–2006): crayon artist. Wawro was diagnosed as "retarded" at birth, and couldn't speak until he was eleven-years-old. At the age of six he began to draw using crayons, and his artistic brilliance was instantly recognized. He had his first formal art exhibition when he was seventeen. The documentary *With Eyes Wide Open* was about Wawro who died of lung cancer at the age of fifty-three.

15. **Jason Padgett** (1970-): number theorist and visualizer. Padgett is a living example of how brain trauma can result in acquired savant syndrome. In 2002, Padgett was attacked by two men who gave him a severe concussion, and when he recovered he was suddenly able to see complex geometrical patterns in everyday objects—and he was able to actually draw the fractals he saw. Padgett is believed to be the only person to draw a graphic representation of $E = mc^2$.

16. **George Widener** (1962): math and calendar calculator and artist. Widener was fascinated as a child to learn that one of the passengers who died on the *Titanic* shared his name. He created a complex art work that listed all the Tuesdays for 700 years beginning on April 16, 1912, the day after the ship sank, and the day on which the mourning began.

17. **Ellen Boudreaux** (1957-): musical savant. Boudreaux is blind due to her premature birth and has thousands upon thousands of songs memorized and can play them

at will. She uses chirping sounds (echolocation) to get around, and since she was eight-years-old, she has been able to tell the time down to the second without ever having seen a clock.

Chapter 2

22 "BAD LUCK" PLAYING CARDS

"Digo, paciencia y barajar."
"What I say is, patience, and shuffle the cards."
—Don Quixote

According to *The Encyclopedia of the Unexplained*, the twenty-two playing cards discussed here are all bad news if they turn up during a fortune-telling card session. Unlike Tarot reading, with its elaborate spreads and complex, labyrinthine interpretations, fortune telling with the five-card deck of regular playing cards is relatively simple and straightforward. The cards are laid out in a favored pattern, and their meanings are then determined, analyzed, and studied.

As an experiment for this feature, I did my own reading using a regular deck of playing cards and one of the simplest methods known. First, I had to determine my "consulter's" card. Because I am a brown-haired male, my consulter's (or "questioner's") card is the King of Clubs. (Diamonds are for blondes and redheads; Hearts, for people with light-brown hair, and Spades, for people with black hair. Males use Kings and women use Queens. Simple, right?)

The divination method I used was to place my consulter's card in the middle, and then deal the deck out into three piles, face down. I then turned up the three top cards, twice, "to give a rough indication of the trends of fortune."

My six cards were the 2 of Spades; the 2 of Diamonds; the 3 of Hearts; the 5 of Clubs; the Ace of Diamonds; and the 2 of Clubs.

According to the *Encyclopedia of the Unexplained*, here's my fortune:

- **The 2 of Spades**: "A move; a change or separation, the break-up of a home or the loss of a friend; an operation or a long journey, possibly a death; the card of the wanderer."

- **The 2 of Diamonds**: "An unhappy love-affair, or an affair opposed by family and friends; take care, something unexpected is in the offing."

- **The 3 of Hearts**: "Poverty, shame, imprudence; beware of rash decisions."

- **The 5 of Clubs**: "A prudent or wealthy marriage; or news from the country."

- **The Ace of Diamonds**: "An engagement or wedding ring; wealth; a letter brings important news."

- **The 2 of Clubs**: "A major disappointment; expect opposition and rely only on yourself."

A bit enigmatic and vague, wouldn't you say? My fortune could be good, or it could be bad. Or it could be both. I guess it all depends on your own state of mind and your own personal interpretation of the reading at the time of the fortune-telling session. If that's the case, then I'll take the wealthy marriage, the wealth, and the news from the country, please. I'll pass on all the others, thank you very much. All kidding aside, there are many people who place great store in what cards tell them, and I'm sure that there are probably some genuinely intuitive (and perhaps psychic?) seers who really try to help people help themselves. Or at least I hope there are.

Here are the miseries attendant to the twenty-two worst cards in an innocent deck of playing cards. (All fortune descriptions are from *Encyclopedia of the Unexplained*, published by Penguin USA.)

- **Ace of Spades:** "A death; illness, bad news, broken relationships, worries, misfortune; cruelty and malice."

- **2 of Spades:** "A move; a change or separation, the break-up of a home or the loss of a friend; an operation or a long journey, possibly a death; the card of the wanderer."

- **3 of Spades:** "Tears; quarrels; a broken love-affair; failure; a journey over water."

- **4 of Spades:** "Illness, sadness; a will; sudden loss of money; poverty; envy and jealousy."

- **5 of Spades:** "Anger, quarrels; try to keep your temper and your patience will be rewarded."

- **7 of Spades:** "Loss of money, or loss of a close friend; suffering and sorrow; danger of quarrels."

- **8 of Spades:** "Be very careful, danger threatens in connection with some current project; expect opposition and treachery; keep a sharp eye out for damaging errors; consider changing your plans."

- **9 of Spades:** "Said to be the most ominous card in the pack, signifying ruin, failure, poverty, sickness and death, hopes and plans frustrated, families broken up; particularly threatening if close to other black cards."

- **10 of Spades:** "Bad luck; trouble; disgrace; prison; it cancels the effects of fortunate cards near it; be cautious and trust no one."

- **3 of Hearts:** "Poverty, shame, imprudence; beware of rash decisions."

- **4 of Hearts:** "Sadness, anxiety, jealousy, domestic difficulties; a broken engagement or a marriage postponed, or a marriage delayed till late in life."

- **7 of Hearts:** "Delusions; dreams that fail to come true; a disloyal or mischief-making friend; a betrayal, broken promises; doubts, puzzlement."

- **2 of Diamonds:** "An unhappy love-affair, or an affair opposed by family and friends; take care, something unexpected is in the offing."

- **3 of Diamonds:** "Domestic disagreements and unhappiness; possible separation or divorce; legal entanglements."

- **4 of Diamonds:** "A secret betrayed, or an unfaithful friend; interfering neighbors or relatives; a short journey; a legacy."

- **6 of Diamonds:** "An early marriage likely to fail or to be ended prematurely; not a favorable card for anyone contemplating marriage; a gift; caution needed."

- **7 of Diamonds:** "Minor loss of money, or unfriendly gossip; danger of scandal; lie low and keep quiet."

- **8 of Diamonds:** "A late and unhappy marriage."

- **2 of Clubs:** "A major disappointment; expect opposition and rely only on yourself."

- **3 of Clubs:** "Discord; a long-lasting marriage or affair, or more than one marriage; or a period of time, three years, months, weeks or days."

- **4 of Clubs:** "Radical changes, inconsistency, misfortune as a result of some caprice; danger of accident; a land journey."

- **10 of Clubs:** "Drunkenness; bad luck; friction with friends."

Chapter 3

51 BANNED BOOKS & AUTHORS
(INCLUDING 1 CARTOON CHARACTER)

"God forbid that any book should be banned. The
practice is as indefensible as infanticide."
—Dame Rebecca West

In many ways, this feature could be considered one of the most frightening in Dr. Bizarro's archive. For a writer, the mere thought of book banning strikes terror—*and rage*—in the heart. Book banning means blacklisting, book-burning, censorship, and the attempt at thought control.

The novels *Brave New World* and *1984* come immediately to mind, as does *Fahrenheit 451* and the memory of the Nazi book bonfires. As you'll see from reading through this compilation, no period in history has been free from the sinister hand of the censor. Nor any geographical location. Even ostensibly enlightened places (like New York City and England) have had their share of notorious censorship and banning incidents.

What is it about certain people that makes them believe that they know what's best for other people?

What has triggered book banning over the centuries? Ideas. Or better, the fear of ideas. And what kind of ideas? Ideas about government, sex, money, God, philosophical constructs—actually, ideas about just about anything that concerns human beings. Whenever a written idea alarms, offends, frightens, disturbs, upsets, flusters, or angers, there will usually be someone who will want to ban it. Writings that question or challenge the political system (and the politicians), or that portray sex realistically are favorite targets. Hell, even a dictionary can be banned, simply for including words that certain people consider obscene.

The titles of the works listed in this feature and the names of their authors should be carved on the Washington Monument. That way every tourist and politician would see them, and be reminded that freedom of speech does not apply only to those words and ideas that are inoffensive to everyone, but also to those words and ideas that are offensive to almost everyone. After all, the words of the Declaration of Independence were pretty offensive to the monarchy back in England, weren't they? That document pissed off the whole country. And perhaps that's the ultimate point.

NOTE: The many and various attempts to repress the following titles include banning, censoring, burning, expurgating, bowdlerizing, forbidding to be imported, confiscating, and/or persecuting for reading and/or owning.

1. *The Odyssey* (c. 850 B.C.) by Homer

   o   387 B.C., Greece.

   o   35, Rome.

2. The Sayings of Confucius and His Disciples (c. 5th century B.C.) by Confucius

   ○ 250 B.C., China.

   ○ 213 B.C., China.

3. *The Clouds, The Birds,* and *Lysistrata* (c. 4th century B.C.) by Aristophanes

   ○ 423 B.C., Athens, Greece (*The Clouds*).

   ○ 414 B.C., Athens, Greece (*The Birds*).

   ○ 411 B.C., Athens, Greece (*Lysistrata*).

   ○ 1967, Athens, Greece (*Lysistrata*).

4. *The Art of Love* (c. 1st century A.D.) by Ovid

   ○ 8, Rome.

   ○ 1497, Florence, Italy.

   ○ 1928, The United States.

   ○ 1929, San Francisco, California.

5. The Bible

   ○ 553, Rome, Italy.

   ○ 1409, England.

   ○ 1525-1526, England.

   ○ 1538, Paris, France.

   ○ 1551, Spain.

   ○ 1555, England.

   ○ 1560, Switzerland.

   ○ 1611, England.

- 1624, Germany.

- 1631, England. (The word "not" was inadvertently left out of the seventh commandment (changing it to "Thou shalt steal" in an edition of 1,000 copies of The Bible. This edition was immediately banned and became known as The Wicked Bible.)

- 1926, The Soviet Union.

6. The Talmud

- 1190; Cairo, Egypt.

- 1244; Paris, France.

- 1264; Rome, Italy.

- 1490; Salamanca, Spain. (This was during the Spanish Inquisition.)

- o 1926; The Soviet Union.

7. The Koran

   - o 1926, The Soviet Union.

8. *The Divine Comedy* (c. 1300) by Dante Alighieri

   - o 1318, Lombardy, France. (Burned.)
   - o 1497, Florence, Italy. (*The Divine Comedy* was one of the works burned by Savonarola in the notorious censorious "bonfire of the vanities.")
   - o 1559, Rome, Italy.
   - o 1581, Lisbon, Portugal.

9. *The Decameron* (1353) by Giovanni Boccaccio

   - o 1497, Florence, Italy. (*The Decameron* was one of the works burned in the "bonfire of the vanities.")
   - o 1559, Rome, Italy.
   - o 1922, The United States.
   - o 1926, The United States.
   - o 1927, The United States.
   - o 1933, Australia.
   - o 1934, Detroit, Michigan. (The criteria was that the book was "salacious.")
   - o 1935, Boston, Massachusetts.
   - o 1953, England.
   - o 1954, Swindon, England.

10. *The Sistine Chapel* by Michelangelo

  o 1933, The United States. (An art book comprised of plates of the ceiling of the Sistine Chapel was confiscated by U.S. Postal Authorities because one of the plates, "The Last Judgement," had naked people in it. The Postal Service was so ridiculed and reviled by both the press and the American people that they rescinded their confiscation and pending prosecution.)

11. *Works* (1517) by Martin Luther

  o 1517, Wittenberg, Germany.

  o 1521, France.

  o 1521, Rome, Italy.

  o 1521, Germany.

  o 1930, Rome, Italy.

12. *Dialogo sopra i due Massimi sistemi del Mondo* (1632) by Galileo Galilei

  o 1616, Rome, Italy. (Banned by Pope Paul IV for defending the Copernican theory that the planets did not revolve around the earth.)

13. William Shakespeare

  o 1597; England. (*The Tragedy of King Richard II;* political reasons.)

  o 1788-1820; England. (*The Tragedy of King Lear;* political reasons.)

- 1931; The United States. (*The Merchant of Venice;* objection by Jewish groups to the character Shylock.)

14. *Robinson Crusoe* by Daniel Defoe

- 1720, Spain.

15. *Gulliver's Travels* by Jonathan Swift

- 1726, England.

16. *Tom Jones* by Henry Fielding

- 1749, Paris, France.

17. *Fanny Hill* by John Cleland

- 1749, England.

- 1821, Boston, Massachusetts. (This was the first known obscenity case in the United States.)

- 1965, Illinois.

18. *Critique of Pure Reason* by Immanuel Kant

- 1827, Rome, Italy.

- 1928, The Soviet Union. (All of Kant's writings were banned.)

- 1939, Spain. (Kant was considered a "disgraceful writer.")

19. *The History of the Decline and Fall of the Roman Empire* (1776-1788) by Edward Gibbon

- 1783, Rome, Italy. (Banned because its scholarship conflicted with church teachings.)

- 1826, England. (Only a bowdlerized edition was allowed to be published. [See the sidebar on Thomas Bowdler, M.D.])

20. *The Age of Reason* by Thomas Paine
- 1797, England.

21. *Justine* (1791) by the Marquis de Sade
- 1791, France.
- 1948, Rome, Italy.
- 1955, Paris, France.
- 1962, London, England.

22. *Faust* (1790) by Jonathan Wolfgang von Goethe
- 1808, Berlin, Germany.
- 1939, Spain. (Goethe was considered a "disgraceful" writer.)

23. *Les Miserables* (1862) by Victor Hugo
- 1850, Russia. (All of Hugo's works were banned.)
- 1864, Rome, Italy.

24. *The Scarlet Letter* (1850) by Nathaniel Hawthorne
- 1852, Russia.

25. *Wonder Stories* (1835) by Hans Christian Andersen
- 1835, Russia.
- 1954, Illinois. (This book was stamped "For Adult Readers" by the authorities to make it "impossible for children to obtain smut.")

26. *On the Origin of Species* (1859) by Charles Darwin

   o   1859, Cambridge, England.

   o   1925, Dayton, Tennessee. (This book banning prompted the famous Scopes evolution trial in which teacher John Scopes was found guilty of teaching evolution by using Darwin's book in his classroom. He was fined $100 for his "crime." The verdict against him resulted in an actual law on Tennessee's books that prohibited teaching anything in the state's classrooms except creationism. This law stood for forty-two years, until 1967, before it was repealed.

27. *Uncle Tom's Cabin* (1852) by Harriet Beecher Stowe

   o   1852, Russia.

   o   1855, The Papal States, Italy.

28. *Leaves of Grass* (1855) by Walt Whitman

   o   1881, Boston, Massachusetts.

29. *Madame Bovary* (1856) by Gustave Flaubert

   o   1857, Paris, France.

   o   1864, Rome, Italy.

   o   1954, The United States.

30. *Alice's Adventures in Wonderland* (1865) by Lewis Carroll

   o   1931, China. (The reason the Chinese censors cited for banning this children's classic

was because "animals should not use human
language.")

31. *The Adventures of Huckleberry Finn* (1885) by
Mark Twain

o 1885, Concord, Massachusetts.

o 1905, Brooklyn, New York.

o 1930, The Soviet Union.

o 1957, New York City. (The frequent use of the
word "ni**er" prompted the ban in 1957.)

32. *Tess of the D'Urbervilles* (1891) by Thomas Hardy

o 1891, England.

33. *Man and Superman* (1903) by George Bernard
Shaw

o 1905, New York City.

o 1929, Yugoslavia. (All works by Shaw were
banned in Yugoslavia.)

34. *The Adventures of Sherlock Holmes* (1892) by Sir
Arthur Conan Doyle

o 1929, The Soviet Union. (The Soviet censors banned Inspector Holmes because of the
many references to "occultism" and "spiritual-
ism" in his *Adventures*.

35. *Sister Carrie* (1900) by Theodore Dreiser

o 1900, New York City.

o 1958, Vermont.

36. *The Call of the Wild* (1903) by Jack London

o 1929, Italy.

o 1929, Yugoslavia.

o 1932, Germany. (*The Call of the Wild* was banned by the Nazis.)

37. *The Jungle* (1906) by Upton Sinclair

o 1929, Yugoslavia. (All of Sinclair's works were banned.)

o 1933, Germany. (*The Jungle* was burned in the Nazi book bonfires.)

o 1956, Berlin, East Germany. (All of Sinclair's works were banned.)

38. *Ulysses* (1922) by James Joyce

o 1922, The United States. (Confiscated copies were burned.)

o 1922, Ireland. (Copies were burned.)

o 1922, Canada. (Copies were burned.)

o 1923, England. (Copies were burned.)

o 1929, England.

o 1930, New York City.

39. *Lady Chatterley's Lover* (1928) by D.H. Lawrence

o 1929, The United States.

o 1930, Washington, D.C.

o 1932, Ireland.

- 1932, Poland.

- 1953, England.

- 1960, Montreal, Canada.

40. *Elmer Gantry* (1927) by Sinclair Lewis

- 1927, Boston, Massachusetts.

- 1931, Ireland.

41. *Desire Under the Elms* (play, 1924) by Eugene O'Neill

- 1925, New York City.

42. *Tropic of Cancer* (1934) and *Sexus* (1949) by Henry Miller

- 1934, The United States (*Tropic of Cancer*).

- 1950, France (*Sexus*).

- 1956, Norway (*Sexus*).

43. Ernest Hemingway

- 1929, Italy (*A Farewell to Arms*).

- 1930, Boston, Massachusetts (*The Sun Also Rises*).

- 1933, Germany. (The Nazis burned many of Hemingway's works in their book bonfires.)

- 1939, Ireland (*A Farewell to Arms*).

- 1953, Ireland (*The Sun Also Rises*).

- 1960, San Jose, California (*The Sun Also Rises*).

44. *Lolita* (1955) by Vladimir Nabokov

   o 1956, Paris, France.

   o 1960, New Zealand.

45. Mickey Mouse (1932) by Walt Disney

   o 1932, The United States. (One of Mickey's cartoons was banned because there was a scene in it in which a cow was seen in a pasture reading Elinor Glyn's erotic romance novel, *Three Weeks*.

   o 1937, Belgrade, Yugoslavia. (A Mickey Mouse cartoon was banned for its alleged "anti-monarchical" plot line.)

   o 1938, Rome, Italy. (Mickey was deemed "unsuitable for children.")

   o 1954, East Berlin, Germany.

46. *The Grapes of Wrath* (1939) by John Steinbeck

   o 1939, St. Louis, Missouri.

   o 1939, Kansas City, Missouri.

   o 1939, California.

47. *The Naked Lunch* (1959) by William Burroughs

   o 1959, Boston, Massachusetts. (How times change: The 1992 film version of Burroughs's *Naked Lunch* didn't even raise an eyebrow in Boston.

48. Tennessee Williams

  o 1965, Portugal. (All of Williams's work was banned.)

49. *From Here to Eternity* (1951) by James Jones

  o 1951, Holyoke, Massachusetts.

  o 1951, Springfield, Massachusetts.

  o 1951, Denver, Colorado.

  o 1953, Jersey City, New Jersey.

  o 1954, The United States. (*From Here to Eternity* was placed on the disapproved list of the National Organization of Decent Literature.)

  o 1955, The United States. (The Postal Service declared the book "unmailable" even though it had been a bestseller for four years.)

50. *Soul On Ice* (1968) by Eldridge Cleaver

  o 1969, California. (The book was banned from California schools.)

51. The American Heritage Dictionary (1969 edition)

  o 1978, Missouri. (The Dictionary was banned because it contained thirty-nine "objectionable" words.)

Thomas Bowdler, MD (1754-1825) is a man whose name is now irrevocably associated with censorship. Apparently, Dr. Bowdler felt that parts of some of the works of the immortal William Shakespeare were too dirty for most (especially children), and thus, took it upon himself to remedy this deplorable situation. In 1818, at the age of sixty-four, Bowdler published *The Family Shakespeare*, an edition of the Bard's works that had been sanitized, purified, refined, sterilized, and generally chopped to smithereens by that self-righteous and self-defined literary critic and moral guardian, Bowdler himself. Upon tackling this sacred project, Bowdler decided to omit "those words and expressions which cannot with propriety be read aloud in the family." To this day, the verb "bowdlerize" has become synonymous with the abhorrent practice of expurgating literary works.

Chapter 4

THE 5 BIGGEST GARBAGE-PRODUCING COUNTRIES ON THE PLANET

This table lists the top garbage-producing countries in the world. As you can see, the United States doesn't even make the top five. Nonetheless, any and all attempts at reducing solid waste output and increasing recycling must continue apace, or else we'll all be crawling through crud and dog-paddling through detritus before too long.

Country	Pounds of Waste per Capita per Year
Kuwait	4,603
Antigua and Barbuda	4,427
St. Kitts and Nevis	4,387
Guyana	4,289
Sri Lanka	4,103

Chapter 5

4 BIZARRO AMERICAN CULTS OF DEATH

What is so desperately lacking in people's lives that they would be willing to give up everything, including their lives, for some charismatic, psychotic, sociopathic "leader?" American history is stained with the bloody explosions of cults gone bad. This feature looks at four of the worst.

1. The Symbionese Liberation Army

Leader: Donald "Cinque" DeFreeze.
Date: Friday, May 17, 1974.
Place: Los Angeles, California.
Method of Death: Gunfire.
Body Count: Six SLA members, including DeFreeze.

They all died during a violent, bloody shootout with five hundred Los Angeles cops. The SLA kidnapped heiress Patty Hearst on February 4, 1974, and after incessant brainwashing and thought control, she joined their organization and helped them rob a bank. She eventually was captured in 1975 and ended up serving twenty-two months in prison for her part in the robbery.

2. The People's Temple

Leader: Jim Jones, who claimed to be God.

Date: Saturday, November 18, 1978.

Place: Jonestown, Guyana, South America.

Method of Death: Mass suicide by drinking cyanide-laced punch*.

Body Count: 913 followers, including Jim Jones.

All his "worshippers" committed suicide at Jones's request. Parents fed the poison to their children.

*NOTE: It was initially believed that the punch Jones used was Kool-Aid, yet packets of Flavor Aid punch were found and it was determined that even though both beverage mixes were used, there was significantly more Flavor Aid than Kool-Aid. However, "drink the Kool-Aid" has become a well-known metaphor and idiom for blind obedience.

NBC-TV newsman Don Harris (left) and photographer Greg Robinson (right) are shown in film taken by NBC cameraman Robert Brown moments before they and Rep. Leo Ryan (D-Calif.) were shot to death in Guyana. —Stories on page 3; other pictures in centerfold

3. MOVE

Leader: John Africa.
Date: Monday, May 13, 1985.
Place: Philadelphia, Pennsylvania.
Method of Death: Fire.
Body Count: Eleven MOVE members.

Their West Philadelphia row house (and sixty-one other houses in a two-block radius) burned to the ground after police dropped a bomb from a helicopter in an attempt to destroy a MOVE rooftop bunker.

4. The Branch Davidians

Leader: David Koresh, who claimed to be Jesus Christ.

Date: Wednesday, April 19, 1993.

Place: Waco, Texas.

Method of Death: Fire.

Body Count: Eighty-six, including David Koresh and an estimated two dozen children.

After a fifty-one-day standoff, the Branch Davidians who were still holed up in a three-story compound outside of Waco apparently set fire to the place when FBI agents used tanks to knock holes in the building and insert tear gas canisters in an attempt to force them to come out. Four Federal agents were killed on February 28, 1993 when the FBI attempted to serve a search warrant on Koresh, who reportedly had $200,000 worth of arms and ammunition in the compound.

Chapter 6

4 BIZARRO LAWS PERTAINING TO WOMEN'S FEET

Which women's body parts would you consider to be blatantly sexual? (And that is not a sexist question, but a necessary one that reflects on the focus of this list.)

Most people would cite the breasts, buttocks, pubic region, and the bare legs on the short list of parts which, while they have other functions to be sure, are major erotic turn-ons for most.

But how about feet? For centuries, women's feet have been considered sexual parts in many cultures, and laws pertaining to their exposure have been written and enforced.

Professor Robert Pelton, in his seminal book, *Loony Sex Laws*, tracked down a few "foot" laws from all over the world, and here are four of the oddest.

1. **Laotia:** There is a foot law in Laotia that dictates that a woman cannot show her toes in public.

2. **China:** There is an interesting interpretation of nudity and eroticism "on the books" in rural China. The law there prohibits a male from looking at the bare feet of another man's wife. Other men are allowed, however, to see anything else they want, including the wife's completely nude body if so desired. But if a neighbor or relative catches a glimpse of her toes, then the offended husband has to kill him.

3. **Europe:** During the Renaissance, painters could not show a woman's toes or bare feet in their works. The women could be stark naked if the artists desired, but feet were verboten.

4. **Europe:** In nineteenth century Europe, female stage performers were banned from showing foot. Almost anything else could be flashed, but again, toes were considered indecent exposure.

Chapter 7

11 BODY PARTS
PEOPLE PIERCE

Body mutilation has always been popular.

Tattoos, piercings, brandings, and other forms of casually violent adornment have been common cultural rituals since man and woman have walked upright. This feature looks at body parts into which people willingly put holes—and then jewelry. The parts are listed in order of bodily descent and for certain parts, some tidbits on who favors each particular mutilatory site are provided.

1. **The Ears, of course:** Countless people of all genders have pierced ears. Having your ears pierced is a rite of adolescence for teen or pre-teen girls and many have a girlfriend do it with an ice cube, a needle, and a piece of cork. (Although the modern spring-loaded "gun" method is quick, cheap, and relatively painless and should be the way you have it done.) Today, many pierce the entire length of the ear—even up into the quite thick (and therefore very sensitive) cartilage.

2. **The Nose:** The most common question asked of people with pierced noses (either nostril wall is pierced and either a hoop or a stud earring is worn) is "What do you do when you get a cold?" The answer is the same as for people with non-pierced noses: You blow your nose. Your viral body fluids just slide right on by the post and clutch arrangement of the earring.

3. **The Philtrum:** The philtrum is the wall of cartilage that separates your right and left nostril. It is usually pierced horizontally through the wall, and a hoop earring is worn so that it hangs onto the upper lip.

4. **The Cheeks:** Piercing the cheeks involves wearing an earring in either facial cheek, with the earring clutch inside the mouth.

5. **The Tongue:** The tongue is pierced approximately halfway up its length, and the earring is worn on the top of the tongue, with the clutch underneath. Recipients claim it is not painful, and that it does not interfere with eating.

6. **The Lower Lip:** When this site is pierced, usually a hoop earring is worn so that the earring goes through the front and back of the lip. Stud earrings are also worn here, but if it's not a dermal piercing, then the clutch on the back of the earring can scrape the lower teeth and make it quite uncomfortable, not to mention remove tooth enamel.

7. **The Nipples:** This is a favorite of both men and women and the consensus is that it's painful to have done.

8. **The Navel:** People put an earring through it.

9. **The Fingernails:** Women with long nails drill a hole
   in the nail and either wear a hoop or a stud through
   the hole.

10. **The Labia:** The labia majora (the external lips of the
    female vagina) are used as a piercing site. This is quite
    a turn-on for many people, although for heterosexuals,
    the male must be careful not to cut open his erection
    by scraping himself with the earring as he's thrusting.

11. **The Penis:** Some men pierce the head of their penis,
    as well as the entire length of the organ. When pierc-
    ing the head, it's usually done above the urethra and
    traverses the head from side to side. When the body of
    the organ itself is done, the earrings can run the entire
    length of the penis.

Chapter 8

THE CHURCH OF SATAN'S 9 SATANIC STATEMENTS

The United States Government recognizes Anton LaVey's Church of Satan as an official church, entitled to all the protection and rights of any other structured religious establishment in America. The Church of Satan worships Satan.

They hold Satanic Black Masses, rituals which some have reported use the body of a naked virgin as the altar, include inserting the name of Satan into prayers where God or Christ is mentioned, as well as defilement of "sacred" artifacts like the Host and wine.

In his writings, Anton LaVey has defined his Church's beliefs and goals and has coalesced their tenets into nine "Satanic Statements."

1. Satan represents indulgence instead of abstinence.

2. Satan represents vital existence instead of spiritual pipe dreams.

3. Satan represents undefiled wisdom instead of hypo-critical self-deceit.

4. Satan represents kindness to those who deserve it instead of love wasted on ingrates.

5. Satan represents vengeance instead of turning the other cheek.

6. Satan represents responsibility to the responsible instead of concern for psychic vampires.

7. Satan represents man as just another animal—sometimes better, more often worse than those that walk on all-fours—who, because of his "divine spiritual and intellectual development," has become the most vicious animal of all.

8. Satan represents all of the so-called sins, as they all lead to physical, mental, or emotional gratification.

9. Satan has been the best friend the Church has ever had, as he has kept it in business all these years.

©1966 Anton Szandor LaVey.

Chapter 9

68 EUPHEMISMS FOR THE DEVIL

There are many ways of naming the ultimate Bad Guy. Here are 68 of them.

1. The Arch Fiend.
2. Auld Hornie.
3. The Author of Evil.
4. The Bad Man.
5. Beelzebub.
6. Belial.
7. The Black Gentleman.
8. The Black Spy.
9. The Buggar Man.
10. The Black Man.
11. The Black Prince.
12. The Dark One.
13. Diablo.
14. Diabolus.
15. Diavolo.
16. Dickens.
17. The Duece.
18. The Evil One.
19. The Fallen Angel.
20. The Father of Lies.
21. The Gentleman in Black.
22. Goodman.

23. His Satanic Majesty.

24. Hobb.

25. Lord Harry.

26. Lucifer.

27. Mephistopheles.

28. Nicholas.

29. Nickey.

30. The Noseless One.

31. Old Bendy.

32. Old Billy.

33. Old Blazes.

34. Old Boots.

35. The Old Boy.

36. Old Cain.

37. Old Cootie.

38. Old Dad.

39. The Old Driver.

40. The Old Gentleman.

41. The Old Gooseberry.

42. Old Harry.

43. Old Horny.

44. The Old Lad.

45. Old Ned.

46. Old Nick Bogey.

47. Old Nick.

48. The Old One.

49. The Old Poker.

50. Old Roger.

51. Old Roundfoot.

52. Old Ruffin.

53. Old Scratch.

54. The Old Serpent.

55. Old Split Foot.

56. Old Toast.

57. The Prince of Darkness.

58. Queed.

59. The Ragamuffin.

60. The Ragman.

61. The Ruffian.

62. Saint Nicholas.

63. Sam Hill.

64. Satan.

65. Scratch.

66. Skipper.

67. Toast.

68. The Wicked One.

Chapter 10

16 CREATIONIST CLAIMS AND WHY BOTH THE CREATIONISTS THEMSELVES AND THEIR SPURIOUS PSEUDOSCIENTIFIC CLAIMS ARE UNEQUIVOCALLY WRONG

The following list of sixteen creationism debunking arguments originally appeared in Dr. Tim M. Berra's brilliant 1990 book, *Evolution and the Myth of Creationism*. In his lucid, reasoned, and enlightened Preface, Dr. Berra said:

> *Creationists, for the most part, are fundamentalist Christians whose central premise is a literal interpretation of the Bible and a belief in its inerrancy. In adopting a literal interpretation of the Bible, they differ from nearly all other Christians and Jews. Scientists, many of whom are*

religious, have no wish to deny fundamentalists their own beliefs, but the creationists are determined to impose their views on others. In particular, they are lobbying to have science classes teach the ideas of: a sudden creation from nothing by God; a worldwide flood; a young Earth; and the separate ancestry of humans and apes. These ideas constitute the biblical story of creation and, as such, are inherently religious. And because they depend on supernatural intervention, not natural law, they are also unscientific. There is no scientific evidence, or even an appeal from common sense or experience, to support the creationists claims. The few claims that are susceptible to testing, such as a young Earth, are shown by the scientific evidence to be false. Yet creationists do not remove demonstrably false ideas from their pantheon of beliefs. Unlike scientists, they do not subject their assertions to revision based on evidence. Since this pattern of thought is not scientific—does not require or even condone testing and retesting—it should not be taught in science classrooms in public schools. The creationists are determined to force their will on society and the schools, through the courts if possible. Their strategy— ironically enough, considering the moral precepts of Christianity—is founded in deception, misrepresentation, and obfuscation designed to dupe the public into thinking that there is a genuine scientific controversy about the validity of evolution. No such controversy exists, but it is difficult for the lay public to distinguish the scientists, who often disagree on the nuances of evolutionary theory (but not on evolution's existence), from the creationists, who stick together and cloak absurd claims in scientific terminology.

Dr. Berra goes on to explain his motives for writing his book: Education, explanation, and ammunition. He is to be lauded for his attempt to shine a light into a dark corner of ignorance and deceit. Dr. Berra provides a much-needed voice of reason with his book.

Dr. Berra is Professor Emeritus of Evolution, Ecology and Organismal Biology at The Ohio State University. He received the Ph.D. in Biology from Tulane University in 1969. He is a three-time recipient of Fulbright Fellowships to Australia in 1969, 1979, and 2009. He taught at the University of Papua New Guinea before joining the faculty of OSU in 1972. Over the last forty years he has spent over nine years doing fieldwork in Australia. He is the author of over seventy-five scientific papers and six books including *Evolution and the Myth of Creationism* published by Stanford University Press in 1990.

Some Creationist Claims: Do They Raise Any Legitimate Doubts?

Dr. Tim M. Berra

1. **The Claim:** Evolution violates the second law of thermodynamics. Entropy (disorder) is always increasing. Since order does not arise out of chaos, evolution is therefore false.

   The Truth: These statements conveniently ignore the fact that you can get order out of disorder if you add energy. For example, an unassembled bicycle that arrives at your house in a shipping carton is in a state of disorder. You supply the energy of your muscles (which you get from food that came ultimately from sunlight) to assemble the bike. You have got order from disorder by supplying energy. The Sun is the source of energy input to the earth's living systems and allows them to evolve. The engineers in the CRS [Creation Research Society] know this, but they permit this specious reasoning to be published in their pamphlets. Just as the more structured oak tree is derived from the less complex acorn by the addition of energy captured by the growing tree from the Sun, so sunlight, via photosynthesis, provides the energy input that propels evolution. In the sense that the sun is losing more energy than the Earth is gaining, entropy is increasing. After death, decay sets in, and energy utilization is no longer possible. That is when entropy gets you. What does represent an increase in entropy, as biologists have pointed out, is the diversity of species produced by evolution.

2. **The Claim:** The small amount of helium in the atmosphere proves that the Earth is young. If the Earth were as old as geologists say, there would be much more helium, because it is a product of uranium decay.

   The Truth: Helium, used to suspend blimps in air, is a very light gas and simply escapes into space; like hydrogen, it cannot accumulate in Earth's atmosphere to any great extent.

3. **The Claim:** The rate of decay of the Earth's magnetism leads to the calculation that the Earth was created about 10,000 years ago.

The Truth: The Earth's magnetic field does indeed decay, but it does so cyclically, every few thousand years, and it is constantly being renewed by the motion of the liquid core of the Earth. The "fossil magnetism" recorded in ancient rocks clearly demonstrates that polar reversals (shifts in the direction of the Earth's magnetic field) have occurred both repeatedly and irregularly throughout Earth history; the calendar of these reversals was established over two decades ago, and quickly became the linchpin in the emerging theory of plate tectonics and continental drift.

4. **The Claim:** If evolution were true, there would have to be transitional fossils, but there were none; therefore evolution did not occur.

The Truth: There are many transitional fossils, including the ape-human transitional form, Australopithecus. Eusthenopteron shows marvelous intermediate characteristics between the lobe-finned fishes and the amphibians. The transitional fossils between amphibians and reptiles are so various and so intermediate that it is difficult to define where one group ends and the other begins. Archaeopteryx is clearly intermediate between reptiles and birds. In spite of such reptilian affinities as a long bony tail, toothed jaws, and clawed wings, creationists declare that because Archaeopteryx had feathers, it was a bird, not a transitional stage between reptiles and birds. Having no explanation of their own, the creationists attempt to deny the transitional fossils out of existence.

5. **The Claim:** Fossils seem to appear out of nowhere at the base of the Cambrian; therefore, they had to have been created.

The Truth: The earliest microfossils date back, in fact, to the Precambrian, about 3.5 billion years ago. A variety of multicellular life appears in the fossil record about 670 million years ago, which is eighty million years before the Cambrian. The Cambrian does seem to explode with fossils, but that is simply because the first shelled organisms, such as the brachiopods and trilobites, date from the Cambrian; their resistant shells fossilize far more readily than their soft-bodied ancestors of the Precambrian. What is more, Precambrian rocks are so old that they have been subjected to a great deal of deformation. We are thus fortunate to have any Precambrian fossils of soft-bodied animals. Still more fossils are discovered every year, and each one further weakens the creationist position.

6. **The Claim:** All fossils were deposited at the time of the Noachian flood.

The Truth: There is not a shred of evidence in the geological record to support the claim of a single, worldwide flood. Geological formations such as mountain ranges and the Grand Canyon require millions of years to form, and the fossil record extends over several billion years. The time required for continents to have drifted into their present positions is immense. These things cannot be accounted for by a single flood lasting a few days or years.

7. **The Claim:** There are places where advanced fossils lie beneath more primitive fossils.

   The Truth: Earth movements such as faulting and thrusting produce these discontinuities; the older rock has simply been pushed over on top of the younger rocks, as we sometimes see even along highway cuts. These places are easily recognized and explained by geologists. They cannot be explained away by the creationists' belief that all fossils are the result of the Noachian flood. Thus the creationists' attempt to fault evolutionary theory by these means end up demolishing one of their own pet claims.

8. **The Claim:** The chances of the proper molecules randomly assembling into a living cell are impossibly small.

   The Truth: Simulation experiments have repeatedly shown that amino acids do not assemble randomly. Their molecular structure causes them to be self-ordering, which enhances the chances of forming long chains of molecules. Simulation experiments also demonstrate that the formation of prebiotic macromolecules is both easy and likely and does not require DNA, which is a later step in the evolution of proteins. The stepwise application of cumulative natural selection acting over long periods of time can make the improbable very likely.

9. **The Claim:** Dinosaur and human footprints have been found together in Cretaceous limestone at Glen Rose,

Texas. Therefore, dinosaurs could not have preceded humans by millions of years.

The Truth: This Fred Flintstone version of prehistory is one of the most preposterous and devious claims that the fundamentalists make, and they have made it in both books and films. The "man-tracks" seen by creationists stem from two sources. One is wishful imagination, whereby water-worn scour marks and eroded dinosaur tracks are perceived as human footprints. The other source is deliberate fraud. Creationist hoaxers obscure the foot pads of dinosaur tracks with sand and photograph what remains, the dinosaur's toe impressions. When reversed, the tip of the dinosaur toe or claw becomes the heel of a "human" print. These prints are shown in poor-quality photographs in creationist literature and films. Because the stride length (seven feet) and foot length (three feet) exceed any possible human scale, the fundamentalists call these the giants mentioned in Genesis. In addition to doctored dinosaur tracks, there are other hoaxed prints circulating in this area of Texas. In fact, carved footprints were offered for sale to tourists in curio shops during the Great Depression. These caught the eye of the paleontologist Roland T. Bird, who recognized them as fakes, but they eventually led him to the legitimate dinosaur footprints at Glen Rose. This area has since been extensively studied by paleontologists, and numerous species of reptiles and amphibians have been catalogued. No genuine human tracks exist there, but by leading to genuine new discoveries, the hoax became a boon to science.

10. The Claim: Biologists have never seen a species evolve.

The Truth: On a small scale, we certainly have. Using allopolyploidy and artificial selection, scientists have manufactured crop plants and horticultural novelties that are reproductively isolated from the parental stock. In addition, one can see stages of incipient speciation in nature by looking at clinal variations and subspecies, that is, gradual change in the characteristics of a population across its geographical range. Major evolutionary changes, however, usually involve time periods vastly greater than man's written record; we cannot watch such changes, but we can deduce them by inference from living and fossil organisms.

11. The Claim: Evolution, too, is a religion, and requires faith.

The Truth: Creationists are beginning to admit that their "science" is not science at all, and that it depends on faith, but, they are quick to add, so does evolution. Not so. Biologists do not have to believe that there are transitional fossils; we can examine them in hundreds of museums around the world, and we make new discoveries in the rocks all the time. Scientists do not have to believe that the solar system is 4.5 billion years old; we can test the age of Earth, Moon, and meteoritic rocks very accurately. We do not have to believe that protocells can be easily created from simple chemicals in the laboratory; we can repeat the experiments, with comparable results. We can also create artificial species of plants and animals by applying selection, and we can observe natural speciation in action. That is the big difference between science and religion. Science exists because of the evidence, whereas religion exists upon faith—and, in the case of religious fundamentalism and creationism, in spite of the evidence.

12. **The Claim:** The numbers of humans today would be much greater if we have been around as long as evolutionists say we have.

   The Truth: This notion makes some very naive assumptions about birth and death rates, and the fecundity of early humans, and assumes that populations are always growing, when in fact most animal populations are at a level somewhat lower than the carrying capacity of their environment. Such stable populations remain stable for long periods of time, held in check by environmental constraints. It is only our own species' recently acquired ability to modify our environment that has allowed our numbers to get dangerously out of control. Ironically, it is our ability to master the environment—as the Bible commands us to do—that may yet do us in.

13. **The Claim:** The current rate of shrinkage of the Sun proves that the Earth could not be as old as geologists say, because the surface of the Sun would have been near the Earth's orbit just a few million years ago.

   The Truth: This simplistic view neglects the fact that stars, such as out Sun, have life cycles during which events occur at different rates. The characteristics of a newly formed star are quite different from those of stars near death. Astronomers can see these differences today by observing young, middle-aged, and old stars. By now, we know a great deal about the Sun, and we know that it has not been shrinking at a constant rate.

14. **The Claim:** A living freshwater mussel was determined by Carbon 14 dating to be over 2,000 years old; therefore Carbon 14 dating is worthless.

   The Truth: When used properly, Carbon 14 is a very accurate time-measuring technique. The mussel in this example is an inappropriate case for 14C dating because the animal had acquired much of its carbon from the limestone of the surrounding water and sediment. These sources are very low in 14C, owing to their age and lack of mixing with fresh carbon from the atmosphere. Therefore a newly killed mussel in these circumstances has less 14C than, say, a newly cut tree branch. The reduced level of 14C yields an artificially older date. The 14C technique has no such problems with the tree branch that gets its carbon from the air, or with the campfire sites of ancient peoples. As with arcwelding or Cajun cooking, one must understand the technique to use it properly. This is another example of the self-correcting nature of science.

15. **The Claim:** The influx of meteoritic dust from space to Earth is about fourteen million tons per year. If the Earth and Moon were 4.5 billion years old, then there should be a layer of dust fifty to 100 feet thick covering their surfaces.

The Truth: This estimate of dust influx is simply out of date. Space probes have found that the level of dust influx from space is about 400 times less than that. Creationists are aware of the modern measurements, but they continue to use the incorrect figure because it suits their purpose. Such is their honesty and scholarship. Do these people believe that the astronauts would have been allowed to land on the Moon if NASA thought they would sink into 100 feet of dust?

16. **The Claim:** Prominent biologists have made statements disputing evolution.

The Truth: The out-of-context quote is one of the most insidious weapons in the creationists' arsenal, and reflects the desperation of their position. Biologists do not deny the fact of evolution. We do, however, debate its mechanisms and tempo. The debate reflects the vigorous growth of a major scientific concept; it is what goes on routinely in all healthy, growing branches of scholarship. Creationists dishonestly portray this as a weakness of the theory of evolution. These sixteen points are just a few of the creationists' arguments. There are others, but they are all of the same character—scientifically inaccurate, willful, or devious.

Reprinted from *Evolution and the Myth of Creationism: A Basic Guide to the Facts in the Evolution Debate* by Tim M. Berra with the permission of the publishers, Stanford University Press, ©1990 by the Board of Trustees of the Leland Stanford Junior University.

Chapter 11

16 CRUCIFIED SAVIORS OTHER THAN JESUS CHRIST

*"We can believe what we choose. We are answerable
for what we choose to believe."*
—Cardinal Newman

*"It is always easier to believe than to deny. Our
minds are naturally affirmative."*
—John Burroughs, *The Light of Day* (1900)

A Cautionary Note: This feature is not for the religiously vulnerable. If you are an ardent Christian who will not entertain, or are offended by, questions and concepts that challenge your beliefs and strike at the very core of Christianity, then you should probably eschew the reading of this feature. It will likely not ensorcell you.

This chapter explicates author Kersey Graves's "Oriental/ Heathen Origins of Christianity" thesis—which he claims disproves the majority of Christianity's most fervently held tenets. Readers will perhaps come away from this feature a "questioning Thomas," if not a "doubting Thomas."

In 1875, religious scholar and historian Kersey Graves pub-lished a book that gave the Christian clergy nightmares. It was called *The World's Sixteen Crucified Saviors or Christianity Before Christ*, and it claimed to prove—calmly, rationally, and with some apparent scholarship—that Christianity was essentially based on legends and myths from centuries past, and that the "legend" of Jesus Christ bore dozens (in some cases, hundreds) of similarities with pagan gods from as far back as the year 2,000 B.C.

The book's subtitle read as follows:

Containing New, Startling, and Extraordinary Revelations in Religious History, Which Disclose the Oriental Origin of All the Doctrines, Principles, Precepts, and Miracles of the CHRISTIAN NEW TESTAMENT and Furnishing a Key for Unlocking Many Of Its Sacred Mysteries, Besides Comprising the HISTORY OF 16 HEATHEN CRUCIFIED GODS

Graves began the book with an "Explanation":

The World's Sixteen Crucified Saviors. What an imposing title for a book! What startling developments of religious history it implies! Is it founded on fact or fiction? If it has a basis of truth, where was such an extraordinary mine of sacred lore discovered? Where were such startling facts obtained as the title of the work suggests? These queries will doubtless arise as soliloquies in the minds of many readers on glancing at the title page… [I deem] it only necessary to state that many of the most important facts collated in this work were derived from Sir Godfrey Higgins' Anacalypsis, a work as valuable as it is rare—a work comprising the result of twenty years' labor, devoted to the investigation of religious history.... With the facts and materials derived from this source, and two hundred other unimpeachable historical records, the present work might have swelled to fourfold its present size...

Graves then actually took the time to offer an "Address to the Clergy," such was his awareness of just how devastating the alleged facts he was planning on revealing could be to the faithful.

Friends and brethren—teachers of the Christian faith: will you believe us when we tell you the divine claims of your religion are gone—all swept away by the "logic of history," and nullified by the demonstrations of science? (I'll bet that got their attention, eh?) The recently opened fountains of historic law...sweep away the last inch of ground on which can be predicated the least show for either the divine origin of the Christian religion, or the divinity of Jesus Christ.

He then ran through a list of common elements of many, many ancient religions and pagan gods, including such things as:

- being foretold by prophets
- a virgin birth
- being born on December 25th
- a sin-atoning crucifixion (often between two thieves)
- rising from the dead after three days buried
- physical ascension into heaven

- the presence of magi, or "wise men"

- being considered part of a divine trinity

- being referred to as "Savior," "Redeemer," "Messiah," and the "Son of God."

He also claimed evidence that at least twenty ancient religions had holy books which had Old and New Testaments, and that the Christian Bible can easily be traced to heathen, rather than divine, sources. He concluded his "Address" with this remarkable statement:

In conclusion, permit us to say that the numerous and overwhelming facts...render it utterly impossible that the exalted claims you put forth for [Christianity] and its assumed author (that of a divine character) can be true. And posterity will so decide, whether you do or not.

Reading *The World's Sixteen Crucified Saviors* is an amazing experience, and is must-reading for anyone interested in the origins of our sociocultural and religious belief systems. One cannot help but wonder what cultural, social, religious, and political machinations have prevented the wide dissemination of this information. On second thought, it might not even be anything that devious: We all know that no one reads anymore, right? A recent poll found that over 50% of the American public goes an entire year without ever buying a book. Such deliberate cultural illiteracy does a far more efficient job of keeping bold and inflammatory information away from the masses than any imagined (or real) bureaucratic censorship. Apathy rules, and we have TV to thank for that, I suppose.

In any case, the following feature coalesces Kersey Graves's research and offers capsule summaries of the "16 Crucified

Saviors Other Than Jesus Christ" and the 100 incredible similarities Graves claims exist between their lives and teachings and those of Jesus Christ. Just reading the alleged similarities between Jesus Christ and the first god on the list, Chrishna, is intimidating for people who have grown up (as did I) immersed in the specifics of the Christ story.

DISCLAIMER: I must make the point that this feature is solely based on the research and material found in Graves's 1875 book. I have not attempted to duplicate his research nor do I vouch for it. I include this feature here for the sake of intellectual advancement, to stimulate discourse, and for entertainment. (I reject the old adage about never discussing religion or politics.) If you are interested in reading firsthand Kersey Graves's astonishing assertions, then I recommend you buy his book. It can be ordered from Amazon.

The name of the god is in ALL CAPS, BOLD, followed by the geographical location where they hailed from (or racial/ethnic background), and the approximate year of their crucifixion.

1. CHRISHNA (India; 1200 B.C.)

- His presence on earth and his death were to atone for the sins of Man.

- He was crucified to appease God.

- He was worshipped by his disciples as God.

- He has often been depicted in drawings as having a divine halo over his head.

- He has often been depicted in drawings as having a "Sacred Heart."

- The cross became a religious symbol and icon after his death.

- His full name was Chrishna Zeus, which some spelled as "Jeseus."

- He performed miracles, including healing the sick, curing lepers, restoring sight, sound, and speech, raising the dead, and casting out demons.

- A "divinely-inspired" book (*The Bhagavad-Gita*) told of his coming and his miraculous works.

- He was born of a virgin, and the mother and new-born child were visited by shepherds.

- He spent a period of reflection in the desert.

- He was baptized in the River Ganges. (Christ was baptized in the River Jordan.)

- He once miraculously enabled his hungry followers to catch many nets full of fish.

- He taught by parable and sermon.

- There is similarity in the two names, "Chrishna," and "Christ."

- The name of Chrishna's mother was "Maia," which is similar to "Mary."

- Chrishna was born on December 25th.

- He had an earthly adoptive father.

- He proclaimed to his followers, "I am the Resurrection."

- He had a last supper with his disciples before being crucified.

- He was crucified between two thieves.

- He was crucified around the age of thirty-three.

- He rose from the dead after three days buried.

- He physically ascended into heaven.

- He taught, "Seek and ye shall find."

- He spoke of the "blind leading the blind."

- He regarded carnal and earthly pleasures were evil.

- He taught that "Faith can move mountains."

- He taught his followers to love their enemies.

- He prophesied his return to earth, which he called a "Second Coming."

- He taught, "It is better to give than to receive."

2. SAKIA (Hindu; 600 B.C.)

- His emblem was a cross.

- One of the crimes for which he was crucified was that he illegally plucked a flower. (One of the charges against Christ was that he plucked an ear of corn on the Sabbath.)

- Legend has it that he was born to atone for man's sins.

- After he was crucified, Sakia was buried for three days, and then rose from the dead.

- He physically ascended into heaven.

- His titles included "Savior of the World," and "The Light of the World."

- His mother was known as "The Holy Virgin, Queen of Heaven."

- He was once tempted by the devil.

- He healed the sick and performed miracles.

- He preached "commandments" which included, "Thou shalt not kill," "Thou shalt not steal," "Thou shalt not commit adultery," "Thou shalt not lie," and "Thou shalt not become intoxicated."

The dates for the remaining fourteen gods are approximate.

3. THAMUZ (Syria; 1160 B.C.)

- He was called "The Risen Lord" and "The Savior."

- He was crucified to atone for man's sins.

- He rose from the dead after being buried.

4. WITTOBA (Telingonese; 552 B.C.)

- He was crucified for man's sins.

- He is usually depicted in drawings as having nail holes in is hands and in the soles of his feet.

- His icon is a cross.

5. IAO (Nepal; 622 B.C.)

- He was known as "The Savior."

- He was crucified on a tree.

- He was accepted by his followers as God incarnate.
- "Iao" (or "Jao") is thought to possibly be the root of "Jehovah."

6. HESUS (Celtic Druid; 834 B.C.)

- He was crucified with a lamb on one side and an elephant on the other. The elephant was thought to represent all the sins of the world and so, we have the "Lamb of God" dying to take away the sins of the world.

7. QUEXALCOTE (Mexico; 587 B.C.)

- He was crucified on a cross to atone for man's sins.
- He was crucified with two thieves.
- He rose from the dead after three days buried.
- He was born of a virgin mother from an "immaculate conception."
- He endured forty days of temptation and fasting.
- He rode a donkey.
- He was purified in a temple.
- He was anointed with oil.
- He forgave sins.
- He was baptized in water.

8. QUIRINUS (Rome; 506 B.C.)

- He was called "Savior."

- He was immaculately conceived and born of a virgin.

- His life was threatened by the reigning king.

- He rose from the dead after being crucified and buried.

- He physically ascended into heaven.

9. PROMETHEUS (Greece; 547 B.C.)

- He was nailed to a cross.

- His critical theological precept was that of "blood atonement."

- The earth shook when he died.

- He was known as "Our Lord and Savior."

- He rose from the dead.

10. THULIS (Egypt; 1700 B.C.)

- He was crucified at the age of 28.

- He rose from the dead after his crucifixion.

- He physically ascended into heaven.

- His death was supposed to benefit mankind.

11. INDRA (Tibet; 725 B.C.)

- He was known as "God and Savior."

- He was nailed to a cross.

- His side was pierced.

- His mother was a virgin.

- He had to die to atone for man's sins.

- He rose from the dead.

- He physically ascended into heaven.

- He could walk on water.

- He knew the future.

- He was believed to be eternal.

12. ALCESTOS (Euripides; 600 B.C.)

- Alcestos was the only female god who was crucified to atone for mankind's sins.

- She was part of a divine trinity.

13. ATYS (Phrygia; 1170 B.C.)

- He was believed to be the Messiah.

- He was crucified to atone for man's sins.

- He rose from the dead after being buried.

14. CRITE (Chaldea; 1200 B.C.)

- He was known as "The Redeemer."

- He was also known as "The Ever-Blessed Son of God"; "The Savior of the Race"; and "The Atoning Offering for an Angry God."

- The earth shook when he was crucified.

15. BALI (Orissa; 725 B.C.)

- He was believed to be God, as well as the Son of God.

- He was crucified in atonement.

- He was the second part of a divine trinity.

16. MITHRA (Persia; 600 B.C.)

- He was crucified to take away the sins of the world.

- He was born on December 25th.

Mithra

Chapter 12

12 ITEMS OF INFORMATION NOTED ON A DEATH CERTIFICATE

"Matters of fact...are very stubborn things."
—Matthew Tindal, *The Will of Matthew Tindal* (1733)

A death certificate must be filed whenever someone dies. Either the attending physician or the coroner fills it out and signs it, and it is filed in the county where the death occurred. Death certificates are public records and anyone can look at a filed death certificate at any time. A death certificate must be filed before the body is dispatched to its final abidance. As you can imagine, most death certificates are fairly routine legal documents, but there are a few questions on them that are intriguing and revealing.

For instance, one death certificate reviewed had a separate block for the question, "Was Decedent of Hispanic Origin?" and if so, it requires specifying Mexican, Puerto Rican, Cuban, etc.. There was only one block however, for every other race, including American Indian, Black, White, and so forth.

This feature abstracts some of the more interesting questions on a typical death certificate, and discusses some of the possible reasons for the particular inquiries.

1. **Age:** This is to be expected, right? Of course, but within the "Age" section are two poignant sections: "Under 1 Year" and then it requests the number of months and days the child lived, and even more heartbreaking, "Under 1 Day," which requests the number of hours and minutes the newborn survived.

2. **Was Decedent of Hispanic Origin?:** As noted above, this odd question is included on some official death certificates.

3. **Decedent's Education:** What does this have to do with a person's death and disposition?

4. **Method of Disposition:** This section offers five choices: Burial, Donation, Cremation, Removed from State, and Other. I assume the "Other" category would include Burial at Sea and, perhaps, Being Picked Clean By Birds, a body disposal custom favored by the Parsis of India.

5. **Name of Embalmer:** Accountability.

6. **Time of Death:** This information could play an important role in homicide investigations.

7. **Date Pronounced Dead:** The date of death could also be critical, especially to the IRS.

8. **Immediate Cause of Death:** This section is part of the overall "Cause of Death" section and this ques-

tion acknowledges that there is an immediate cause of death, but that often the underlying cause of death is more important. For instance, a young person could be found dead of cardiac arrest. This is the immediate cause of his demise. But it may then be determined that the cardiac arrest was caused by an overdose of crack, thus, the underlying cause. There is a relevant line from Jimmy Breslin's hilarious book about the Mafia, *The Gang That Couldn't Shoot Straight*. In it, one of the wiseguys is explaining the death of a rival organized crime soldier. He tells his colleagues that the guy died of "natural causes": "His heart stopped when I put a knife into it."

9. **Underlying Cause of Death:** Respiratory and cardiac arrest caused by lung cancer, for example.

10. **Was an Autopsy Performed?:** The State wants to know if one was, and if so, what was determined.

11. **Were Autopsy Findings Available Prior to Completion of Cause of Death?:** If they weren't, the message is that the "Cause" of death had better concur with the actuality and if it doesn't, there must be a good reason why it doesn't.

12. **Manner of Death:** This section offers six choices and they essentially cover all bases. They are Natural, Accident, Suicide, Homicide, Pending Investigation, and Could Not be Determined.

Chapter 13

DEATH WISHES: 7 SUICIDAL SPORTS

*"The thought of suicide is a great source of comfort:
with it a calm passage is to be made across many a
bad night."*
—Friedrich Nietzsche

It could be somewhat difficult to understand participating in a sport in which death is one possible outcome.

Participants say it's the thrill. The cheating of death. The endorphin rush. The personal satisfaction of actually doing it. Perhaps. But it says something about a person's personality that they really don't feel quite alive unless they're testing fate and daring death to take its best shot.

These seven activities don't all technically qualify as sports per se, but they are things that people do that could wind up killing them.

1. **Boxing:** This is a sport where you deliberately fight someone, and willingly allow yourself to be pummeled about the face and body by your opponent. Boxing

aficionados talk about the "technical" aspects of the "game," the arm extension, the weight differentials, the blows scored, etc. But all that aside, boxing comes down to a sanctioned brawl. Men have died in the ring, and that's what makes this a suicidal sport. It is also not the healthiest thing in the world to have your head bashed repeatedly.

2. **Bungee Jumping:** Tie an elastic rope to your ankles and then jump off a bridge. People have died while bungee jumping when their bungee cord snapped. Lately, air bags have been used when practical, but when the jump takes place over water or rocks, such a precaution is not always possible.

3. **Car Racing:** Drive around a narrow track in a tiny matchbox car at speeds almost faster than a speeding bullet, with a whole bunch of other guys trying to run you off the road. The accepted wisdom is that everyone goes to car races just to see the crashes. That should probably be a message to the drivers.

4. **Marathon Running:** Run twenty-six miles without stopping. People have died participating in marathons. Those endorphins must be worth it.

5. **Mountain Climbing:** This is a test of endurance that ultimately begins to kill the climber the higher they go. To this day there are unburied bodies on Mt. Everest of those climbers who couldn't survive the climb.

6. **Running with the Bulls:** People running through the streets of Pamplona, Spain are chased by a herd of en-

raged bulls. People are gored, trampled, and killed. The "festival" lasts nine days and includes eight bull runs.

7. **Sky-Diving:** Go up in an airplane and jump out. That is the essence of the sport of sky-diving. Sometimes the parachute fails to open. Then you die. But it is likely that your loved ones will get a refund.

I suppose there's always the possibility, when playing any sport, that one can be killed. Better to stay home and read a good book instead!

Chapter 14

68 EUPHEMISMS FOR DYING

No one wants to play in the last scene of this weird stage play called life, and yet, along with taxes, it is the only thing in our lives we can be absolutely, positively, bet-the-house sure will happen.

Here are 68 ways to say the curtain has come down (and perhaps you know others).

1. Answer the Final Summons
2. Answer the Last Call
3. Answer the Last Muster
4. Beam Up
5. Bite the Big One
6. Bite the Dust
7. Breathe Your Last
8. Buy Your Lunch
9. Buy the Farm
10. Cash In Your Chips
11. Climb the Golden Staircase
12. Cock Up Your Toes
13. Coil Up Your Ropes
14. Come Over
15. Croak
16. Cross Over

17. Cross the Great Divide
18. Depart to God
19. Drop Off the Hooks
20. Expire
21. Fade Away
22. Give Up the Ghost
23. Go Home
24. Go On To a Better World
25. Go the Way Of All Flesh
26. Go Tits Up
27. Go To Heaven
28. Go To Meet Your Maker
29. Go To Sleep
30. Go West
31. Hand In Your Chips
32. Join the Angels
33. Join the Great Majority
34. Kick Off
35. Kick the Bucket
36. Kiss the Dust
37. Lay Down the Knife and Fork
38. Pass Away
39. Pass In Your Chips
40. Pass In Your Marble
41. Pass On
42. Pass Out
43. Pass Over
44. Perish
45. Pop Off
46. Pop Off the Hooks
47. Pull a Cluck
48. Raise the Wind
49. Shit the Bed
50. Shuffle Off This Mortal Coil
51. Skip Out
52. Sling Your Hook
53. Slip Your Breath
54. Slip Your Cable
55. Slip Your Wind
56. Snuff It
57. Squiff It

58. Step Into Your Last Bus
59. Step Off
60. Step Out
61. Stick Your Spoon In the Wall
62. Sun Your Moccasins
63. Take An Earth Bath
64. Take the Long Count
65. Tap Out
66. Tip Over
67. Turn Your Face to the Wall
68. Yield Up the Ghost

Chapter 15

12 DEVICES, TOOLS & PRACTICES USED FOR SEXUAL ENHANCEMENT & DIVERSITY

Humankind as a species has spent a lot of time trying to improve its sex life. To wit:

1. **Anal Plugs:** Rubber or plastic plugs that are shaped like fingers or cones and are inserted into the anus to stimulate the rectal nerve endings. In males, the plugs also stimulate the highly sensitive prostate region. In females, the plugs tighten up the vagina. The plugs are used during intercourse or other sexual activity with a partner, or alone as an enhancement to masturbation. The plugs are between four and eight inches in length and fit most rear entrances. Sometimes the cone-shaped plugs get stuck. The rectum and anus have a series of sphincter muscles that tighten and expand during defecation or stimulation and occasionally, if a cone plug does not have a thick flange or rim at its wide end,

the butt will suck the cone up into its depths. This is not pleasant. Removal of anal plugs is not an uncommon procedure at hospital emergency rooms all over the world.

2. **Artificial Vaginas:** Hand-held latex or rubber masturbation tools that look exactly like a female vagina, complete with clitoris and pubic hair. Some of these ersatz orifices can be filled with warm water to give them a flesh like feel, and some are battery-powered and vibrate as well. Some are molded from porn stars' private parts.

3. **Ben Wa Balls:** Traditional Ben Wa Balls are an ancient and clever Oriental sex toy designed for females only. They are two small stainless steel balls that are inserted into the vagina and then left there for a period of time. The balls rub against the lining of the vagina and can cause continual sexual arousal. Many women report constant pleasure from Ben Wa Balls, but orgasm is uncommon since most women need some type of clitoral stimulation to achieve a climax.

4. **Catheters:** Thin, flexible tubes that are inserted into the male or female urethra and primarily used to drain the urinary bladder. Catheters, which have been used in sex play for close to 4,000 years, are of interest mainly to S & M enthusiasts primarily because use of a catheter gives the inserter total control over the insertee. Many S & M zealots find the obvious dominant/submissive nature of the encounter incredibly exciting. The catheter is actually inserted all the way into the bladder and

then urine flow is started and stopped at the whim of the dominant participant. Ejaculation during catheterization is not uncommon. According to sexologists and medical experts, the catheter stimulates the nerve-rich urethra/prostate/bladder region, and this stimulation is the appeal of this potentially dangerous practice.

5. **Cock Rings:** Rubber or leather rings that fit around the base of an erect penis and exert just enough pressure to help maintain an erection by constricting blood flow.

6. **Dildos:** Fake penises. They come in a variety of extremely lifelike shapes, sizes, and colors, and many have a scrotum, complete with individual testicles, attached. They are used by women for masturbation and to mount another woman in lesbian intercourse, and by both men and women to mount a male in anal intercourse. They are also used by impotent men as a means of satisfying their partner. They can be strapped on with a waist belt or used by hand. Two-headed penises are available for mutual lesbian intercourse. Some male porno stars have sat for plaster castings of their erections and testicles and then marketed the dildo under their own brand name. Women in X-rated films can be seen fellating dildos. They pretend to enjoy this but the primary purpose of such activity is visual stimulus.

7. **Electric Shock:** Used during sex to stimulate the genitals and other organs. Battery- and AC-powered prods and devices (like TENS units) are used to apply small electrical charges to the penis, testicles, vagina, clito-

ris, and anus. These devices should never used on the nipples (or anywhere above the waist for that matter) because the electrical current could interfere with the heart's normal rhythm and cause arrhythmia, palpitations, and in some cases, heart attack and death. There have been reported cases of electrocution when devices were used improperly or fell into water. Advocates claim electric shock intensifies and prolongs sexual arousal and orgasm.

8. **Enemas:** An enema is the insertion of liquid into a person's rectum. Enemas, which have been common in sex play since Egyptian times, have long been used for constipation and before anal sex to completely clean the anus. Today, wine and coffee enemas are popular because of the alcohol and caffeine content of the fluids.

9. **Footware:** Foot fetishism is an industry unto itself. Legs, feet, and toes have long been esteemed as sex objects, even though they have absolutely no connection with the genitals whatsoever (although foot reflexologists will argue that point). I guess this proves that the most powerful sex organ is the brain. A big part of foot fetishism is footware, which includes all kinds of shoes, as well as legware like nylon stockings, garter belts, socks, and pantyhose. The big favorite, of course, is high heels. These shoes have a devoted, occasionally fanatical following.

There are several theories as to why high heels are so popular, one of which is that men like the way women have to walk when they're wearing heels. The shoes' construction (especially the really high heels, 3 inches or more) change a woman's gait so that the hips sway more, the calf and thigh are emphasized, and the buttocks is prominent. This might be partially true but it does not explain the popularity of magazines in which women are posed in a reclining position wearing nothing but high heels. The nudity is a certainly a factor, of course, but the shoes themselves tend to be the focus of attention in these photos. Some psychologists claim that the potential threat of the stiletto-like heel of the shoe is a turn-on to men who have latent masochistic and submissive tendencies.

10. **Love Dolls:** Inflatable dolls that have open mouths, vaginas, and anuses. Men use these dolls as surrogate sex partners. Dolls are sold in sex shops and online and some X-rated film actresses have modeled for dolls marketed under their own brand name. Today, a popular, albeit expensive love doll is the Real Doll, hailed as the most realistic sexual experience short of doing it with a human being.

11. **Male Masturbators:** These are latex tubes into which the erect penis is inserted. When stroked up and down an erection, the tubes are supposed to simulate fellatio. Fleshlight is probably the most popular male masturbator.

12. **Vibrators:** Penis-shaped electrical (A/C or battery) devices that are used to stimulate the genitals, the anus, and the nipples. Women often insert a vibrator into the vagina, and men use it to penetrate the anus. There are

other types of vibrators that do not look like penises but vibrate electronically and are used for stimulation but not penetration.

Chapter 16

DR. ESE'S 11 SIGNS OF DEMONIC POSSESSION

Dr. Ese, a noted medieval researcher of the paranormal, came up with the following eleven indications that a person might be possessed by a demon or by Old Scratch himself. Some of these are scary: Centuries past, living alone and being ugly were enough to convince people that you were possessed. With those criteria, it wouldn't be too hard today for an awful lot of people to qualify for discount exorcisms.

1. Imagining yourself possessed.

2. Leading an evil life.

3. Living alone.

4. Chronic ailments, unusual symptoms, a deep sleep and/or the vomiting of strange things (although no specifics are offered as to what exactly the suspected possessee had to vomit in order to qualify).

5. Blaspheming and/or making frequent reference to the Devil.

6. Making a pact with the Devil.

7. Being controlled by spirits.

8. Having a face that inspires horror and fear. (This meant that you were suspected of being possessed by the Devil if you were ugly.)

9. Being tired of living and giving up all hope.

10. Being enraged and/or being violent.

11. Making the cries and noises of a beast.

Based on information in *An Encyclopaedia of Occultism* by Lewis Spence (University Books, 1960).

Chapter 17

63 BIZARRO FORMS OF DIVINATION

Lewis Spence, in his *An Encyclopaedia of Occultism* (University Books, 1960), defines divination as "The method of obtaining knowledge of the unknown or the future by means of omens." And just what exactly is an omen? An omen can be anything from entrails to arrows, and they are used in ways that go beyond being simply creative. Many of these practices move into the realm of being truly bizarro.

This listing of forms of divination ranges from "Aeromancy," which is using atmospheric phenomena such as thunder, lightning, comets, etc. to tell the future; to "Xylomancy," which is the Slavonic method of telling the future using the position of randomly found small pieces of wood that you happen to come across during a journey. For brevity, most forms of divination will be defined by the objects used. For instance, for "Anthropomancy," it will not say "The entrails of men and women are studied to tell the future," but rather, "Male and female entrails." You can assume that the things listed were all used in some manner to foretell future events.

1. **Aeromancy:** Observation of atmospheric phenomena such as thunder, lightning, clouds, comets, storms, etc.

2. **Alectryomancy:** A rooster pecked seeds of grain off letters drawn in a circle and spelled out the name of a person.

3. **Aleuromancy:** Messages written on paper were wrapped in balls of flour and then mixed up nine times and distributed. The person's fate was revealed by the flour ball they received. (This perhaps could have been the ancestral forefather of the Chinese fortune cookie.)

4. **Alomancy:** Salt.

5. **Alphitomancy:** Barley was given to people suspected of crimes and whoever got sick from eating it was guilty.

6. **Amniomancy:** The flesh "caul" membrane found on the faces of some newborns.

7. **Anthropomancy:** Male and female entrails.

8. **Apantomancy:** Chance meetings, especially with animals.

9. **Arithmancy:** Numbers.

10. **Armomancy:** Examination of the shoulders.

11. **Astrology:** Using the positions of the sun, the moon, and the planets in the Solar System to tell the future of specific individuals.

12. **Automatic Writing:** Messages from dead spirits channeled in writing through a medium who usually has to be in a trance to receive the writing.

13. **Axinomancy:** An axe or a hatchet.

14. Belomancy: Arrows.

15. Bibliomancy: A person suspected of being a wizard or sorcerer was weighed. If he weighed less than the local church's Bible, he was innocent.

16. Botanomancy: Carved-in questions appeared on burned brier branches.

17. Capnomancy: The observation of smoke. (Sometimes smoke from the burning of poppy seeds.)

18. Catoptromancy: Use of a mirror.

19. Causimomancy: Fire.

20. Ceraunoscopy: Examination of the air.

21. Ceroscopy: Melted wax disks were read by a magician.

22. Clairaudience: Spirit voices would speak to the person with clairvoyance and reveal information.

23. Clairvoyance: The ability to see people and events distant in time and/or space.

24. Cleromancy: The throwing of lots, using black and white beans, bones, stones, etc.

25. Clidomancy: The name of a person who figures into some situation is written upon a key which is then hung onto a Bible. The Bible is then hung on the finger nail of the ring finger of a virgin. The direction in which the swaying book turns determines the fate of the person in question.

26. Coscinomancy: A sieve, a pair of scissors, and the thumb nails of two people are used in concert to determine innocence or guilt. The sieve is hung by a thread from the shears which are supported on the thumb nails of the two people in question. The direction of the sieve's spin determined the guilty party.

27. **Critomancy:** Cakes.

28. **Crystalomancy:** Also known as crystal gazing, this form of divination involves a seer looking into a crystal ball or some similar object to tell the future.

29. **Dactylomancy:** Rings.

30. **Daphnomancy:** Throwing a laurel branch into a fire.

31. **Demonomancy:** Turning to demons for occult knowledge.

32. **Direct Writing:** This is similar to **Automatic Writing**, except that in **Direct Writing**, the writing appears on its own, with no intervention from a human medium.

33. **Eromanty:** The use of air. The Persians devised this method of divination in which they would breathe over a vase filled with water. Bubbles in the water meant that the objects of their desire would come to them.

34. **Gastromancy:** Seers would hear voices emanate from a person's belly and answer questions. This was often just a fraudulent form of ventriloquism.

35. **Gyromancy:** A small circle was drawn on the ground and the letters of the alphabet were written on its circumference. The person who wanted an answer to a question stood inside the circle and was spun around repeatedly until he was too dizzy to stand up. The letters he stumbled over as he fell out of the circle spelled out his answer.

36. **Hippomancy:** The movement of certain sacred white horses divined the future.

37. **Hydromancy:** Refers to various uses of water as a means of divination, including throwing things into water, and suspending things on a string over water.

38. **Kephalonomancy:** This is one of those ancient practices that makes us curious about just how bizarro those ancients actually were. This practice involved burning a piece of carbon on the head of an ass (or sometimes a goat) and reciting the name of suspected criminals. If a crackling sound was heard when a certain person's name was mentioned, the guy was guilty as charged.

39. **Lithomancy:** Any number of forms of divination using stones.

40. **Margaritomancy:** A pearl was placed beneath an upside down vase. As in many other forms of divination, the names of suspected bad guys were then recited. When a guilty person's name was mentioned, the pearl would purportedly fly upwards and shatter the bottom of the vase.

41. **Muscle-Reading:** A form of fortune-telling in which a seer reads the muscles of a person who is suspected of knowing some truth that needs to be revealed. It was based on the principle that muscles (especially throat muscles) will shape themselves into the position of a name thought of by a person and a qualified seer could then interpret the movements as words.

42. **Myomancy:** The behavior of rats or mice.

43. Necromancy: The spirits of the dead reveal the future and answer questions.

44. Onimancy: Divination by observation of a manifestation of the angel Uriel after oil of walnuts mingled with tallow is placed on the fingernails of an "unpolluted" boy or a young virgin.

45. Onomancy: The spelling of and distribution of vowels and consonants in a person's name.

46. Onychomancy: Divination by observing the sun's reflection in a person's fingernails.

47. Ooscopy: Eggs.

48. Oomantia: Eggs.

49. Ornithomancy: The flight and/or song of birds.

50. Phyliorhodomancy: Rose leaves.

51. Psychomancy: This is similar to necromancy in that the spirits of the dead are invoked for purposes of divination.

52. Psychometry: Telling the future by holding something possessed by a person.

53. Pyromancy: Telling the future by reading fire.

54. Rhabdomancy: Using a rod or a staff for divination.

55. Rhapsodamancy: This method of divination involved opening a book of randomly selected poetry and reading the first verse the eye fell upon.

56. Seances: People sit in a circle with a seer and attempt to communicate with the dead.

57. Slate Writing: A form of Direct Writing.

58. Spodomancy: Divination by reading the ashes and cinders of any number of different sacrificial fires.

59. Stolcheomancy: A form of **Rhapsodamancy** in which the works of Homer or Virgil are used.

60. Stolisomancy: The way a person dresses him or herself.

61. Sycomancy: The leaves of the fig tree.

62. Tephremancy: A form of **Spodomancy** in which the fire had to have consumed certain sacrificial victims.

63. Xylomancy: The Slavonic method of telling the future using the position of randomly found small pieces of wood that you happen to come across during a journey.

Chapter 18

6 FORMS OF PENIS MODIFICATION

Penis modification is one of the most extreme forms of bizarro sexual behavior known to man.

Why change your penis? Penis modification is used to enhance the organ for sex. With penis modification, the penis is almost looked upon not as an organ with which we should accept and use, but rather as a tool that should be improved, if possible.

1. **Bihari Surgery:** During Bihari Surgery, a ligament in the groin above the penis is surgically severed. This allows what is essentially a dangling erection. This makes men who have the surgery look better endowed than they actually are, usually adding one-and-one-half to two inches in length. It also allows for a wider variety of sexual positions, since the post-surgery penis has a wider range of motion than the normal erection, which is suspended upright from the groin. This procedure was named after an Egyptian doctor named Bihari.

2. **Foreskin Restoration:** There are two types of Foreskin Restoration, surgical and non-surgical. One non-surgical technique, known as tissue expansion, involves stretching the skin of the flaccid penis a little at a time until enough new skin has grown to cover the head of the penis. Each stretch tears the skin and the body responds by growing more. This process could take years.

Another—a skin graft procedure using scrotal skin—is a bit more bizarre.

Mark Waring, author of the 1988 book, *Foreskin Restoration*, described this type of procedure in his book and it was discussed in Brenda Love's *The Encyclopedia of Unusual Sex Practices:*

"[The skin graft method] consists of cutting the ring of skin approximately an inch below the glans penis, pulling the top skin forward so that it covers the glans, then cutting two parallel openings into the scrotum that are perpendicular to the penis. The penis is then inserted into this open pocket so that the cut area on the penis is covered, yet the top of the glans still extrudes far enough for urination. The man is sent home and after almost a year returns for the second surgical procedure which consists of detaching the skin surrounding the penis from the scrotum and securing it into place. Complications with this type of surgery include scarring, disfiguring, and possible growth of scrotal hair on the new foreskin."

Foreskin Restoration is apparently so popular that it even had its own magazine for a time, *Foreskin Quar-*

terly, and its own organization, Brothers United for Future Foreskins (BUFF).

3. **Meatotomy:** The deliberate enlargement of the urethra. The way it's done is by inserting progressively larger and larger diameter catheters into the urethra during masturbation, each time tearing and widening the urethral tube and then allowing it to heal in the larger size. Each time the urethra is torn, new skin grows to fill in the tear until after many deliberate enlargements, the urethra is huge. There are men who have enlarged their urethras so much that they can accept the head of another man's penis into the opening.

4. **Penis Implants:** This modification is not to be confused with the procedure of implanting a rod or inflatable tube in an impotent man's penis in order to allow him to have intercourse. This type of implanting has as its goal making the penis look like a French tickler condom. (The ones with all the bumps.) Men who are into this type of "improvement" slice open the skin of their penis shaft, insert balls, stones, beads, pearls, and other solid, hard, usually round objects into the slits and then allow the incisions to close and heal. There are some women who greatly enjoy this type of erection enhancement, although it could be somewhat uncomfortable for the "modified" man when he is not having sex.

5. **Penis Inserts:** This is like piercing (see the list on Body Parts People Pierce) only a bar or a ring is inserted

into the head of the penis, configured so that it enters through the urethra and comes out beneath the head.

6. **Penis Splitting:** This involves actually cutting the penis in half, lengthwise, like splitting open a sausage. The organ is sliced down the shaft, from the head to the groin, and when done properly, the two halves can heal into two distinct, fully-functioning penises.

One man who took years to complete the process, described the results in *The Encyclopedia of Unusual Sex Practices*:

"My decision to surgically remodel my genitals was deliberate, of deep satisfaction to me, highly exciting, sexually adventurous, and erotically exhilarating... Full erections are still maintained as previously, but now in two complete, separate halves. The erotic zones of my penis are still the same, with orgasms and ejaculations functioning perfectly. Entry into the vagina requires a little extra effort for insertion, but once my penis is inside, its opened effect on the vagina's inner lining is more pronounced, giving better female orgasmic feelings."

Chapter 19

7 BIZARRO PHYSICAL THINGS THAT CAN GO WRONG WITH THE HUMAN BODY

"Est modus in rebus, sunt certi denique fines, Quos
ultra citraque nequit consistere rectum."
"Things have their due measure; there are ultimately
fixed limits, beyond which, or short of which,
something must be wrong."
—Horace, *Satires*

Barnum & Bailey used to advertise their freak show as "The Peerless Prodigies of Physical Phenomena and Great Presentation of Marvelous Living Human Curiosities." It may have been hyperbolic, but it sure as hell worked to draw the crowds. (An analogue to the old freak shows are today's show's like Discovery Life's *Body Bizarre*, which looks at physical anomalies, but always focuses on "fixing" the person and presents their stories with compassion.)

Throughout man's time on this planet, things have consistently gone wrong with the development of the fetus in utero, or later, with growth and/or the health of some particular body part or function. In the past, before modern medicine, often these "freaks of nature" died. In many cases, however, they survived and had to earn their keep by exhibiting their deformities in circus freak shows. (Tod Browning's classic 1932 film, *Freaks*, chronicles life in a freak show.)

Here are seven things that can go wrong with the human body both before and after birth. (Often things like weird abilities or skin disorders don't manifest themselves until later in life.) We've all seen the new mommy and daddy counting their babies toes and fingers to first, make sure they're all there, and finally, to make sure they're aren't any extra. There's good cause for that practice, as you'll see from the following.

1. **Bizarre Eyeball and Ear Abilities:** Some people can pop their eyeballs out of their sockets and blow smoke through their eyes and out of their ears.

2. **Bizarre Skin Disorders:** Strange types of human skin have included alligator-like skin, skin that can be stretched like rubber, and hard, elephant-like skin. People have developed massive wart-like growths that look like tree branches or wood and completely entomb hands and/or feet.

3. **Enormous Testicles:** This is actually a medical condition called elephantiasis. The *Bantam Medical Dictionary* defines the disease as "a gross enlargement of the skin and underlying tissues caused by obstruction of the lymph vessels, which prevents drainage of lymph from the surrounding tissues. Inflammation and thickening of the walls of the vessels and their eventual blocking is commonly caused by the parasitic filarial worms. The

parts most commonly affected are the legs but the scrotum, breasts, and vulva may also be involved. Elastic bandaging is applied to the affected parts and the limbs are elevated and rested."

Elephantiasis is mostly found in tropical countries and explicit photos of afflicted natives are common in many books about freaks and human oddities. In some men, their scrotum enlarges to the size of a large watermelon and bigger. In some cases, the scrotum becomes so large, it is big enough to be sat upon like a hassock. The treatment for elephantiasis is the drug diethylcarbamazine, which kills the worm larva that are in the bloodstream.

4. **Huge or Extra Breasts:** Extra breasts or nipples is called polymastia or pleomastia. In 1886, two women lived who both had ten breasts each, all of which secreted milk. In 18th century France, a polymastic woman named Madame Ventre lived in Marseilles. Madame Ventre had a fully-functioning, lactating breast sticking out of her left thigh just below her waist. In 1894, a case was reported of a man who possessed eight breasts.

In modern times, one of the most common forms of polymastia is three nipples. Celebrities who have shown or admitted to having three nipples include Mark Wahlberg, Bill Paxton, Tilda Swinton, and Carrie Underwood.

Huge breasts is another condition involving women's mammary glands. (Enlarged breasts in males has its own name. gynecomastia.) Some women suffering from this condition are so big their natural breasts hang down to their waist. One case involved a woman whose breasts weighed forty-four pounds and measured thirty-three inches in circumference.

5. **Huge Buttocks:** This is called steatopygia and is characterized by the accumulation of huge amounts of fat in the buttocks. It is also called the "Hottentot Bustle," named after the Hottentot Tribe of Africa where this condition was first noted. Today, this grotesque enlargement of the buttocks is thought by the medical establishment to be possibly an evolutionary development that allows the storage of large amounts of body fat without impeding heat loss from the rest of the body. Another characteristic of steatopygia is really long labia minor that hang down between the knees.

6. **No Arms:** People born without arms become incredibly adept at doing things with their feet and toes. Some astonishing abilities manifested by these limbless wonders include painting, playing the violin and guitar, shooting a rifle, driving a carriage, writing "longfoot," driving a car, playing the mandolin, playing cards, and doing carpentry work. One British man with no arms was such a talented foot pianist that he performed on concert tours and earned his living as Tommy Toes Jacobsen. Mark Goffeney, the guitarist for the band Big Toe, was born without arms and plays guitar and bass in the band with his feet.

7. **Siamese Twin Syndrome:** Siamese twins, which today are properly called conjoined twins, are twins born

joined together at some body part, and sometimes sharing common internal organs. The term "Siamese twin" came from the twins Chang and Eng who were born conjoined at the stomach in Siam in 1874. Two terms used to describe conjoined twins are "Cephalopagi," which means joined at the top of the head, and "Ischiopagi," meaning joined at the groin. Sometimes the twin is alive and functioning and lives a long life; sometimes the twin is just a parasitic non-viable appendage that juts out from somewhere on the host's body.

Here is a look at eighteen notable conjoined twins:

- **Betty Lou Williams:** Betty Lou had a twin growing out of her waist that had buttocks and a pair of legs.

- **Bill Durks:** Bill was two-faced. Literally. He possessed two noses and two eyes and, for commercial purposes, painted a third eye in the middle of his forehead. Bill's mouth was split at the middle of his upper lip and looked like two mouths.

- **Daisy and Violetta Hilton:** These conjoined girls were stunningly beautiful and both were talented musicians. They were joined at the hips and yet both had very active sex lives. They claimed to be able to separate themselves mentally when the other was having sex.

- **Donni and Ronnie Galyon:** These two males were joined at the stomach.

- **Edward Mordrake:** Mordrake had a second face on the back of his head that could laugh and cry but not eat or speak.

○ **Frank Lentini:** Frank was born in 1889 in Sicily and had three legs and two complete sets of sex organs. Photographs exist of Frank showing the camera his extra leg and two penises.

○ **Laloo:** Laloo was a Hindu who was born in Oudh in 1874. He had a headless twin attached to his body at the neck. The twin had two arms and two legs, and a functioning set of genitals. The twin could urinate and get an erection.

○ **Liou-Tang-Sen and Lious-Seng-Sen:** Two males who were joined by a thin strip of skin at the stomach.

○ **Macha and Dacha:** These guys had two complete upper bodies and two heads, and shared one lower body.

○ **Margaret and Mary Gibb:** These girls were joined at the buttocks and refused to separate even though doctors believed the operation would be successful. They died together in 1967.

○ **Margarete Clark:** She had a small twin growing out of her belly. It looked as though the twin's head was stuck in Margarete's belly, face down, with the buttocks facing away from Margarete's body.

○ **Millie and Christina:** These were conjoined slave girls who were born in 1851 in North Carolina. Their father was an American Indian, and their mother was a mulatto slave. They were joined at the back.

○ **Myrtle Corbin:** Myrtle had a twin growing out from between her legs. Myrtle had four legs, twenty toes, and two vaginas. During her life, she had five children, four girls and one boy. Three of her children were born from one body, and two were born from the other. Myrtle's husband usually had intercourse in the twin's vagina.

Myrtle Corbin

○ **Pasquel Piñon:** Pasquel was born in Mexico in 1917 and had an extra head on his forehead.

○ **Rita and Christina:** These conjoined twins were born in 1829 in Sassari, Sardinia, and had a double body above the waist. They had two heads, four arms, four lungs, two hearts, two stomachs, one bladder, and two legs.

○ **Rosa and Josepha Blazek:** These twins were born in Bohemia in the late 18th century and were joined at the waist. They had one anus, but two vaginas. In 1910, Rosa got pregnant and had a baby. Josepha claimed not to have been aware of her sister having sex although many Siamese twins claim that their nervous systems are somehow linked to their twins and that they feel what the other feels.

○ **The Tocci Brothers:** These Italian twins were born in 1877 and had two heads and two upper torsos, but shared one set of legs.

○ **Abby and Brittany Hensel:** These twins were born in 1990 and are dicephalic parapagus twins. They each have a separate head, heart, stomach, spine, and lungs. They share digestive and reproductive systems, have two breasts and three kidneys.

Chapter 20

THE 35 HIGHEST-CHOLESTEROL FOODS KNOWN TO MAN

One of the drawbacks of meat consumption is cholesterol. Cholesterol is a fatty substance that is only found in animal protein that clings to your artery walls like the thick brown gunk that lined the walls of people's houses in the Midwest after the 1993 Mississippi River floods finally receded. (The Midwesterners call the stuff "gumbo.")

The difference, however, is that cholesterol can't be scraped off your arteries all that easily, and if enough of it builds up, it's goodbye guy or gal.

Here are 35 foods and dishes that, if partaken of on a regular basis, will make your cardiologist shake her head and start talking about the wisdom of "pre-need" funeral planning. Bon appetit!

FOOD	CHOLESTEROL
3 oz. of cooked pork brains	2,169 mg
3 oz. of cooked beef brains	1,746 mg
1 cup of stabilized dry eggs	1,714 mg
1 cup of plain dry eggs	1,615 mg
6 oz. of cooked beef sweetbreads	1,560 mg
1 cup of egg salad	1,124 mg
7 oz. of braised lamb sweetbreads	932 mg
1 cup of stewed chicken liver	884 mg
1 cup of stewed turkey liver	876 mg
6 oz. of braised pork spleen	856 mg
1 cup of scrambled eggs	854 mg
1 whole fried chicken with skin, batter-dipped	810 mg
2 slices of braised beef kidney	750 mg
1 whole duck, roasted with skin	640 mg
1 jar Gerber's Egg Yolks Baby Food	622 mg
6 oz. of braised pork liver	604 mg
1 2-egg omelet	536 mg
3 oz. of cooked pork kidney	408 mg
1 cup of braised beef heart	398 mg
2 cups of cheese soufflé	392 mg
3 oz. of fried beef liver	372 mg
1 cup of stewed turkey gizzards	336 mg
1 serving of chicken giblets, floured and fried	335 mg
1 cup of stewed turkey heart	328 mg
2 slices of Quiche Lorraine (9" pie)	318 mg
12 oz. of roasted turkey breast with skin	310 mg
4 tablespoons of Hollandaise sauce	298 mg
1 hard-cooked egg	274 mg
6 oz. of cooked pork tongue	248 mg

6 oz. of cooked pork chitterlings	244 mg
1 raw duck liver	227 mg
1 6 oz. pork fritter	222 mg
1 cup of turkey fat	209 mg
8 oz. of eggnog	150 mg
1 cup of cooked pork sausage	124 mg

Postscript

8 oz. of human breast milk	34 mg

Chapter 21

25 HORRIFIC TORTURES AND PUNISHMENTS THROUGH THE AGES

This looks at some of the techniques humans have devised to inflict pain upon fellow humans.

What is it about certain people that causes them to be so creative and inventive when it comes to finding new ways to cause suffering? Is it a brain chemistry kind of thing? Or is it purely environmental? The guy having his testicles removed by having them tied off and "strangulated" probably doesn't really care that much about how his castrator came to his dream career. Some of these vile acts are still being practiced today.

1. **Bamboo Under the Fingernails:** This Chinese torture is agonizingly painful and would often guarantee the confession the torturers wanted. Long thin shoots of sharp bamboo would be inserted beneath the fingernails of the victim, usually all the way back to the cuticle, and then left there. If the prisoner resisted sur-

rendering the wanted information, another finger was done. And another. And then another. If all ten fingers didn't do the trick, there were always the toenails.

2. **The Brank:** This was a mean one. Here we have an English device designed to punish women who talked too much. The Brank, which was also known as The Scolder's Bridle, consisted of a steel cage that was worn on the head like a helmet. Inside the cage was a protruding steel plate that either had sharp spikes on it or which was cruelly sharpened. This plate was placed in the offending woman's mouth so that if she even moved her tongue she would do major damage to her mouth and tongue and experience excruciating pain. The woman had to wear this contraption in and about town and occasionally a chain was attached to the front of the Brank so that she could be led around like a dog on a leash.

3. **Castration:** A wire or cord was wrapped around the base of the victim's scrotum and the testicles were either cut off or pulled off.

4. **The Chinese Water Torture:** A prisoner was tied to a table and his head was strapped in place so that he couldn't move anything but his eyes. Water was then dripped onto his forehead, one inexorable drop at a time. Apparently this was absolutely maddening, and after a period the victim would reveal the secret, confess to the crime, or agree to do anything his or her captors requested to get them to stop the drip, drip, drip. This doesn't sound as if it would be too hard to take,

but reports from people who have undergone it con-firm it to be devilishly effective. This was particularly favored in circumstances where torture was necessary, but no evidence of physical damage could show.

5. **Disemboweling:** This could ostensibly be considered a form of execution since not too many people can sur-vive having their upper and lower transverse colons and their stomachs surgically removed (without anesthesia of course) and not put back, but we've included it here because disembowelment was often used as a means of torture/punishment during which the victim just hap-pened to die. Victims of this horrible torment were usually tied to a post or a tree and then their abdomen was sliced open and their innards were pulled out and either left hanging or cut out completely and thrown on the ground. Sometimes the victim was forced to watch his guts set on fire while he was still alive. Need-less to say, because of the violent trauma to the body, it did not take long for this form of torture to turn into an execution. Vlad the Impaler was a big fan of disem-bowelment.

6. **The Drunkard's Cloak:** If an Englishman was found guilty of public drunkenness, he was often obligated to wear a Drunkard's Cloak, which was essentially a huge, heavy barrel which covered the offender from knees to neck, and from which only his arms, legs, and head protruded. Sometimes weights were hung off the barrel or off the wretch's wrists to make it even more difficult to walk about. This was considered one of the most hu-

miliating forms of punishment that could be inflicted on an evil-doer.

7. **The Ducking Stool:** This was mainly used to punish "scolding women" and women of "bad repute" in England and Scotland although brewers of bad beer and bakers of bad bread were also punished in this manner. The Ducking Stool device was either on wheels and mobile or permanently erected by the side of a river. An arm chair (which was actually quite comfortable) was fastened to the end of a long (twelve to fifteen feet) wooden beam which was attached by a bolt in the center of the beam to a cross bar so as to allow the arm to be raised and lowered at will like a see-saw. A rope was hung off the shore end of the bar and the "guilty" woman was repeatedly lowered into the cold water for varying amounts of time "to cool her immoderate heat." Sometimes the man in charge of administering the punishment (and it was always a man) would get carried away and leave the woman beneath the water too long and accidentally drown her. The Ducking Stool was being used as recently as the late 1800s both in England and the colonial United States.

8. **The Finger Pillory:** This was what it sounds like: a mini-Pillory designed for one or more fingers. The oak top bar would be closed tightly at the knuckle onto a finger which had been bent into a right angle pointing down. There was no way for the finger to be removed until the bar was opened and after a short time, the pain was excruciating.

9. **Foot Roasting:** This one must have hurt like hell. Literally. Foot Roasting was one of Tomás de Torquemada's favorite Spanish Inquisition tortures and was greatly feared. The procedure for this torment consisted of exactly what it says: A prisoner's feet were covered with lard and then slow-roasted over a fire for hours.

10. **The Garrote:** This torture involved binding a prisoner to a rack and tying ropes around his arms and legs. The rope was then slowly tightened and tightened until it ate through first skin, then layers of muscle, until it finally reached the bone. If a person was left tied up long enough on the rack, gangrene and blood poison-

ing would often set in. But by the time that happened the victim was usually either in shock or dead.

11. **The Garrucha:** This was one of the three most-favored Spanish Inquisition tortures. A prisoner's hands were bound behind his back and he was then picked up off the floor by his wrists by a chain suspended from the ceiling. When his body reached a certain height, his captors would begin slowly lowering him to the floor with jerky, bouncy pulls on the chain. By the time the victim reached the floor, both of his arms were usually pulled out their sockets.

12. **Hacking To Pieces:** Depending on what and how many body parts were hacked off determined whether this was a torture/punishment or a form of execution. If a hand or a foot (or more than one) was lopped off with a sword or an ax, the victim could survive, and then hacking was considered to be a punishment. Runaway slaves in pre-Civil War America were often hobbled by having one foot chopped off if they were caught. Larcenous workers in African diamond mines were also punished in like manner. Some Far Eastern countries (Iraq and Iran in particular) still use amputation of the hands as punishment for certain crimes, especially stealing.

13. **Hat Nailing:** Vlad Dracul the Impaler, the inspiration for the Dracula legend, came up with this one. Two Italian ambassadors once refused to take off their hats in his presence. Their punishment was having their hats nailed to their heads.

14. Impalement: Impalement was a particular favorite of Vlad the Impaler. This form of torture/execution involved impaling people on wooden spikes and leaving them to die a horrible and painful slow death. The impalement was often done up the rectum, or sometimes through the stomach or heart. Occasionally, for variety, Vlad would impale people upside down through the skull. Sometimes just the head was impaled, but this was more a form of decorating than torture since the owner of the head was usually long dead by the time he was put on display. In Cambodia, Pol Pot's barbarous Khmer Rouge was particularly enamored of head impaling.

15. The Jougs: This English device was nothing more than an iron collar that opened in the back and had a ring for a padlock in front. The jougs were usually attached by chain to a public site such as a church door or a pole or tree in the town center. Its primary purpose was to serve as a means for public humiliation, but, as was often the case with our oh-so-inventive forefathers, additional torments were often added to confinement in the jougs.

16. The Pillory: The Pillory was a form of standing stocks. A 17th century historian named Holloway described the Pillory at Rye, England: "It measures about six feet in height, by four in width. It consists of two up-posts affixed to a platform, and has two transverse rails upper one of which is divided horizontally, and has a hinge to admit of the higher portion being lifted, so as to allow of the introduction of the culprit's head and hands."

Offenders were put into the pillory for public humiliation and often the evidence of the crime (bad meat,
stolen bread, etc.) was hung around their neck. Some
towns combined a Pillory with Stocks and a Whipping
Post, providing convenient one-stop punishment. The
Pillory in and of itself wasn't too bad, but it was the
"add-on" punishments that turned this into a genuine
torture. Citizens convicted to stand in the Pillory often had to also endure having their ears nailed to the
Pillory, having their ears sliced off after their sentence
was served, and having their noses slit open and then
burned with a hot iron.

17. **Rape:** Women have always known that rape is not a
crime of sexual passion, but rather, a crime of violence,
and throughout the ages, the rape of women has been
utilized as a particularly heinous and devastating form
of torture. For example, the Serbs use rape as a weapon
of war. There are reports that Serb troops have been
ordered to rape Muslim women at will, even going
so far as to chain young girls in "rape rooms" where
entire battalions of soldiers gang-rape them in numb-
ing succession. Variations on rape as a form of torture
include using sexual congress as the ultimate form of
humiliation: After the invading soldiers have had their
way with the women, fathers are forced to rape their
daughters while the mothers watch; sons are forced to
rape their mothers; brothers are forced to have sex with
their pre-adolescent sisters. Aside from the horrifying
dehumanizing effect of being raped, another, more insidious reason for the practice is that it contributes to

"ethnic cleansing." The raped women often give birth to children sired by the invading soldiers, thus essentially diluting the victimized enemies' blood line.

18. **The Repentance Stool:** This old form of Scottish punishment wasn't very violent but it was considered especially humiliating since it was carried out in a church before all the other worshipers. The Repentance Stool was an elevated stool with a foot rest. Persons guilty of adultery were forced to sit on the stool in the front of the church during services and be gazed upon by all the other holier-than-thou parishioners. Sometimes a black hood was put over the person's head.

19. **Riding The Stang:** This was a particularly ridiculous form of punishment that once again resorted to public humiliation for maximum deterrent effect. If a man was suspected of beating his wife or being "henpecked," his fellow townsfolk would ride the stang for three consecutive night. Riding the Stang basically involved making fun of the suspected husband. The wittiest man in the town would be carried through the streets on a chair carried on the shoulders of some of the other local males. He would beat a drum and make up insulting rhymes about the husband. One (rather humorous) rhyme from Yorkshire, England went as follows (the language has been modernized for reading ease):

Heigh dilly, how dilly, heigh dilly dang,
It's neither for your part nor my part
That I ride the stang;
But it is for Jack Soloman—

His wife he does bang.
He banged her, he banged her,
He banged her indeed;
He banged the poor woman,
Though she stood him no need.

20. **Scalding:** This consisted of pouring large quantities of boiling water onto a victim's bare skin. One of the most notable sufferers of this torture was a Japanese man named Anthony Ixida, who was once scalded for thirty-three days because of his adherence to Catholicism. He was beatified after his death but never canonized as a saint.

21. **Skinning:** This involved slowly stripping thick layers of skin off the victim's body while they remained conscious. Sometimes salt was poured onto the raw exposed flesh.

22. **The Spanish Water Torture:** This was a particularly horrifying torture that was mainly used to extract confessions from suspected criminals. Also known as The Toca, this insidious procedure was used during the Spanish Inquisition and was as feared as Foot Roasting. A suspect was tied to a rack that swiveled in the middle so that his head could be positioned lower than his feet. The man's head was strapped in place with an iron band and his nose was sealed shut. A thick piece of cloth was then stuffed into his mouth and a slow, steady stream of water was poured into the cloth. The effect combined drowning and suffocation, all while

the victim remained completely conscious. This torture was one of anti-Semite Tomás de Torquemada's inventions. A form of this torture is still practiced today and is known as "waterboarding."

23. **The Stocks:** The stocks were a wooden device that had holes in it for the offender's legs. The criminal was locked in the stocks for many hours at a stretch, outdoors, and often had to submit to verbal humiliation as well as confinement. "Bathroom breaks" were not allowed, and after a couple of hours, there would be considerable back and leg pain and stiffness.

24. **Teeth Pulling:** The torturer would take an iron pincers and, one by one, wrench the victim's teeth out of their mouth. One of the most notable historical personages to undergo this particularly nasty form of persuasion was St. Apollonia, who died in the year 249. Her teeth were yanked for her refusal to renounce her Christianity. She is now the patron saint of dentists. (Not kidding.)

25. **Whipping:** Flogging was a very popular form of punishment in Olde England, and the scourge of the lash was meted out to both men and women in equal measure. There were two ways a whipping sentence was carried out. One was on a "whipping cart," which was wheeled about the town to the sites where a flogging was needed. The guilty party was stripped naked in the street and tied to the back of the cart and then whipped publicly until his or her body was bloody. The nudity of both men and women alike was a favorite attraction

of flogging. The second type of whipping was done at a "whipping post," a sturdy piece of pole in the center of a town that the offender was tied to naked and, as on the cart, whipped until bloody. Eventually the nudity requirement was modified for convicted women: They were only undressed to the waist, much to the dismay of the sadistic voyeurs who attended all public floggings. A particularly nasty English judge named Jeffreys is on record as once saying, "Hangman, I charge you to pay particular attention to this lady. Scourge her soundly, man; scourge her till her blood runs down! It is Christmas, a cold time for a madam to strip. See that you warm her shoulders thoroughly!" On many occasions, a person was whipped until they died.

Chapter 22

48 RELIGIOUS PHENOMENA, INCLUDING WEEPING & BLEEDING STATUES AND SIGHTINGS OF THE VIRGIN MARY

Atheists don't believe that there is anything other than this world. Their ideology states that there is no God; miracles are impossible; and the purpose of organized religions is to keep the masses intellectually and emotionally sedated. They dismiss religious experiences such as Virgin Mary sightings or other unexplainable spiritual phenomena as mass hallucinations or hoaxes. They believe that by turning to, or depending on, an outside force for help, judgment, and forgiveness, we deny our essential humanity and refuse to accept reality. The bottom line of their philosophy is that belief in God is a crutch, and that until mankind as a species outgrows the need to depend on such fairy tales, we will never solve the very real problems of real people in our very real world.

All are entitled to believe as they wish. But what about the *real* miracles, if there is such a thing? What about documented cases of seemingly impossible events? What about the following 48 cases—all of which have occurred since 1969—of religious phenomena? The atheists will dismiss these events as delusions or natural phenomena that we cannot yet understand. The faithful will look to them as a sign that there is indeed a supernatural power and that life does indeed go on after our brief stint here on Earth. The specific meanings, or lack thereof, of these 48 purported paranormal occurrences is in the eyes, heart, and soul of the beholder.

1968

Cairo, Egypt
Our Lady of Zeitoun appears above a church in Cairo, Egypt.

Can you see the Virgin Mary to the left of the dome?

December 1969
Tarpon Springs, Florida, USA
An icon of St. Nicholas weeps.

1970
Lanciano, Italy
Bread and wine that miraculously turned to real flesh and blood
in the 8th century are examined scientifically and determined
to still be human flesh and blood twelve centuries later.

May 1970
Chicago, Illinois, USA
Blood oozes from the 1700-year-old remains of St. Maximina.

The 1970s
Havana, Cuba
The Virgin Mary appears several times standing on the water
of Havana Bay.

January 3, 1971
Maropati, Italy
A painting of the Virgin Mary weeps real blood.

1972
Madrid, Spain
A statue of the Virgin Mary weeps blood from the eyes and
heart a total of eleven times.

1972
Syracuse, Sicily, Italy
A limestone crucifix bleeds.

December 19, 1972
Ravenna, Italy
A Fatima statue of the Virgin Mary weeps.

January 1972
Monterrey, Mexico
A statue of the Infant Jesus breathes, sweats, and weeps every day for 15,000 people.

1973
Akita City, Japan
A statue of the Virgin Mary weeps from its right hand.

August 1973
Naples, Italy
A picture of Jesus bleeds.

December 1973
Tarpon Springs, Florida, USA
An icon of St. Nicholas weeps.

January 1974
Pescara, Italy
A plate with an image of Pope John XXIII (and JFK) weeps blood.

1975
Akita City, Japan
The statue from 1973 now weeps and sweats.

1975-Present
Queens, New York, USA
The Virgin Mary regularly appears and speaks through a Long Island grandmother.

April 1975
Boothwyn, Pennsylvania, USA
A statue of Christ bleeds at the hands.

May 26, 1976
Port-au-Prince, Haiti
A statue of the Virgin Mary weeps.

1977
Damascus, Syria
A statue of the Virgin Mary weeps.

May 25-26, 1979
Roswell, New Mexico, USA
A portrait of Christ bleeds.

1980-1983
Grauhlet, Tarn, France
In a cemetery chapel, burning napkins appear at the foot of a statue of the Virgin Mary sixteen times in three years.

August 30, 1980
Niscima, Sicily, Italy
A statue of the Virgin Mary weeps blood.

1981
Thornton, California, USA
A statue of the Virgin Mary weeps oil and moves thirty feet.

1981-1986
Madrid, Spain
The Virgin Mary appears in a tree and gives messages.

June 24, 1981
Medjugorje, Yugoslavia
The Virgin Mary appears regularly to teenagers. Apparitions continue today.

August 15,1983
Beit Sahour, Jordan
The Virgin Mary appears at the Lady's Well grotto.

February 1983
Baguio City, Philippines
A statue of the Virgin Mary with her heart exposed visibly bleeds from the heart.

November 18, 1983
Rmaïch, Lebanon
A statue of the Virgin Mary flows blood and olive oil.

December 24, 1984
Bakersfield, California, USA
Our Lady of Guadalupe appears in a La Loma barrio.

May 1984

Chicago, Illinois, USA

A statue of the Virgin Mary weeps.

September 1984

Montpinchon, Manche, France

The Virgin Mary appears to townsfolk.

August 16, 1985

Melleray, Cappoquin, County Waterford, Ireland

A statue of the Virgin Mary comes to life and gives the faithful messages.

February 14, 1985

Asdee, County Kerry, Ireland

Statues of Jesus and Mary move.

July 1985

Ballinspittle, County Cork, Ireland

A statue of the Virgin Mary moves.

March 15, 1985

Concord, Sydney, Australia

A statue of the Lebanese saint, St. Charbal, oozes oil that causes a crucifix to drip blood when touched by it.

December 6, 1986

Chicago, Illinois, USA

A painting of the Virgin Mary weeps.

March 1986
Shoubra, Cairo, Egypt
The Virgin Mary appears on the roof of the church of St. Damiana in Papadoplo and the apparitions are witnessed by thousands of people.

1987
Bessbrook, County Antrim, Northern Ireland
The Virgin Mary appears regularly to two people in a church.

April 26, 1987
Grushevo/Hrushiv, Ukraine
The Virgin Mary appears to an eleven-year-old girl.

July 1987
Mutwal, Sri Lanka
A statue of the Virgin Mary moves.

October 1987
Ramallah, Jordan
A plastic statue of the Virgin Mary oozes olive oil.

October 17, 1987
Wynne, Arkansas, USA
A cross appears on a glass door after a woman prays for her dead husband.

1988
Manila, Philippines
The Virgin Mary appears to crowds of people.

August 1988
Lubbock, Texas, USA
The Virgin Mary appears in the sky above a church.

Good Friday, 1989
Ambridge, Pennsylvania, USA
A statue of Jesus closes its eyes.

1992
New Haven, Connecticut, USA
A figure of the crucified Christ appears in the limbs of a tree in Wooster Square Park. The apparition becomes known locally as "The Jesus Tree."

1992
Marlboro Township, New Jersey, USA
The Virgin Mary appears to Joseph Januskiewicz in his backyard on the first Sunday of every month.

2015
Marietta, Georgia
An image of the Virgin Mary appears on a window of the Transfiguration Catholic Church on December 12th, the Feast Day of Our Lady of Guadalupe.

Postscript: The Vatican has steadfastly refused to sanction the vast majority of religious manifestations and alleged miracles. To date, they have only vouched for less than twenty Virgin Mary apparitions, including Fatima and Lourdes. For more information see the book, *Encountering Mary*. [Bibliographic details are in the "Works Consulted" section.]

Chapter 23

ESOTERICA & ARCANA ABOUT VICTORIAN ASYLUMS AND WORKHOUSES

8 Criteria for Being Committed to a Victorian Asylum

This is a sampling of some of the criteria Victorian-era doctors used to determine if someone was a lunatic. Manifest a couple of these and the odds are you'd be put away.

1. Incessant chatter and the use of inappropriate or over-familiar language, laughing or singing without obvious cause or motive.
2. A loss of strength or will, resulting in a failure to be active in choice or employment or to interact with those around you.
3. A belief that fraudulent enemies unknown are depriving you of something that is rightfully yours, or are trying to poison or otherwise attack you. Typically, a patient in this condition may have made threats to harm

someone they know or to destroy their property, believing them to be part of the conspiracy against them.

4. Being found wandering without seeming to have an aim or direction, and usually in a state of inadequate dress.

5. A fear or dread of something being about to befall you, no matter how unlikely, such as your bed catching fire or being infected by some fanciful disease.

6. Holding some unusual desires or notions, such as the need to act as a messenger or a belief that you can predict high tides.

7. Unusual facial expressions, such as constant grimacing, twitching or other violent movements or the acting out of imaginary fancies.

8. If a parent, especially a mother, ceasing to show interest in the care of your children. In extreme cases, you may have threatened or attempted to harm your child.

Source: *Life in the Victorian Asylum* by Mark Stevens

A Typical Daily Schedule in a Victorian Workhouse

The Workhouse was for the destitute in Victorian England. It provided clothing, food, and shelter, but it wasn't free. It was institutional living and everyone had to contribute however they could.

6:00 A.M.—Awakening

- Rise.
- Chamberpots are emptied, and people who soiled themselves during the night are taken to the baths.
- People who can be trusted with a toothbrush (and who still have their own teeth) are allowed to brush their teeth. People with dentures are instructed to put them back in their mouth.
- Hair is combed and brushed.
- People dress, with assistance if needed.

7:00 A.M.—Breakfast

- Grace is said.
- Breakfast menu consists of eight ounces of buttered bread and tea or coffee.

8:20 A.M.—Morning Prayers

- Anyone can attend, but participation is not required. The fear was that religious services could trigger religious mania in the susceptible.

Work

- Inmates who work received extra privileges, including more food and additional items of clothing.
- Jobs at the asylum included:
  - Shredding newspapers
  - Cleaning, scrubbing, polishing fixtures
  - Mopping
  - Polishing furniture
  - Beating rugs
  - Gardening
  - Mowing
  - Kitchen work
  - Livestock work
  - Churning butter
  - Collecting eggs
  - Digging in the fields
  - Spreading manure on crops
  - Sowing
  - Reaping
  - Harvesting crops
  - Tending to livestock
  - Landscaping
  - Draining the cess pit
  - Painting
  - Laundry work

Skilled Work

- Inmates, if they were lucid and capable, also helped the following skilled workers:

  - Shoemaker
  - Tailor
  - Upholsterer
  - Carpenter
  - Seamstress

Those Who Could Not Work

- There were inmates who could not work for a range of reasons, including psychological, physical, and medical. But these people were not allowed to simply sit around or lie in bed all day. There were activities for them, too.

- Walking—male and female groups always walked in different directions so they would not come upon each other.

- Exercising
- Stretching
- Outdoor Games
- Cricket
- Football (non-contact)
- Lawn tennis
- Croquet
- Bowling

- Indoor Games & Pursuits
- Reading
- Cards
- Dominoes
- Draughts
- Bagatelle
- Billiards

12:30 PM—Dinner

- The philosophy regarding feeding lunatics was as follows: Lunatics commonly have excess energy so foods served are intentionally limited to foods lacking in an abundance of nutrients, i.e., carbohydrates, starches, etc. Protein and fats are limited because they provide energy.

An Australian Mental Asylum Menu

Food was a big deal in asylums, and meat was usually a staple. This menu covers a week in the Gladesville Mental Hospital in Australia in 1926.

"Mince-Meat" is a mixture of chopped dried fruit, distilled spirits and spices, and sometimes beef suet, beef, or venison. Originally, Mince-Meat always contained meat.

"Blanc Mange" is a sweet dessert commonly made with milk or cream and sugar thickened with gelatin, cornstarch or Irish moss, and often flavored with almonds.

DAY	BREAKFAST	DINNER	TEA
Monday	• Fried sausages • Oatmeal • Tea	• Pea Soup • Roast Beef • Mince-Meat • Vegetables in Season • Baked Rice Custard • Rice Pudding	• Cold Beef • Tea
Tuesday	• Irish Stew • Oatmeal • Coffee	• Roast Mutton • Mince-Meat • Vegetables in Season • Plum Pudding • Date Pudding	• Sweet Scones • Tea
Wednesday	• Curried Sausages • Oatmeal • Coffee	• Steak & Kidney Pie • Mince-Meat • Vegetables in Season • Rice Pudding	• Silverside of Corned Beef • Tea
Thursday	• Stewed Steak & Bacon • Oatmeal • Tea	• Vegetable Soup • Roast Beef • Mince-Meat • Vegetables in Season • Bread & Butter Pudding • Rice Pudding	• Sweet Scones • Tea
Friday	• Fried Sausages • Oatmeal • Coffee	• Fried Fish • Baked Fish • Mince-Meat • Vegetables in Season • Date Pudding • Plum Pudding • Sweet Sauce	• Cheese • Tea
Saturday	• Fried Loin Chops • Oatmeal • Tea	• Baked Rabbit • Roast Beef • Mince-Meat • Vegetables in Season • Tapioca • Vermicelli Custard	• Brawn • Tea
Sunday	• Brazed Mutton • Oatmeal • Coffee	• Cold Corned Beef • Cold Mutton • Mince-Meat • Vegetables in Season • Blanc Mange	• Tea-Cake • Tea

The 9 Consequences of Masturbation in 1850s Victorian England

According to the Victorian medical establishment, the consequences of a male pumping his pickle or a female buttering her muffin were dire. The results could be catastrophic and included the following.

1. Softening of the brain
2. Insanity
3. Epilepsy
4. Dementia
5. Asthma
6. Nervousness
7. Depression
8. Hysteria
9. Suicide

7 Facts about Bedtime at the Victorian Asylum

At 7:30, the bedtime ritual at a Victorian asylum began. Everything was done expeditiously and all patients were settled in their beds by 8:00 PM.

1. Patients who needed bathing or desired a bath were placed in a tub and washed and supervised.

2. Bath water was always 90-96 degrees Fahrenheit.

3. One tub of water was allocated and used per patient. Females were allowed more time because of their longer hair. In workhouses, which were often a much harsher living arrangement, residents often bathed in the prior person's dirty water.

4. A vermin check of hair was conducted.

5. Fingernails and toenails were clipped.

6. Men were shaved.

7. Some dorms were watched all night, specifically the ones containing epileptics, soilers, and self-harmers.

Chapter 24

7 INVASIVE MEDICAL TESTS ALL OF WHICH INVOLVE INSERTING SOMETHING INTO ONE BODILY ORIFICE OR ANOTHER

"I find the medicine worse than the malady."
—John Fletcher, *The Lover's Progress*

"You're going to put that thing where?
—Anonymous patient

Most people hate going to the doctor. The only saving grace to a doctor's visit is being told that there's nothing wrong. The Annoyance Factor triples, however, when your friendly medico orders one or more innocuously-monikered "tests."

These seven medical tests are some of the "worst" known to mankind, although that somewhat damning and frightening judgment must be taken with a grain of salt. With today's anesthesias and small and flexible endoscopic scopes and tubes, even the worst medical tests are often far less painful than their reputation would have you believe. It is quite true that the fear is often worse than the actual procedures.

The point is not to panic when one of the following tests are ordered. The medical establishment is well aware that most people today (particularly men) are terrified of anything medical and so are extremely well-prepared with a wonderful arsenal of tranquilizers, anesthetics, and painkillers. Do not be afraid (or too proud) to ask for them. That's why they were invented.

1. **Bone Marrow Aspiration:** Ordered when doctors are looking for severe anemia, leukemia, bone cancer, other blood diseases, and when they want to track the toxic effects of certain drugs used during chemotherapy treatment for cancer.

   A sample of your bone marrow (about a teaspoon) is taken by syringe from either the back of your hip bone or from your breast bone, and the test is always performed by a doctor. Reportedly, the most painful part of the procedure is when the marrow is being drawn up into the syringe, but as always, this is a very subjective experience.

   A woman interviewed for this book had CLL (Chronic Lymphocytic Leukemia, a chronic malignancy of the blood that is much less serious than the usually fatal Acute Leukemia). She had a Bone Marrow Aspiration done on the spur of the moment due to a potentially serious blood test report. She had it done in her doctor's office and was stunned at how little she felt.

A lot has to do with the doctor's expertise and technique when it comes to the insertion of the syringe and the drawing of the marrow. Other patients, on the other hand, have described this procedure as excruciatingly painful, one report describes the feeling as someone cracking open the bone that is being aspirated. Because of the seriousness of this test, it is usually only ordered when something correspondingly serious is suspected.

Bring someone with you: If this test is done on an out-patient basis, you will not be able to drive yourself home, and you will probably have soreness for several days afterwards. The good news is that whatever is wrong with you will probably be revealed and confirmed by this test. And after all, isn't is sometimes worse not to know what's wrong with you? Also, there is very little risk with this test and, if performed in the doctor's office, is not that expensive. If performed in a hospital, though, then as always, money is no object and the cost will skyrocket. The actual test is very brief, about as long as it takes to draw blood, but you will probably be in the office for close to an hour when you add in the pre-test preparations and the post-test rest period.

2. **Renal Angiography:** Ordered when doctors are looking for tumors of the kidney or narrowing of the kidney arteries.

After local anesthesia, a catheter is inserted into the femoral artery in the groin and maneuvered until it is near the suspect kidney. A dye is then injected into the catheter and when it enters the kidney arteries, X-rays are taken. The catheter insertion can be painful. The dye burns when it is being injected and can occasionally cause nausea.

One of the dangers of this test is the possibility of the catheter dislodging a blood clot that can then travel to another artery and cause a blockage. The upside of the procedure is that it is very accurate and will probably provide your doctor with the answers she needs to properly treat you. Today, this test is usually done on an outpatient basis because of the prohibitive costs of hospitalization. Depending on how long your doctor looks around up there, this test could take anywhere from a half hour or so to over an hour or more.

3. **Cardiac Catheterization:** Similar to Renal Angiography except that the catheter and dye are inserted into the heart instead of the kidney. This test is performed to diagnose heart disease and coronary artery disease. Unlike Renal Angiography, this test is always performed in a hospital.

   The bad news about this test is that approximately one in a thousand patients undergoing cardiac catheterization suffer a fatal heart attack during the test or immediately after. The good news is that if they do find some kind of heart or arterial disease, the test probably saved your life. As with Renal Angiography, this test could take anywhere from a half hour or so to over an hour or more, depending on how long your doctor looks around.

4. **Cystoscopy:** During a Cystoscopy, a tube is inserted into the urethra in order to get a look at the bladder, the ureters, and occasionally to take a urine sample directly from one of the kidneys. The test is performed to look for kidney and/or bladder tumors and stones, and to determine the cause of bladder infections, pain on urination, bleeding, and prostate trouble (in males).

The insertion of the catheter can be really uncomfortable, and when the tube reaches the bladder, there could be a strong (and disconcerting) urge to urinate. After the test (which lasts about twenty minutes), urination may be painful and the urine may be bloody. There may also be back pain and bladder spasms. This test can be performed either in the hospital or on an outpatient basis.

Reports from several men and women who have had this test are encouraging: Not one of them said that it was anywhere near as unbearable as they imagined. One gentleman had to have it done weekly because of a cancer scare and he eventually eschewed even the local anesthetic to numb the urethra. Another interviewee needed this test to determine the severity of a tear in his urethra. After the test he went out for breakfast and he polished off a stack of pancakes, eggs, and home fries. He was obviously no worse for wear. So, again, much of the pain associated with this test may actually be from tension stemming from pre-test apprehension and anxiety.

5. **Bronchoscopy:** Ordered when doctors want a look at, or a culture from the bronchi, which are the main air passageways of the lungs. It is used when cancer of the lung or some other type of lung disease is suspected.

A fiber optic Bronchoscope, which is essentially a viewing scope attached to a tube, is sent down into the patient's lungs via the nose. (It is sent through the nose because when it was sent down the throat by the mouth, patients tended to bite down on the tube because of fear or anxiety.)

Once the Bronchoscope is in the bronchi, pictures may be taken, samples may be harvested, or the doctor can just look around. The biggest problem with this test for the patient is the feeling that they are suffocating. After all, there is a big tube lodged in the throat and the natural reflex is to feel as though your airways are being blocked. But air flows freely into and out of the lungs throughout this test and if a patient is calm and relaxed, everything goes much easier.

The Bronchoscope drips a local anesthetic onto an area before it touches it, so the actual pain is minimal. The peculiar and unnatural feeling of having something foreign in your nose, throat, and lungs is what makes this test so disturbing. (This test was seen being performed in the 1991 William Hurt film, *The Doctor*. Hurt was called into a colleague's operating room to look down the Bronchoscope and confirm a tumor that the doctor had seen.)

6. **Colonoscopy:** Ordered when a patient has serious gastrointestinal trouble such as chronic diarrhea, bleeding,
or prolonged and severe abdominal pain that is not rec-
tified by other non-invasive treatments such as dietary
manipulation and/or antibiotics.

This procedure is used to diagnose such conditions as
ulcerative colitis, inflammatory bowel disease, several
forms of cancer, and other gastrointestinal troubles.
Once again, a tube is inserted into an orifice, only this
time, it's the southern exposure the medicos want a
look at. Yes, a tube is inserted into your rectum and
sent north all the way up through your large intestine. Occasionally air is sent through one of the tubes
of the Colonoscope in order to inflate the intestine so
the doctor can get an unobstructed look. This feels like
gas pains, only you can't expel it the way you normally
would.

Sometimes the doctor will snip a tissue sample, a procedure that usually goes largely unnoticed by the patient. (Remember how often it seemed that former
President Reagan had his polyps removed via this procedure?) Embarrassment plays a big part in making this
test a real pain in the ass, so to speak, although actual
pain is minimal. You lie on your left side and are essentially naked under a hospital gown. It's an awkward
and uncomfortable position and the test can last up to
an hour or more. You will be completely emptied out
before the test by fasting, laxatives, and sometimes a
morning enema, so you will not be feeling full of vim
and vigor—just plastic hosing and air. The test can be

done on an outpatient basis and is usually extremely conclusive in determining the problem.

7. **Barium Enema:** Ordered when any of a number of lower gastrointestinal diseases are suspected. Cancer, ulcerative colitis, diverticulitis, and polyps are some of the things they will be looking for.

This test involves pumping a liquid called barium into your lower intestine via a tube inserted into your rectum. When the liquid has completely filled your colon, X-rays are taken and obstructions, tumors, and polyps can be clearly seen. Since the doctors don't want to see anything other than what they're looking for, it is necessary that the patient be completely emptied out. Completely. You will not be allowed to eat anything for a full twenty-four hours before the test. That means that if the test is scheduled for 9:00 A.M. in the morning, you will not be able to eat a thing from 9:00 A.M. the previous morning. That can be a long time without food. And to make matters worse, you will not be able to drink anything for at least eight hours prior to the test, which, in our illustrative case, would mean from around midnight the night before.

Another added attraction to this test is that the night before you have to show up at the hospital, you will have to swallow a bunch of laxatives, and possibly give yourself an enema. (A "wet and wild" experience, as Kramer on *Seinfeld* once described an enema.)

So what this all means is that you will be up quite early the morning of the test and in addition to have to shower and do your hair (while hungry and thirsty), you will probably be spending quite a bit of time on the toilet. Once at the hospital, you will be told to undress and put on one of those charming gowns that let the immediate world see the cellulite you've been trying to get rid of for the past two decades.

The test (which takes about a half hour) begins with the lubrication of your anus and the insertion of the tube. The barium is then pumped into you and occasionally a nurse will have to press on your abdomen to make sure that the liquid fills all the nooks and crannies of your nether regions. Sometimes air is pumped in with the barium. X-rays are taken and you will be told to hold the barium in. This admonishment does not always work and occasionally leaks occur. Don't sweat it: It happens all the time.

After enough X-rays have been taken, you will be allowed to go to the bathroom and empty out. You will probably be relieved at this point, believing it is all over. Don't be. While there is still a light coating of barium in your intestine, more X-rays will be taken. After this, they will probably set you free.

There isn't any actual pain with this test, but there is discomfort. You will feel like you've got gas and can't let it out, and you will feel like you have to move your bowels and can't find a toilet. Since we've all experienced those feelings throughout our lives, a Barium Enema could be looked upon as a nostalgic change to re-experience old memories. (Then again, maybe not.)

For a couple of days after the test you will probably be constipated. Drink huge amounts of water and it will clear up in time. Also, when you do finally move your bowels, your stool will be "a whiter shade of pale." This is normal, and not something you see every day, wouldn't you say?

Chapter 25

19 LAST MEALS

As the last taste of sweets, is sweetest last,
Writ in remembrance more than things long past."
—William Shakespeare
The Tragedy of King Richard II

What would you choose if you had one meal left to eat in this life? That is the question Death Row occupants must answer.

This feature looks at the last meal requests made by 19 executed prisoners. In the majority of cases, their requests were filled. When they were not, or when the offered meals were refused, it is so noted.

1. **Unnamed Jewish Convict**
   Prison: Sing Sing.
   Last Meal: This gentleman decided to use the opportunity of his final meal to challenge ancient Jewish rules against the eating of pork. He ordered a full-course kosher dinner...and a ham sandwich.

2. **Prisoner Number 77681**

   Prison: Sing Sing.

   Last Meal: His pending death certainly did not affect this prisoner's appetite. For his last meal, 77681 ate a stew made of Long Island duck, peas, and olives. He ate the stew with dumplings, four slices of bread, and boiled white rice on the side. He also had a tomato salad, and for dessert, he enjoyed a nice piece of strawberry shortcake and a pint of vanilla ice cream. He topped all this off with a good cigar.

3. **Joshua Jones**

   Prison: Coudersport, Pennsylvania Prison.

   Date: 1839.

   Last Meal: Joshua Jones selected a symbolic last meal. On the day of his hanging, he found that he had exactly one dollar left to his name. He ate the bill between two slices of bread.

   Method of Execution: Hanging.

4. **Chauncey W. Millard**

   Prison: Utah State Prison.

   Date: 1869.

   Last Meal: Millard apparently wanted to be sailing on a sugar rush when he confronted the business end of his executioners' rifles. Millard's last meal consisted of nothing but candy.

   Method of Execution: Firing Squad.

5. **William Rose**

   Prison: Minnesota State Prison.

   Date: 1891.

Last Meal: Rose ordered a rather elegant last meal of oysters and eggs.

Method of Execution: Hanging.

6. Gee Jon

Prison: Carson City State Prison.

Date: February 8, 1924.

Last Meal: Old habits die hard. Gee Jon's execution was scheduled for early morning and, thus, Jon ordered a typical breakfast as his last meal. He ate ham and eggs, toast and coffee.

Method of Execution: Gas Chamber.

7. Isidore Zimmerman

Prison: Sing Sing.

Date: January 26, 1939.

Last Meal: Isidore was another big eater. His last meal consisted of a large steak, a salad, and potato pancakes. Zimmerman had originally requested cheese blintzes, but that was one specialty the Sing Sing kitchen could not provide without longer notice. The pancakes were substituted instead. For dessert, Izzy ate two orders of Jell-O with ice cream, and he finished everything off by smoking cigarettes and cigars.

Method of Execution: Electrocution.

8. Leslie B. Gireth

Prison: San Quentin.

Date: 1943.

Last Meal: Gireth chose drive-in food as his last meal. He ordered two hamburgers and two Cokes.

Method of Execution: Gas Chamber.

9. **Barbara Graham**

   Prison: San Quentin.

   Date: June 3, 1955.

   Last Meal: Graham forsook her last meal and instead decided on a "last dessert." She ordered and ate a hot fudge sundae.

   Method of Execution: Gas Chamber.

10. **Eugene Hickock & Perry Smith**

    Prison: Kansas State Penitentiary.

    Date: April 14, 1965.

    Last Meal: The two *In Cold Blood* murderers' eyes were apparently bigger than their stomachs. As their last meal they ordered shrimp, French fries, garlic bread, and for dessert, ice cream and strawberries with whipped cream. They didn't touch a bite of it.

    Method of Execution: Hanging.

11. **Gary Gilmore**

    Prison: Utah State Prison.

    Date: December 17, 1976.

    Last Meal: For Gilmore's last meal (which was eaten the night before his sunrise execution), he ordered a hamburger, hard-boiled eggs, a baked potato, milk and coffee, but reportedly only consumed the milk and coffee. Accounts vary.

    Method of Execution: Firing Squad.

    Note: Gary Gilmore's trial and execution was a media event. His name became a household word and his sordid story was immortalized by Norman Mailer in the best-selling book, *The Executioner's Song*, which was later made into a movie.

12. Stephen T. Judy

Prison: Indiana State Prison.

Date: 1981.

Last Meal: Stephen Judy skipped the food completely for his last meal and instead decided on a "last round." He ordered and drank four bottles of cold beer.

Method of Execution: Electrocution.

13. Charlie Brooks

Prison: Texas State Prison in Huntsville.

Date: December 7, 1982.

Last Meal: Brooks was obviously a meat and potatoes kind of guy. His last meal consisted of a steak, french fries and, for dessert, peach cobbler.

Method of Execution: Lethal Injection.

14. Margie Velma Barfield

Prison: Central Prison in Raleigh, North Carolina.

Date: November 2, 1984.

Last Meal: Barfield chose a "last snack" over a "last meal," selecting junk food as the last thing she would ever eat in this life. She enjoyed a last repast of Cheez Doodles and Coca-Cola.

Method of Execution: Lethal injection.

15. Ted Bundy

Prison: Florida State Penitentiary.

Date: January 24, 1989.

Last Meal: Bundy refused to order a last meal so the prison brought him the standard meal of steak and eggs. He refused to eat it, so they sent him to his

death on an empty stomach.
Method of Execution: Electrocution.

16. John Wayne Gacy

Prison: Stateville Correctional Center in Illinois
Date: May 10, 1994.
Last Meal: 12 deep fried shrimp, a bucket of
Original Recipe chicken from KFC, a pound of fresh
strawberries, French fries, and a Diet Coke.
Method of Execution: Lethal Injection
Note: Gacy's last words reportedly were "Kiss my ass."

17. Scott Dawn Carpenter

Prison: Oklahoma State Penitentiary
Date: May 8, 1997
Last Meal: Barbecued beef ribs, corn on the cob,
baked beans, potato salad, hot rolls, sweetened
lemonade and pecan pie with whipped topping.
Method of Execution: Lethal Injection
Note: Carpenter refused to appeal his Guilty verdict
and requested the death penalty. He was twenty-two
when he was put to death.

18. Allen Lee Davis

Prison: Florida State Prison
Date: July 8, 1999
Last Meal: Lobster tail, a half pound of fried shrimp,
six ounces of fried clams, a half-loaf of garlic bread,
thirty-two ounces of A&W Root Beer
Method of Execution: Electrocution
Note: Davis's execution was so bloody that one judge

said the photos taken after showed a man being tortured to death by the state of Florida.

19. Brandon Joseph Rhode

Prison: Florida State Prison

Date: December 27, 2010

Last Meal: A chili dog, tater tots, carrots, cole slaw, a slice of cake, and fruit punch.

Method of Execution: Lethal Injection

Note: Rhode attempted suicide six days before his scheduled execution and then tried to get his rescheduled execution cancelled by claiming the suicide attempt had left him brain-damaged.

Chapter 26

2 TYPES OF IQ EVALUATION IN THE PRE- AND POST-PC ERA

Pre-PC* Era

IQ	Evaluation
0-25	Idiot
25-50	Imbecile
51-70	Moron
71-80	Borderline
81-90	Dull
91-110	Normal
111-140	Superior
141+	Genius

Post-PC Era

IQ	Evaluation
<70	Definite feeble-mindedness
70-80	Borderline deficiency
80-90	Dullness
90-110	Normal or average intelligence
110-120	Superior intelligence
120-140	Very superior intelligence
140+	Genius or near genius

*PC= Politically Correct

Chapter 27

14 METHODS OF EXECUTION THROUGH THE AGES

"I hate victims who respect their executioners."
—Jean-Paul Sartre

Society has always had to deal with bad guys.

Sometimes they're fined; sometimes they're locked up; and sometimes they're killed. Finding new and improved ways to do away with the condemned has occupied great (and not-so-great) minds for centuries and, as is common with human endeavors, the many and devious ways of ending someone's life have been inventive, to say the least.

This feature looks at 14 of man's favorite ways of saying, "Here's your hat, what's your hurry?" and really meaning it.

1. **Beheading:** This was a popular form of execution in Greece and Rome before Christ where an ax or sword were the tools of the trade. In the eleventh century, beheading as a form of execution came to England and quickly replaced hanging as the favored method of doing away with the condemned criminal (The well-

placed condemned criminal, that is. The poor were still hanged for quite some time.).

Beheading was clean and quick and most believed that it was painless. In 1792, Beheading became modernized: On April 25, the first beheading by the guillotine took place. The guillotine was invented by Dr. Antoine Louis and Tobias Schmidt, and popularized by Dr. Joseph Guillotin. The condemned's head was placed at the bottom of a grooved channel and a sharpened, extremely heavy blade was dropped onto his neck. Gravity added urgency to the speed of the blade's descent and, voila, head in a basket.

The guillotine prompted bizarre experiments to ascertain whether or not the decapitated head retained any sensory awareness at all. For a while, French doctors were grabbing the disembodied heads and sticking pins in them and burning their eyeballs to see if there was any response. One doctor reported that "The face bore a look of astonishment."

THE GUILLOTINE.

2. **Boiling to Death:** The condemned would be placed in a giant pot filled with boiling water and hung over a fire. He would remain there until he was dead.

3. **Broiling to Death:** This method involved tying the victim to a red-hot griddle and broiling him or her until they died. The most notable broilee was St. Lawrence, who was subjected to this because he wouldn't turn over the Church's treasures to Rome. (He showed up with the poor, the sick, and the intellectually disabled when ordered to bring to Rome the church's fortune and told the Emperor that these poor souls were the Church's treasures.) After a time tied to the griddle (during which he bore the agony with incredible stoicism), Lawrence asked to be flipped over, as he was cooked enough on one side. His executioners were reportedly not amused.

4. **Burning to Death:** This was used as a method of execution for centuries throughout Europe and in America. The condemned was tied to a stake, wood and kindling were placed around his or her feet and ignited. This form of execution was agonizing and yet there are many reports of Christian martyrs "staked" who bore their pain with stoic silence, and with their eyes fixed on heaven. Probably the most well-known victim of burning to death was Joan of Arc, who was burned at the stake in France in 1431 for heresy.

5. **Crucifixion:** The Romans essentially invented crucifixion as a form of execution and in their quest for homicidal excellence, they came up with not one or two, but four ways to crucify someone.

The four ways were all variations on the shape of the cross on which the person was hung. These were the

"Y", the "X", the "T", and the "H." (With the "H," the person was hung by one arm and one leg.)

Usually the victim was either hung with ropes to the cross or nailed through the hands and wrists, as was Jesus Christ. (Jesus is most often shown crucified on a "T" cross, but there are also paintings that show him on a "Y", with the legs bent at the knee. Both were in common usage during Christ's life and it is possible that he may have died on one of the other forms.)

Crucifixion was a slow form of death. Usually the person died from suffocation and/or exposure, but occasionally the executioners would break the crucified's legs and/or stick a sword in their side to hasten the process. The Romans often included the added attraction of a pre-crucifixion scourging and in some cases they would take the time to insert sharp little pieces of bone under the victim's skin before they raised him on the cross. (Christ's crown of thorns seems to have been a torture designed specifically for him as a way of mocking his claim of being the king of the Jews.)

In feudal Japan, crucifixion was also used as a means of execution but they expedited the process: They would tie the condemned man to a cross and then shoot arrows into him until he was dead.

6. **Drawing and Quartering:** There were two types of Drawing and Quartering, The Russian version, and the English version, and both were used in the 12th century and earlier.

The Russian version (the more well-known) involved tying the condemned's arms and legs to four horses. The horses were then whipped and forced to flee in four different directions. The victim's arms and legs were summarily ripped from their sockets. Since this did not immediately kill the condemned, his torso was then decapitated to finish him off.

The other type of Drawing and Quartering—also incredibly vicious—was developed in England. In this version, the condemned was dragged behind a horse to the site of his execution. There he was hanged, but not to the death. He was simply strung up by the neck and allowed to slowly suffocate. This was the "Drawing" part.

While he was hanging and still conscious, though, he was also disemboweled and his intestines were burned in a fire while he watched. This was the "Quartering" part. After his guts were ashes, he was decapitated and then his corpse was cut into pieces.

Notable Drawn and Quartered historical figures (many of whom were hung first) include Thomas Abel, in 1540 (for denying ecclesiastical supremacy of the King of England); Henry Walpole, in 1595 (for being a Catholic priest); Thomas Garret, in 1608 (for refusing to take the Oath of Supremacy); Ambrose Barlow, in 1641 (for refusing to renounce his priesthood); and John Kemble, in 1679 (for being a Catholic priest).

7. **Electrocution:** In a typical execution by electrocution, the prisoner is strapped into the electric chair with eight heavy leather straps: two on the ankles, the chest, the upper and lower arms, and the waist. In most cases, a leather mask is placed over the face and secured to the back of the electric chair. Electrodes are attached to the prisoner's head and leg. The amount of voltage and length of the charges differ from state to state, although most executioners will start with a minimum charge of 2,000 volts for up to ten seconds, drop down to 500 volts or so for upwards of thirty seconds, and then finish things off with another 2,000 volts. Death is *usually* fairly speedy (see the chapter on Botched Executions) with this amount of voltage sailing through the condemned's veins. Death occurs within three seconds or

so and the condemned is usually unconscious in less than 1/240 of a second.

8. **Firing Squad:** Today, a firing squad usually consists of five men, all of whom are expert marksmen. Four of their rifles are loaded with live shells; one is loaded with a blank round. This allows each executioner to never be completely sure that he killed a man. (According to Frederick Drimmer in *Until You Are Dead...* however, experienced riflemen can always tell which gun had the blank in it: it's inevitably cooler than the others.)

The prisoner is strapped into a chair and blindfolded. The prison physician listens for his heart and places a paper target over it. Upon the warden's signal, the shooters shoot at the heart. The five executioners are concealed behind a wall that has an opening for the rifle barrels. Death is usually immediate. The firing squad was long a popular form of execution in the United States for a long time. A recent notorious execution by firing squad in the U.S. was that of Gary Gilmore in 1977. Today only three states—Mississippi, Oklahoma, Utah—still offer the Firing Squad as an option for condemned prisoners. Lethal Injection is their primary method of execution.

9. **Hanging:** This form of execution still used today in three states (Delaware, New Hampshire, Washington), originated when someone threw a rope over a tree limb and slowly pulled the condemned (or the lynched) up by his neck until he died. Later, the doomed were placed on a ladder and stood upright in a cart, both of

which were quickly pulled away so that the body could be allowed to swing.

According to the National Coalition to Abolish the Death Penalty and Amnesty International, there are four stages to a death by hanging. 1) At the moment of the drop, the body's weight violently tears the neck muscles, the skin, and blood vessels. If the length of the drop has been calculated correctly and the knot placed properly, the person's neck should break. 2) Because of the constriction of the noose, the veins that move blood to the heart are closed off. 3) Arteries that send blood to the head and brain, however remain open, and the condemned experiences an excruciating head-ache. 4) Eventually, breathing and heart rate slow, and within ten to twenty minutes after the drop, the person is usually pronounced dead.

People urinate and defecate when they are hung and, in the case of males, will often get an erection and actually ejaculate at the moment of impact. These aspects of hangings were quite stimulating to 16th and 17th century public hanging groupies. Today, hanging is a common form of execution in dozens of countries around the world, although there are not many groupies.

10. **Impalement:** The executioner would seat the condemned on a stake—a thick, sharp, long stake. The point of the stake would be inserted into the rectum and the victim would be "assisted" in pushing himself down until the stake punctured his intestines and ultimately killed him. This was slow, torturous, and excruciatingly painful.

11. **Lethal Gas:** This has been used in the United States as a method of execution since the 1920s. It is a gruesome mode of death and many people who have witnessed a death by "the big sleep" never want to see another.

The condemned, wearing a stethoscope tube taped to his chest, is strapped into a chair in the gas chamber. Beneath the seat of the chair hangs a bag filled with one pound of cyanide pellets. In the floor beneath the chair is a well that has a pipe feeding it from outside the death chamber. After the prisoner is strapped into the chair and the room is ascertained to be airtight, a liquid mixture of distilled water and sulfuric acid is piped into the well beneath his chair. When the warden signals the executioner, the bag of cyanide pellets is lowered into the acid. The cyanide instantly dissolves and the death vapors begin filling the execution chamber.

Death from lethal gas is not immediate. It could take up to fifteen minutes for the heart to stop beating and the prisoner is conscious for much of that time. San Quentin Prison physician, Dr. Stanley, quoted in *Until You Are Dead...* by Frederick Drimmer, once remarked, "The idea that cyanide kills immediately is hooey. These men suffered as their lungs no longer absorbed oxygen and they struggled to breathe. They died of an internal suffocation against which they had to fight and from which they must have suffered."

Death Row prisoners sentenced to die in the gas chamber are usually not given any drugs or sedatives before being executed, although in some prisons, the condemned man is allowed a shot of whiskey before taking that long walk. After the prison physician pronounces the man dead and the gas is drawn out of the death chamber, the prisoner's body, as a precaution for prison personnel, is sometime sprayed with liquid ammonia to neutralize any gas on the clothing.

12. **Lethal Injection:** Injection has of late been looked to as the ultimate humane method of execution. You lay the condemned prisoner on a gurney, inject him with a smorgasbord of deadly chemicals, he goes to sleep, and fifteen or twenty minutes later, he's on his way to the morgue for his autopsy. Basically, that is pretty much the way it works in modern western society, but in the Middle East, the term "Lethal Injection" takes on a whole new meaning. There, a particularly vile form of Lethal Injection, involving embalming fluid, is neither painless, nor humane. A common form of execution for perjurors in the Middle East is Intravenous Embalming while still alive. (See Chapter 28, "Botched Executions," for details on Lethal Injections executions gone wrong.)

13. **Pressing to Death:** This was a common form of execution during the Middle Ages, which involved tying the condemned to four stakes, spread-eagled on the floor. A large board was then placed on the person's body and heavier and heavier weights were placed on top of the board until the life was literally crushed right out of the poor loser.

This was an extremely slow process, quite torturous, and could last for several days before the condemned gladly expired. One famous "pressee" was Margaret Clitherow, who was pressed to death at York, England on March 25, 1586. Her executioners used an 800 pound weight to slowly crush the life out of her.

14. **Stoning to Death:** The condemned would be brought to an open area and stood in the center of a circle formed by his "executioners." They would then hurl heavy stones, rocks, and boulders at his body. They would consciously avoid throwing stones at his head so that he would remain conscious. The stoning would continue until the victim was dead on the ground. Sometimes the victim would be placed waist deep in a hole, which would prevent him or her from falling over as he was pummeled.

Chapter 28

47 BOTCHED EXECUTIONS FROM 1982-2016

It is reasonable to assert that none of these executions were actually botched since, in the end, the condemned did die. However, the word "botched" in this context means any execution process that veers in any way from *calm, quick, humane*, and *painless*. If we apply those criteria to these executions, it becomes clear that it is perfectly justified to describe them as "botched."

1. Frank J. Coppola
Date: August 10, 1982
State: Virginia
Method of Execution: Electrocution.
Coppola's head caught fire and it took two jolts of electricity to kill him. The execution chamber filled with smoke, too.

2. John Evans
Date: April 22, 1983
State: Alabama

Method of Execution: Electrocution

The leg electrode caught fire and flew off Evans' leg; his temple sparked and smoked (his head may have caught fire under the hood), and it took three blasts of electricity to finally kill him. His body was charred and smoldering when it was over.

3. Jimmy Lee Gray
Date: September 2, 1983.
State: Mississippi
Method of Execution: Asphyxiation (via the gas chamber)

The executioner was drunk. Gray gasped for air for eight minutes. He may have helped his death along by banging his head against a steel pole until he died.

4. Alpha Otis Stephens
Date: December 12, 1984
State: Georgia
Method of Execution: Electrocution

The first jolt didn't kill him. As Stephens continued to gasp for breath, the execution team waited six minutes for his body to cool enough for them to examine him. The second blast killed him.

5. Stephen Peter Morin
Date: March 13, 1985
State: Texas
Method of Execution: Lethal Injection

It took forty-five minutes of poking and probing to find suitable veins for the needles. Morin was a drug addict and his veins were shot.

6. William E. Vandiver
Date: October 16, 1985
State: Indiana
Method of Execution: Electrocution
Vandiver's execution took five jolts of electricity to kill him. The ordeal lasted seventeen minutes and Vandiver's body smoked and burned throughout the whole time. In one of greatest examples of understatement ever, the Indiana Department of Corrections later stated that the execution "did not go according to plan."

7. Randy Woolls
Date: August 20, 1986
State: Texas
Method of Execution: Lethal Injection
Woolls had to help the execution team find a useable vein with which to kill him.

8. Elliot Rod Johnson
Date: June 24, 1987
State: Texas
Method of Execution: Lethal Injection
Johnson's collapsed veins made the execution take almost an hour.

9. Raymond Landry
Date: December 13, 1988
State: Texas
Method of Execution: Lethal Injection
This one sounds like a black comedy. Two minutes after the drugs started flowing into Landry's veins, the syringe slid out of his arm and the execution chemicals started spraying all over the death chamber. It took them fourteen minutes to reinsert the syringe.

10. Stephen McCoy
Date: May 24, 1989
State: Texas
Method of Execution: Lethal Injection
McCoy had a violent reaction to the drugs and started gasping and heaving himself against the straps on the gurney. A witness fainted, knocked over another witness, and for a period there was the fear that everyone else witnessing the execution would also faint. The Texas Attorney General admitted later that they might have given McCoy heavier doses of the drugs and that they may have administered them too quickly. Good safety tip.

11. Horace Franklin Dunkins, Jr.
Date: July 14, 1989
State: Alabama
Method of Execution: Electrocution
Dunkins was mentally challenged and it took two jolts of electricity nine minutes apart to kill him. Why? Because they hooked the jacks on wrong. That's a quote from a prison guard. "I believe we've got the jacks on wrong." They later admitted

human error and the Alabama Prison Commissioner officially regretted what happened.

12. Jesse Joseph Tafero
Date: May 4, 1990
State: Florida
Method of Execution: Electrocution
Flames erupted from Tafero's head six inches high during the execution, and it took three blasts of electricity to kill him. They admitted human error and said the problem was due to using a synthetic sponge instead of a natural sponge. They stuck a synthetic sponge in a toaster, which caught fire, to prove their point.

13. Charles Walker
Date: September 12, 1990
State: Illinois
Method of Execution: Lethal Injection
This poor fellow suffered like crazy during his execution. The plastic tubing kinked, the needle was pointed in the wrong direction, and he experienced excruciating pain. They called it equipment failure and human error, although the narrative points more toward the human error part than equipment failure. (The needle didn't point itself in the wrong direction, right?)

14. Wilbert Lee Evans
Date: October 17, 1990
State: Virginia
Method of Execution: Electrocution

This one sounds like a scene from a horror movie. The electricity ruptured something in Evans's nose and as he was being electrocuted, blood poured down out of his mask and onto his shirt, drenching it. Witnesses say the blood sizzled. It took two jolts to kill him.

15. Derick Lynn Peterson
Date: August 22, 1991
State: Virginia
Method of Execution: Electrocution
Peterson wouldn't die. "He has not expired," the prison doctor said. They had to give him a second blast of electricity to finally kill him.

16. Ricky Ray Rector
Date: January 24, 1992
State: Arkansas
Method of Execution: Lethal Injection
Rector had brain damage and was a large man. It took fifty minutes to find a vein in which to inject the chemicals. Rector helped. Ultimately, it took five medical personnel working simultaneously to find a vein. Rector moaned loudly throughout the ordeal.

17. Donald Eugene Harding
Date: April 6, 1992
State: Arizona
Method of Execution: Asphyxiation
Harding turned purple and thrashed and wrenched violently against the restraining straps as he was enveloped in the toxic

cyanide gas. It took ten-and-a-half minutes for him to die. Reporters who witnessed the execution were described as "walking vegetables" for days after.

18. Robyn Lee Parks
Date: March 10, 1992
State: Oklahoma
Method of Execution: Lethal Injection
Parks gagged, choked, and spasmed for eleven minutes before being pronounced dead. The sight was horrifying and the words some of the reporters used to describe it were "painful," "overwhelming," "disturbing," "scary," "ugly," and "stunning." Reportedly, reporters couldn't look each other in the eye when it was over.

19. Billy Wayne White
Date: April 23, 1992
State: Texas
Method of Execution: Lethal Injection
It took the execution team forty-seven minutes to find a suitable vein on White, and that was with White's help. He had used heroin most of his life and his veins were in poor shape. He was described as courteous and cooperative during the ordeal and, after being injected at 12:49 AM, he was pronounced dead nine minutes later.

20. Justin Lee May
Date: May 7, 1992
State: Texas
Method of Execution: Lethal Injection

May had a violent reaction to the execution drugs, gasping, and thrashing against the leather restraints. It was not a peaceful death.

21. John Wayne Gacy
Date: May 10, 1994
State: Illinois
Method of Execution: Lethal Injection
Things did not initially go well for the Killer Clown, starting with the execution dugs solidifying in the IV tube inserted into Gacy's arm. It took ten minutes to replace the tube with a new one. He was pronounced dead eighteen minutes later and his brain was removed for study. The problem was blamed on inexperienced prison personnel who were untrained in IV insertion.

22. Emmitt Foster
Date: May 3, 1995
State: Missouri
Method of Execution: Lethal Injection
The lethal chemicals stopped flowing into Foster's body seven minutes after they were administered due to the execution team pulling the leather restraining straps on the table so tight that they cut off his circulation. The coroner checked him out and instructed them to loosen the straps. That did the trick and he was pronounced dead twenty-three minutes later, for a total execution time of thirty minutes.

23. Richard Townes, Jr.

Date: January 23, 1996
State: Virginia
Method of Execution: Lethal Injection

It took twenty-two minutes for the execution team to decide that there was no suitable veins in Townes' arms to accommodate the lethal injection needle. They finally executed him via a vein in the top of his right foot.

24. Tommie J. Smith

Date: July 18, 1996
State: Indiana
Method of Execution: Lethal Injection

It took the execution team forty-nine minutes to achieve access to Smith's veins for the induction of the lethal chemicals. They stuck him all over the place until a doctor gave him a sedative and tried to insert a catheter into his neck. That didn't work either so they finally decided on his foot, which did work. Twenty minutes later he was pronounced dead, for a total unconscionable execution time of one hour and nine minutes.

25. Pedro Medina

Date: March 25, 1997
State: Florida
Method of Execution: Electrocution

It's definitely a botched execution when the witnesses all start gagging. When the executioner flipped the switch and sent electricity coursing through Medina's body, his head caught fire and shot twelve-inch flames up from the top of his headpiece. The resultant stench caused the witnesses to gag and the executioner to cut power to the electric chair. Medina died a few minutes later. This was ultimately blamed on human error. Someone didn't put the electricity-conducting wet sponge into the headpiece correctly. Ya think?

26. Scott Dawn Carpenter
Date: May 8, 1997
State: Oklahoma
Method of Execution: Lethal Injection
It took eleven minutes for Carpenter to die and he did not go gently into that good night, no siree. As soon as the drugs were administered he began gasping, shaking, making guttural sounds and exhibiting violent muscle spasms. Carpenter was only twenty-two when he murdered a store owner by stabbing him in the neck. He refused to appeal his Guilty verdict and requested the death penalty. He said he couldn't see himself spending the sixty or seventy years of his life behind bars. The state of Oklahoma obliged him.

27. Michael Eugene Elkins
Date: June 13, 1997
State: South Carolina
Method of Execution: Lethal Injection
First of all, Elkins' body was a mess. He had serious liver and spleen problems which made his body swell up and impede easy access to his veins. It took the execution team almost an hour to find a vein and at one point, Elkins asked, "Should I lean my head down a bit?" They finally found a suitable vein in Elkins' neck.

28. Joseph Cannon

Date: April 23, 1998
State: Texas
Method of Execution: Lethal Injection
Cannon said his final words, they stuck in the needle, and...
the needle popped out after a vein collapsed in his arm. Cannon politely informed his executioners "It's come undone."
They closed the curtain, and spent fifteen minutes putting the
needle back in. When they opened the curtain, Cannon was
crying, but made his final statement again, and the execution
proceeded to its conclusion.

29. Genaro Ruiz Camacho

Date: August 26, 1998
State: Texas
Method of Execution: Lethal Injection
This execution was unconscionably long because it took two
hours to find a suitable vein on Camacho. This seems to qualify
as cruel and unusual, but the execution team proceeded apace,
no matter how long it took.

30. Roderick Abeyta

Date: October 5, 1998
State: Nevada
Method of Execution: Lethal Injection
Imagine lying strapped to a gurney for twenty-five minutes
while needles are stuck into various veins in an attempt to find
one suitable for lethal injection. That's what happened to Roderick Abeyta.

31. Allen Lee Davis

Date: July 8, 1999

State: Florida

Method of Execution: Electrocution

You know an execution went bad when a Supreme Court Justice later said of the execution photos "the color photos of Davis depict a man who—for all appearances—was brutally tortured to death by the citizens of Florida." Yikes. While still alive, blood from Davis's mouth poured onto his shirt and oozed through the buckle holes of his leather chest strap. Davis weighed 350 pounds and his electrocution was the first in Florida's new electric chair, which had been built to fit Davis' girth. A Republican Florida Congresswoman who witnessed the execution was at first shocked by the blood, but then said she realized it was a sign from God that the execution had been all right with him because the blood formed the shape of a cross.

32. Christina Marie Riggs

Date: May 3, 2000

State: Arkansas

Method of Execution: Lethal Injection

Riggs, who was a Licensed Practical Nurse, refused to appeal her guilty verdict and asked to be executed. She was found guilty of murdering her two young children. Her execution was delayed for eighteen minutes because the team couldn't find a suitable vein. They finally ended up asking Riggs if they could put the needles into her wrist and she said yes, after which the execution proceeded as planned. Her last words were, "I love you, my babies."

33. Bennie Demps
Date: June 8, 2000
State: Florida
Method of Execution: Lethal Injection
You know an execution went bad when the condemned uses the opportunity of his final statement to say, "They butchered me back there. I was in a lot of pain. They cut me in the groin; they cut me in the leg. I was bleeding profusely. This is not an execution, it is murder." It took execution personnel thirty-three minutes to find a vein to use for the lethal chemicals. They found a suitable one relatively quickly, but it took a long time to find a second useable vein, which was a requirement under Florida law. Ultimately, they gave up on the second vein and went ahead and executed him using the original vein.

34. Claude Jones
Date: December 7, 2000
State: Texas
Method of Execution: Lethal Injection
The motto of notoriously botched executions could have been uttered by a member of Claude Jones' execution team who said, "They had to stick him about five times." The execution was delayed for a half hour while they tried to find a vein in the IV drug user. Ultimately they found a suitable vein in his leg but it wasn't really the perfect input: the executioner actually told the warden "not to panic" because he was going to push the drugs through very slowly because, of course, what you want when you're executing someone by lethal injection is to prolong the time it takes for the drugs to take effect.

35. Bert Leroy Hunter

Date: June 28, 2000
State: Missouri
Method of Execution: Lethal Injection
Bert Hunter may, or may not have suffered "a violent and agonizing death." Once the drugs were injected, some accounts
have him gasping, coughing, choking, and convulsing before
dying. A lawyer said he suffered greatly; three reporters down-
played the reaction. Regardless of the severity of the reaction,
the reality is that Hunter did not die peacefully.

36. Jose High

Date: November 7, 2001
State: Georgia
Method of Execution: Lethal Injection
It took High one hour and nine minutes to die. They took close
to twenty minutes trying to find a vein, and then the EMTs
hired to do the injection quit. A tech finally got a needle into
High's hand and then—in a very rare instance of a physician
agreeing to participate in an execution—a doctor came in and
inserted a second needle between his shoulder and his neck.

37. Joseph L. Clark

Date: May 2, 2006
State: Ohio
Method of Execution: Lethal Injection
When the condemned's arm begins to swell like a balloon, and
the doomed man himself starts complaining, "It don't work, it
don't work," you have what could be described as a textbook
example of a botched execution. First, it took twenty-two min-

utes to find a vein. Then when the arm began to swell, the execution team took another thirty minutes to find another vein. During this ordeal, witnesses reported hearing Clark, moaning, shouting, and making guttural noises. Ultimately, he was declared dead an hour and a half after the execution began.

38. Angel Diaz
Date: December 13, 2006
State: Florida
Method of Execution: Lethal Injection

Any execution that causes the governor to suspend all executions in the state can probably be considered the quintessential botched execution. After the first injection of the lethal chemicals, Diaz grimaced, writhed, and tried to mouth words. They gave him a second dose and it took thirty-four minutes for him to expire. Why so long? Because the needles went in one side of the veins and out the other, so the lethal chemicals were injected into soft tissue and muscle rather than his bloodstream. At first, the Florida Department of Corrections said Diaz's long and agonizing death was because he had liver damage. Nope. The Medical Examiner confirmed his liver was fine and the problem had been the perforated veins. *The New Republic* magazine published Diaz's autopsy photos. They were ghastly. Good for Governor Jeb Bush for suspending executions, albeit temporarily. The suspension was lifted in July 2007 and the first execution (Mark Dean Schwab) following the reinstatement was in July 2008.

39. Christopher Newton
Date: May 24, 2007

State: Ohio
Method of Execution: Lethal Injection
It took two hours to declare Newton dead. Because he weighed 265 pounds, the execution team stuck him at least ten times before finding a suitable vein.

40. John Hightower
Date: June 26, 2007
State: Georgia
Method of Execution: Lethal Injection
It took forty minutes to find a vein—and it was team of nurses doing the searching!—in Hightower and it was a total of fifty-nine minutes before he was declared dead.

41. Curtis Osborne
Date: June 4, 2008
State: Georgia
Method of Execution: Lethal Injection
Osborne waited fifty-five minutes on the table while the U.S. Supreme Court reviewed his final appeal, which was rejected. The execution team then took thirty-five minutes to find a vein, and then it took Osborne fourteen minutes to die, for a total execution time of one hour, forty-four minutes. "Cruel and unusual" doesn't even come close to what Osborne endured.

42. Romell Broom
Date: September 15, 2009
State: Ohio
Method of Execution: Attempted Lethal Injection

Romell Broom is the only prisoner to survive attempted Lethal Injection. After two hours of painfully jabbing Broom with needles trying to find a vein, Ohio Governor Ted Strickland ordered the execution to stop. At one point, Broom tried to help the execution team find a suitable vein ultimately covering his face and sobbed. Even though there were plans to try again a week after the first attempt, court appeals—mainly claiming that a second attempt would violate the Eighth Amendment's proscription against cruel and unusual punishment—have kept Broom out of the death chamber and, as of January 1, 2017, he remains alive and well on Ohio's Death Row.

43. Brandon Joseph Rhode
Date: September 27, 2010
State: Georgia
Method of Execution: Lethal Injection
It took medics a half hour to find a vein on Rhode and then it took fourteen minutes for him to die. Rhode had actually bought himself a reprieve of six days when he attempted suicide but failed. A sympathetic guard had given him a razor blade. His lawyers then tried to get the execution cancelled on the claim that the suicide attempt had left Rhode brain damaged. According to court documents, "[Rhode] said he wanted to do it himself so he would not be put down like a dog. He said that they were going to try to put him down like a dog, that what was going to be used on him wouldn't even be used on a dog."

44. Dennis McGuire
Date: January 16, 2014

State: Ohio

Method of Execution: Lethal Injection

The state of Ohio tried to execute Dennis McGuire using hydromorphone and midazolam, known, respectively commercially as Dilaudid, an opioid painkiller and Versed, a pre-surgery sedative. The combination ultimately worked, but during the twenty-five minutes it took for McGuire to die, he experienced "repeated cycles of snorting, gurgling and arching his back, appearing to writhe in pain [and] it looked and sounded as though he was suffocating." That description is from a lawsuit the family filed immediately following the execution.

45. Clayton D. Lockett

Date: April 29, 2014

State: Oklahoma

Method of Execution: Lethal Injection

Law prohibits veterinarians from using for euthanasia the three-drug combination used on Clayton Lockett on the grounds that it's too painful. Did that stop the state of Oklahoma from using them on a human being? No, it did not. The three drugs were the sedative midazolam (Versed), the muscular paralytic vecuronium bromide (Norcuron), and potassium chloride. First, it took an hour for a paramedic to find a suitable vein in Lockett's groin area. Then, the injection protocols were so botched a doctor was called in to assist. He did, immediately violating the Hippocratic Oath the moment he stepped into the death chamber. However, after repeated injections of the chemicals, Lockett remained alive. The thrashing, open eyes suggesting consciousness (at one point Lockett actually said the word "Man"), and apparent resistance to the heart-stopping drugs moved Governor Mary Fallin to stop the execution. Lockett died ten minutes later of a heart attack. (For complete details on Lockett's botched execution, see the article "The Cruel and Unusual Execution of Clayton Lockett" by Jeffrey E. Stern in the June 2015 issue of *The Atlantic Monthly,* The article is also available online at https://www.theatlantic.com/magazine/archive/2015/06/execution-clayton-lockett/392069/)

46. Joseph R. Wood

Date: July 23, 2014
State: Arizona
Method of Execution: Lethal Injection
It took Wood one hour and forty minutes to die because the state of Arizona used only two drugs—Dilaudid and Versed—to execute him. He gasped, writhed, and obviously suffered greatly during the ordeal. The scene was so bad that Wood's lawyers filed an emergency appeal during the execution to put a stop to it. It was not granted, and a reporter later wrote that Wood gasped 640 times before he finally died.

47. Brandon Jones

Date: February 3, 2016
State: Georgia
Method of Execution: Lethal Injection
It took twenty-four minutes to not find a vein in Jones' left arm, and then another eight minutes to not find a vein in his right arm. The execution team then asked a doctor to violate her code of ethics and help. She agreed to, and after poking for thirteen minutes, she finally inserted an IV in Jones' groin. The execution began and six minutes later, Jones's eyes popped

open, before he ultimately died. He was seventy-two years old
at the time of his execution.

Sources: The Death Penalty Information Center, Murderpedia.
org, Dr. Michael L. Radelet, University of Colorado

Chapter 29

10 COMMON ELEMENTS OF A NEAR-DEATH EXPERIENCE

We returned to our places, these Kingdoms,
But no longer at ease here, in the old dispensation,
With an alien people clutching their gods.
I should be glad of another death.
—T. S. Eliot, "Journey of the Magi"

Near-Death Experiences (NDEs) are also known by the term, "The Lazarus Syndrome." The phrase "Near-Death Experience" was first coined by Raymond Moody in 1975 but there are reports of this type of experience in the Bible, and in the writings of the ancient Greeks, Romans, and Egyptians.

A Near-Death Experience is an apparent preternatural event that a person goes through at the point of death. The reason we're even aware of NDEs is because the people who have had them near death were saved, and thus, able to tell about it. This feature will look at the common elements of the majority of NDEs, but first here is a rundown of some possible explanations for the experience.

- Some scientists and doctors look to hypoxia as a cause for an NDE. Hypoxia is a decrease of oxygen to the brain, and, the theory goes, when the brain is oxygen-deprived, hallucinatory sensory experiences occur.

- More spiritually-oriented people such as psychics and clergy choose to believe that a Near-Death Experience is an actual look, and actual experiencing, of the next world and the afterlife. They believe that we all experience exactly what all NDE'ers do, except that the majority of us don't come back to life and, thus, the experience remains within the soul of the deceased.

- Carl Sagan, in his book, *Broca's Brain*, may have the best explanation of all. His theory is that a Near-Death Experience is a re-experiencing of our own birth. This would explain why NDEs are especially common (and similarly remembered and recounted) in three- to nine-year-olds who "die" and are brought back to life. Their latent birth memories are far more "recent" than those of, say, a seventy-five-year-old. Sagan put it this way: "[E]very human being, without exception, has already shared an experience like that of those travelers who return from the land of death; the sensation of flight; the emergence from darkness into light; an experience in which, at least perceived, bathed in radiance and glory. There is only one common experience that matches this description. It is called birth."

It is intoxicating to believe that an NDE is a genuinely supernatural experience. Many people who have had them claim an incredible sense of peace regarding their eventual death, a truly desirable state of mind.

John White, in his book, *A Practical Guide to Death and Dying* describes this epiphany:

"The aftereffects of the near-death experience are striking. In general, there is a marked shift in values toward the spiritual, and the total effect is akin to a spiritual rebirth. Most often people say they completely lose their fear of death, knowing it to be based on illusion. They also find that they are more alive, more aware, more sensitive to beauty in the natural world and to the feelings of others. They tend to become stronger psychologically and to have a greater sense of self-worth. They also feel strongly a need to be of service to society in some way, as if they now have a purpose for being in the world—a purpose that came clear to them only through the near-death experience. They are more willing and able to express love and concern to others, and they're more tolerant of others. Their religious sense is deepened, not especially by going to church or temple so much as by a constant background feeling of a spiritual dimension underpinning life. They have an inward feeling of closeness to God and to their fellow man. Altogether, they tend to express thanks for having had the near-death experience." [pg. 23]

A 1991 Gallup Poll reported that twelve million Americans have had Near-Death Experiences. Based on the percentage (5%) of respondents who claimed the experience, we can extrapolate that approximately sixteen million people have had NDEs by 2016.

Here are the ten most commonly-reported elements of the Near-Death Experience. This information is drawn from Raymond Moody's book, *The Light Beyond*, and are listed in the order of frequency of citation.

1. **Being in Another World or Realm:** This is one of the most commonly reported experiences. People feel that they have somehow crossed over into another plane or level of existence.

2. **An Overwhelming Feeling of Peace:** The sense of peace, serenity, and contentment is so palpable to NDE'ers that many have actually chastised the doctor for pulling them away from the afterlife and bringing them back to life.

3. **A Review of the Person's Life:** This is the archetypal experience of having your life flash before your eyes. This experience has also been reported by people who believed they were dying but who remained conscious throughout. People falling off buildings or drowning have all reported a life review.

4. **An Out-of-Body Experience:** Most NDEs begin with the person's astral body floating up and out of their physical body. Many report then feeling as if they could fly at will.

5. **Accurate Visual Perception:** NDE'ers can often relate details about things they could not have seen while

clinically dead, including scenes and events that take place outside the emergency room or site. Perhaps an NDE allows us to tap into some sort of dormant sensory ability that we're not capable of accessing in the material world?

6. **Encountering Other People:** Many NDE'ers claim to have met and had conversations with deceased relatives and friends on the other side. To some, this is the most bittersweet aspect of a Near-Death Experience.

7. **Audible Voices and Sounds:** NDE'ers can also often relate details about things they could not have heard while clinically dead.

8. **The Light:** A wondrous and, to some, holy light often bathes and beckons people who have a Near-Death Experience. Most feel that the light is the source of all things or, is actually the physical manifestation of God.

9. **The Tunnel:** This is often spoken of as one of the most common elements of a Near-Death experience and yet, in fact only 9% of people who were interviewed by Raymond Moody reported walking or floating down a tunnel.

10. **Precognition:** Precognition, or being able to predict the future, was the least-reported NDE element. Cynics look to this as proof that there is nothing even remotely supernatural going on here, and thus, the paucity of genuinely provable phenomena. But 6% of all of Raymond Moody's NDE'ers reported being able to know at least something of future events after their experience.

Chapter 30

8 PLAGUED PLACES

AN EPHEMERIS OF SELECTED BLIZZARDS, CYCLONES, EARTHQUAKES, EPIDEMICS, FAMINES, FLOODS, HAILSTORMS, HURRICANES, PLAGUES, TIDAL WAVES, TORNADOES, TYPHOONS, AND VOLCANIC ERUPTIONS

Do you like where you live? If you could, would you move somewhere else? Read through this feature and think twice before you answer. There are places on this planet that have had more than their share of bad luck. The history of certain countries and regions reads like a Baedeker of bad news: famines, earthquakes, epidemics, typhoons…all manner of dire occurrences seem to plague certain spots with depressing regularity. This feature looks at a selection of the dreadful things that have occurred in eight places on God's green earth.

1. China

Earthquakes

- January 23, 1556: Northern China; 830,000 die.

- November 30, 1731: Peking; 100,000 die.

- December 16, 1920: Gansu (8.6 on the Richter Scale); 180,000 die.

- July 28, 1976: Tangshan (8.2 on the Richter Scale); between 240,000 and 750,000 die.

Floods

- 1642: Hunan Province; hundreds of thousands die.

- September, 1911: Yangtze River; 200,000 die.

- July, 1915: Kwangtung and Kiangsi; over 100,000 die.

- August, 1931: Yangtze River; 3,700,000 die.

- November, 1939: Northern China; 200,000 die.

- August, 1950: Eastern China; 89 die, 10,000,000 homeless.

- July, 1954: Central China; 40,000 die.

- May, 1991: Southeastern China; 1,700 die.

Typhoons

- July 27, 1862: 40,000 die.

- August 2, 1922: 60,000 die.

Famines

- 1876-1879: 13,000,000 die.
- 1928-1929: 3,000,000 die.
- 1936: 5,000,000 die.
- 1939: 200,000 die, 25,000,000 left homeless.

2. England

Epidemics

- 1485: Sweating sickness; thousands die. Writer Raphael Holinshed described the scene in this manner: "Scarce one amongst an hundred that sickened did escape with life, for in all maner as soone as the sweate tooke them... yielded up the ghost."
- 1346-1353: The Black Death kills upwards of 200 million people
- 1507: Sweating sickness in London; thousands die.
- 1518: Sweating sickness in London; thousands die.
- 1665: Bubonic plague in London; 100,000 die.
- 1684: Smallpox in London; 100,000 die.
- 1851-1855: Tuberculosis; 250,000 die.
- 1853: Cholera epidemic in London; thousands die.

In the 14th century England, a plague took 200 million souls

3. India

Cyclones

- October 7-11, 1737: Calcutta; 600,000 die.

- December, 1789: Coringa; over 20,000 die.

- June, 1822: The Ganges River; 50,000 die.

- May, 1833: Calcutta; 50,000 die.

- October 5, 1864: Calcutta; 80,000 die.

- October 31, 1876: Bengal; 100,000 die.

Famines

- 1769-1770: Hindustan; millions die.

- 1790-1792: Bombay; unknown millions die. As the famine wore on, cannibalism was rife. This famine was known as the "Skull Famine" because of the tens of thousands of unburied corpses piled everywhere.

- 1866-1870: The Bengal Region; 1,750,000 die. The total number of dead includes 250,000 who died from a fever epidemic that spread throughout northern India after the famine was over.

- 1876-1878: Southern India; 5,000,000 die.

- 1896-1897: 1,250,000 die.

Plagues

- 1903-1908: 4,000,000 die.

- 1910-1913: The Black Plague; millions die.

Hurricanes, Tidal Waves, Hailstorms & Floods

- June 5, 1882: Hurricane and Tidal Waves in Bombay; 100,000 die.

- April 30, 1888: Hailstorm in Moradabad; 250 die.

- October 16, 1942: Hurricane in Bengal; 389 die.

- July, 1993: Massive flooding in Calcutta; 4,300 die.

Earthquakes

- May 31, 1935: Quetta (7.5 on the Richter Scale); 50,000 die.

- September 30, 1993: Bombay (6.3 on the Richter Scale);
25,000+ die.

4. Iran (Persia)

Earthquakes

- 1040: Tabriz; 50,000 die.

- 1727: Tabriz; 75,000 die.

- September 1, 1962: 4,500 die.

- August 31, 1968: (7.8 on the Richter Scale); 12,000 die.

- September 16, 1978: Northeast Iran (7.7 on the Richter Scale); 25,000 die.

- June 21, 1990: Northern Iran (7.7 on the Richter Scale); 50,000 die.

5. Italy

Volcanic Eruptions

- 79: Mount Vesuvius; Pompeii and Herculaneum, 16,000 die.

- 427: Mount Vesuvius; scores die.

- 1169: Mount Etna; 15,000 die. The deaths occurred from the earthquake and tidal waves that followed the eruption.

- December 16, 1631: Mount Vesuvius; 4,000 die.

- March 11, 1669: Mount Etna; 20,000 die. This was Mount Etna's worst eruption. (So far.)

- April 24, 1872: Mount Vesuvius; close to 30 die.

Earthquakes

- December 5, 1456: Naples; 35,000 die.

- July 30, 1626: Naples; thousands die.

- 1693: Naples; 93,000 die.

- 1693: Catania; 60,000 die.

- February 4, 1783: Southern Italy; 60,000 die.

- July 26, 1805: Naples and Calabria; 26,000 die.

- August, 1819: Genoa and Palermo; thousands die.

- December 28, 1908: Messina, Sicily (7.5 on the Richter Scale); between 160,000 and 250,000 die.

- November 23, 1980: Southern Italy; 5,000 die.

6. Japan

Earthquakes & Undersea Earthquakes

- December 30, 1703: Tokyo; 37,000 die.

- 1847: Nagano; 34,000 die.

- March 21, 1857: Tokyo; 107,000 die.

- August 31, 1886: Off the Japanese Coast (undersea); 28,000 die.

- October 28, 1891: Central Japan; 7,300 die.

- June 15, 1896: Off the Northeast Japanese Coast (undersea); 28,000 die.

- September 1, 1923: Tokyo; 140,000 die.

- July 12, 1993: Hokkaido (7.8 on the Richter scale); 12 die.

7. The United States

Epidemics & Plagues

- 1699: Yellow Fever epidemic in Charleston, South Carolina and Philadelphia, Pennsylvania, 370 die.

- 1735-1740: Diphtheria epidemic in New England; 80% of the children die.

- 1793: Yellow fever epidemic in Philadelphia, Pennsylvania; 4,044 die.

- 1832: Cholera epidemic in New York City; 4,000 die.

- 1853: Yellow fever epidemic in New Orleans, Louisiana; 7.848 die.

- 1861-1865, The Civil War: Typhoid, dysentery, and other diseases; 187,000 die.

- 1878: Yellow fever epidemic in New Orleans, Louisiana and Memphis, Tennessee; 14,000 die.

- 1878: Smallpox epidemic in Deadwood, The Dakota Territory. A 26-year-old nurse named Martha Jane Canary nurses the sick, ignoring her own health. Because of her efforts, she becomes known as Calamity Jane.

- 1900: Bubonic plague epidemic in Honolulu, Hawaii (still only a U.S. territory); thousands die.

- 1900: Bubonic plague epidemic in San Francisco, California; 117 die.

- 1903: Typhoid epidemic in New York City.

- 1907: Bubonic plague epidemic in San Francisco, California.

- 1907: Bubonic plague epidemic in Seattle, Washington.

- 1914: Bubonic plague epidemic in New Orleans, Louisiana.

- 1916: Polio epidemic; 6,000 die.

- 1919: Bubonic plague epidemic in New Orleans, Louisiana.

- 1924: Bubonic plague epidemic in Los Angeles, California.

- 1931: Diphtheria epidemic; 17,000 die.

- 1952: Polio epidemic; 50,000 infected; 3,300 die.

- 1980-: The AIDS epidemic; 666,000 deaths (through 2016).

Hurricanes

- September, 1841: Saint Jo, Florida; 4,000 die.

- August 27, 1881: Southern U.S. Coast; 700 die.

- August 28, 1893: Southern U.S.; 1,000 die.

- October 1, 1893: Gulf of Mexico states; 2,000 die.

- May 8, 1900: Galveston, Texas; 6,000 die.

- September 17, 1926: Florida 450 die.

- September 10, 1928: West Palm Beach, Florida; 5,000 die.

- September 2, 1935: Florida Keys; 400 die.

- September 21, 1938: New England; 500 die, 14,000 buildings destroyed.

- September 14, 1944: New England; 389 die.

- October 12, 1954: Hazel hits the U.S. East Coast; 411 die, $1 billion in damage.

- June 27, 1957: Audrey hits Texas, Louisiana, Mississippi; 500 die.

- September 6, 1960: Donna hits the U.S. East Coast; 143 die.

- August 17, 1969: Camille hits the Southeastern U.S.; 258 die, $1.5 billion in damage.

- June 21-26, 1972: Agnes hits the U.S. East Coast; 118 die, 116,000 houses destroyed.

- September 7, 1979: David hits the Southeastern U.S.; 2,000 die.

- September 12, 1979: Frederick hits Alabama and the Mississippi Coast; 5 die, $2.3 billion in damage.

- August 24, 1992: Andrew hits Florida, Louisiana, southern U.S. States; 30 die, 250,000 people homeless, over $20 billion in damage.

Earthquakes

- 1755: Boston, Massachusetts; no deaths.

- December 15, 1811: New Madrid, Missouri; few deaths.

- August 31, 1886: Eastern U.S.; 110 die.

- April 18, 1906: San Francisco, California (8.3 on the Richter Scale); 700 dead, 225,000 homeless.

- March 27, 1964: Anchorage, Alaska (8.6 on the Richter Scale); 118 die.

- October 17, 1989: San Francisco, California (6.9 on the Richter Scale); 60 die.

- August 8, 1993: Guam (8.1 on the Richter Scale); millions of dollars in damage.

Tornados & Cyclones

- September 10, 1811: Charleston, South Carolina; over 500 die.

- May 7, 1840: Natchez, Mississippi; 317 die.

- June 16, 1842: Natchez, Mississippi; 500 die.

- February 19, 1884: Southern U.S. (cyclone); 800 die.

- May 27, 1896: St. Louis, Missouri; 306 die.

- May 26, 1917: Southern and Midwestern U.S.; 249 die.

- March 18, 1925: Missouri, Illinois, Indiana; 689 die.

- September 29, 1927: St. Louis, Missouri; 85 die. This tornado lasted five minutes and destroyed 1,800 houses.

- January 9, 1953: Worcester, Massachusetts 90 die, 4,000 buildings destroyed.

- April 11, 1965: U.S. Midwest (35 at one time) 271 die.

- April 3-4, 1974: South and Midwest (over 148 at one time); 315 die.

Blizzards

- November 17-21, 1789: New England; hundreds die.
- March 12, 1888: Eastern U.S. Coast; 800 die.
- November 26-27, 1898: Northeastern U.S. Coast; 455 die.
- January 27-29, 1922: Eastern U.S. Coast; 120 die.
- March 15, 1941: North Dakota and Michigan 151 die.
- January 14, 1952: The Sierra Nevadas; 26 die.

Floods

- May 31, 1889: Johnstown, Pennsylvania 2,200 die.
- April, 1927: The Mississippi Valley; 313 die.
- January, 1937: The Ohio River Basin; 137 die.
- February 26, 1972: Logan, West Virginia; 107 die.
- July, 1993: The Mississippi River and 55 of its tributaries in the upper Midwest (massive flooding), including Iowa, Missouri, Minnesota, Wisconsin; 20 die, 33,700 evacuated, 7,500+ homes damaged, 2 million acres under water, $2.4 billion+ in crop losses, 100+ breached levees, $5 billion+ overall damage.

Devastation from the Johnstown Flood

8. The World

Epidemics

- 1881-1896: Cholera epidemic, millions die.

- 1918-1919: Spanish Flu epidemic; between 22 and 25 million die.

- 1957-1958: Asian Flu epidemic; millions affected, but few deaths.

- 1980-: The AIDS epidemic; 25 million die worldwide; 666,000 die in the U.S. (through 2016)

Chapter 31

73 RENOWNED LITERARY CLASSICS INITIALLY REJECTED AS UNPUBLISHABLE BY A PUBLISHER FROM 1818-1990

Aspiring—but unpublished—writers, take note: This list will be the most encouraging thing you will ever read. You will suddenly—and with piercing clarity—realize that literary rejection is neither personal nor a definitive judgment of your talent. It is simply the nature of the beast. There are far more writers than there are outlets for their work and thus, the enormously depressing publisher rejection rate. But take heart: As this list so dramatically illustrates, you are in good company. In fact, you are in extremely good company. Just think: You, as a writer, have something in common with Jane Austen, William Faulkner, F. Scott Fitzgerald, D. H. Lawrence, Ernest Hemingway, Gustave Flaubert, and even James Joyce and Walt Whitman. Fine company indeed, wouldn't you say?

Spurned Classics

The 1800s

1818 *Northanger Abbey* by Jane Austen

1819 *The Sketch Book* by Washington Irving

1846 *Typee* by Herman Melville

1851 *Moby Dick* by Herman Melville

1855 *Leaves of Grass* by Walt Whitman

1856 *Madame Bovary* by Gustave Flaubert

1857 *Barchester Towers* by Anthony Trollope

1887 *A Study in Scarlet* by Sir Arthur Conan Doyle

1891 *Tess of the D'Urbervilles* by Thomas Hardy

1891 *The Picture of Dorian Gray* by Oscar Wilde

1895 *Poems* by William Butler Yeats

1895 *The Time Machine* by H.G. Wells

1898 *The War of the Worlds* by H.G. Wells

1900-1910

1900 *Sister Carrie* by Theodore Dreiser

1905 *Man and Superman* by George Bernard Shaw

1906 *The Jungle* by Upton Sinclair

1908 *The Wind in the Willows* by Kenneth Grahame

1909 *Three Lives* by Gertrude Stein

1911-1920

1912 *Riders of the Purple Sage* by Zane Grey

1912 *Under the Moons of Mars* by Edgar Rice Burroughs

1913 *Swann's Way* from *Remembrance of Things Past*
by Marcel Proust

1915 *The Rainbow* by D.H. Lawrence

1916 *A Portrait of the Artist as a Young Man* by James Joyce
1918 *Cornhuskers* by Carl Sandburg
1919 *Winesburg, Ohio* by Sherwood Anderson
1920 *The Mysterious Affair at Styles* by Agatha Christie
1920 *This Side of Paradise* by F. Scott Fitzgerald

1921-1930

1922 *Poems* by George Santayana
1922 *Ulysses* by James Joyce
1925 *Gentlemen Prefer Blondes* by Anita Loos
1926 *The Torrents of Spring* by Ernest Hemingway
1928 *Lady Chatterley's Lover* by D. H. Lawrence
1929 *Look Homeward, Angel* by Thomas Wolfe
1929 *Sartoris* by William Faulkner

1931-1940

1931 *Sanctuary* by William Faulkner
1931 *The Good Earth* by Pearl Buck
1934 *Lust for Life* by Irving Stone
1934 *The Postman Always Rings Twice* by James M. Cain
1937 *And To Think That I Saw It On Mulberry Street*
by Dr. Seuss

1941-1950

1943 *The Fountainhead* by Ayn Rand
1944 *The Razor's Edge* by W. Somerset Maugham
1945 *Animal Farm* by George Orwell
1947 *Under the Volcano* by Malcolm Lowry
1948 *The Naked and the Dead* by Norman Mailer
1950 *The Book of Merlyn* by T.H. White

1951-1960

1951 *Malone Dies* by Samuel Beckett

1951 *Molloy* by Samuel Beckett

1952 *Kon-Tiki* by Thor Heyerdahl

1952 *The Diary of Anne Frank* by Anne Frank

1954 *Lord of the Flies* by William Golding

1954 *The Bridge Over the River Kwai* by Pierre Boulle

1955 *Lolita* by Vladimir Nabokov

1955 *Peyton Place* by Grace Metalious

1955 *The Deer Park* by Norman Mailer

1955 *The Ginger Man* by J.P. Dunleavy

1957 *Atlas Shrugged* by Ayn Rand

1957 *The Assistant* by Bernard Malamud

1958 *A Separate Peace* by John Knowles

1960 *Welcome to Hard Times* by E.L. Doctorow

1961-1970

1961 *Catch-22* by Joseph Heller

1961 *Mastering the Art of French Cooking* by Julia Child

1961 *The Tin Drum* by Günter Grass

1963 *The Ipcress File* by Len Deighton

1963 *The Spy Who Came In From the Cold* by John Le Carré

1966 *Giles Goat-Boy* by John Barth

1966 *In My Father's Court* by Isaac Bashevis Singer

1966 *Valley of the Dolls* by Jacqueline Susann

1967 *The Chosen* by Chaim Potok

1971-1980

1973 *Crash* by J.G. Ballard

1976 *A River Runs Through It* by Norman MacLean

1980 *A Confederacy of Dunces* by John Kennedy Toole
1980 *The Clan of the Cave* Bear by Jean Auel

1981-1990

1983 *Ironweed* by William Kennedy

Chapter 32

13 STIGMATICS

"My marks and scars I carry with me, to be a witness
for me, that I have fought his battles, who will now
be my rewarded."
—John Bunyan, *The Pilgrim's Progress*

"The miracle of the Church seems to me to rest not
so much upon faces of voices or healing power coming
suddenly near to us from afar off, but upon our
perceptions being made finer, so that for a moment
our eyes can see and our ears can hear what is there
about us always."
—Willa Cather, *Death Comes for the Archbishop* (1927)

"One miracle is just as easy to believe as another."
—William Jennings Bryan, The Scopes Trial, July 21, 1925

The Encyclopedia of the Unexplained had this to say about the strange physical phenomenon known as stigmata:

[Stigmata are] wounds or marks on the body corresponding to the wounds suffered by Christ on the cross, in the hands, feet, and side; stigmatics may also bear the bruise on the shoulder caused by carrying the cross, rope-marks on the wrists and ankles, the marks of scourging and those of the crown of thorns on the forehead. [p. 240]

Since the first century A.D. there have been over three hundred reported cases of stigmatization. The Catholic Church has been *extremely* cautious about attributing a divine cause for the appearance of stigmata on one of their rank and file faithful. This is in line with their official, usually neutral, position on almost all seemingly supernatural religious phenomena, such as miraculous healings attributed to particular saints and sightings of the Virgin Mary.

Today, skeptics believe that auto-suggestion and religious hysteria are the root causes for stigmatization, but this still leaves us with some apparently unanswerable questions, such as why do stigmatics only secrete blood and water—never pus—no matter how long the stigmatic wounds are open? And why don't the dead bodies of many stigmatics often never decay—even after hundreds of years—and continue to emit a sweet odor even after death and burial? Also, there are reported cases of the stigmatic's blood acting in a weird fashion, such as in the case of Marie-Dominique Lazzari. She bled from her hands and feet, and when lying prone in bed, the blood from her feet would flow up her toes, in an apparent defiance of gravity.

Dermography, or skin writing, is another facet of the stigmata phenomenon. Words and/or symbols appear spontaneously as raised welts or red marks on the believer's skin. A well-known depiction of this type of religious physical manifestation was in the 1973 horror film *The Exorcist*. In that chiller, the words *Help me* appeared as raised welts on Regan's abdomen. Regan was possessed by a demon at the time and it seems that the plea for help came from her own subconscious, rather than from a spiritual entity.

This feature looks at 13 documented stigmatics and provides some details as to the circumstances and nature of their holy wounds.

1. **St. Paul (died c. 67):** The Apostle Paul was the first recorded case of religious stigmatization. Paul revealed the appearance of his wounds in his Epistle to the Galatians: "From henceforth let no man trouble me: for I bear in my body the marks of the Lord Jesus" (6:17). According to legend, Paul was also capable of performing miracles and died on the same day as Saint Peter. Nero beheaded Paul in 67 during his vicious persecution of Christians. The former Pharisee was likely between fifty-two and sixty-two years of age at the time of his death.

2. **Lutgardis (1182–June 16, 1246):** Lutgardis was a Benedictine nun whose body dripped blood when she experienced Christ's Passion during religious ecstasies. Her stigmata and visions spanned the twelve years from 1202 through 1214. She is considered one of the leading mystics of the 13th century and is also reputed to have performed miracles and made prophecies.

3. **St. Francis of Assisi (c. 1181–October 3, 1226):** St. Francis first experienced the stigmata on September 14, 1224, while praying in his cell on Mount Alverna. His stigmata consisted of torn and bleeding flesh at the five sites: hands, feet, and side. The wounds on his hands and feet looked like punctures made by spikes. He suffered severe pain and much bleeding from his stigmata and it is believed that his wounds hastened his death at the relatively young age of forty-five.

4. **Catherine of Siena (March 25, 1347–April 29, 1380):** Catherine of Siena first received the stigmata in 1375 at the age of twenty-eight. (Twenty-eight, as you will notice, appears often as the age for the first manifestation of stigmata.) What was especially odd about her stigmatization was that her wounds remained invisible throughout her lifetime, but appeared on her body after her death. It must be assumed that she suffered from the pain and bleeding in silence throughout the five years of her stigmatization. Her death at the young age of thirty-three (the accepted age of Christ at the time of his crucifixion) revealed her wounds.

5. **Rita of Cascia (born Margherita Lotti; 1381–May 22, 1457):** Rita's stigmata did not appear until late in her life. In 1441, at the age of sixty, Rita heard a sermon about Christ's crown of thorns. Later, a bleeding "thorn" wound appeared on her forehead. Several miracles were attributed to her intervention after her death and she was canonized a saint in 1900.

6. **La Bienheureuse Lucie De Narni (1476–1544):** Lucie manifested the stigmata for seven years beginning at the age of twenty. She died at the age of sixty-eight, almost forty years after the last appearance of her wounds. In 1548, four years after her death, her body was exhumed and it was found to be free from decay and putrefaction. Her corpse exuded a sweet odor and blood still flowed from the wound in her side. In 1710, 162 years later, her body was yet again exhumed and was found to be still be in a perfect state with no decay.

7. **Johanna Della Croce (b. 1524):** Johanna's stigmata appeared every Friday regularly throughout her life and vanished two days later on Sunday. In Catholic theology, Friday is the day Christ died and Sunday the day he rose from the dead.

8. **St. Veronica Giuliani (December 27, 1660–July 9, 1727):** In 1693, at the age of thirty-three, Veronique's stigmata first manifested itself as a crown of thorns. Bleeding wounds appeared on her forehead in the places where Christ wore his crown of thorns. In 1697, at the age of thirty-seven, Veronique manifested the other five common stigmatic wounds: She bled from her side, her two hands, and her two feet. It is also reported that Veronique could levitate at will. She was acknowledged as one of the most astounding mystics of the eighteenth century and was canonized a saint in 1839.

9. **Jeanne de Maria Jesus (18th cen.):** Jeanne's stigmata manifested itself in several uncommon ways. Her skin became dark and blue. Blood pooled beneath her fin-

gernails and toenails. Dark bruises appeared on her arms and legs. Jeanne's most alarming stigmata sign was the sweating of blood from her forehead and elsewhere on her body. Not much other biographical information exists about Jeanne de Marie-Jesus.

10. **Blessed Anne Catherine Emmerich (September 8, 1774–February 9, 1824)**: Catherine was a nun at the Dolmen convent. Her crown of thorns wounds opened regularly every Friday. Throughout her life she manifested eight wounds on her hands and feet (front and back on both hands and feet), which flowed blood continuously with no apparent severe ill effects.

11. **Gemma Galani (March 12, 1878–April 11, 1903)**: It is not known when Gemma first received the stigmata. In addition to the wounds, she also experienced mystical visions of Christ, as well as enduring alleged demonic assaults. She died of tuberculosis of the spine at the young age of twenty-five and was canonized in 1940.

Padre Pio

12. Padre Pio (May 25, 1887–September 23, 1968): Padre Pio da Pietralcini (whose real name was Francesca Forgione) is one of the most well-known of the modern stigmatics. He first manifested the stigmata in 1915, at the age of twenty-eight. He was a Capuchin monk who lived in the convent of San Giovanni Rotondo in Italy. In 1918, the wounds on his hands and feet began flowing blood and water at the rate of a glass a day. His other reputed paranormal/supernatural gifts included clairvoyance (seeing or sensing things not visible with ordinary sight such as apparitions and spirits) and precognition (being able to predict the future). The religious faithful turned to Padre Pio for spiritual guidance, healings, and the Catholic Church canonized him a Saint in 2002.

13. **Teresa Neumann (April 8 or 9, 1898–September 18, 1962):** Teresa Neumann, who was born at Konnersreuth, Germany, is another modern stigmatic around whom a devotive cult has developed. Like Padre Pio, Teresa's stigmata appeared at the age of twenty-eight during Lent in the year 1926. She would go into a trance and have visions of Christ's Passion, during which she would bleed from her hands, feet, and forehead, and also cry tears of blood. She rarely ate. As with Padre Pio, Catholics turned to her for all manner of spiritual guidance and intervention, but again, the Church remained neutral as to whether or not her manifestations had a divine source.

Chapter 33

7 SEXUAL BONDAGE PRACTICES

Bondage practices are sexual acts that usually involve some form of domination and submission. Whips, straps, gags, and harnesses are the most common artifacts used in S & M sex play, but there are also other, stranger devices and practices much beloved by aficionados.

1. **Cages:** These are what you imagine they might be: A box of some sort—usually wire, iron, or wood—that the slave is imprisoned in for a period of time. Sometimes males are anchored to the bar of a cage by a ring through the head of their penis.

2. **Genital Encasement:** Encasement involves putting a "cage" of metal or some other material over the penis, thus preventing contact with the organ and consequently, prohibiting orgasm. Reportedly, sensitivity is greatly increased when the encasement device is eventually removed.

3. **Impaling:** This involves hammering stainless steel needles through the webbing of the fingers, the head of the penis, or through a woman's breasts and into a piece of stationary wood, thereby "imprisoning" the person and allowing total sexual access.

4. **Lacing:** Lacing is putting a needle and thread through a person's skin and then securing the needle to the wall or some other stationary object. Once again, prohibition of movement and complete sexual access are the ultimate goals.

5. **Speculum Play:** This involves using the device used for gynecological exams for sex play.

6. **Spreader Bars:** These are long bars that have cuffs on the ends that are secured to the wrists and/or ankles. The bar prevents a person from closing their legs and eliminates the need to tie someone's arms to the bedposts. Spreader bars allow total sexual access.

7. **Three-Legged Bloomers:** These are thin pants that have two leg holes and an opening for the crotch. A hood hangs over the crotch hole and the wearer straddles their lover's head, covering his or her face with the hood. This ensures unavoidable, maximum oral/genital contact.

Chapter 34

11 CELEBRITY UFO SIGHTINGS

1. **Muhammad Ali:** The Champ admits to having seen at least sixteen UFOs during his life. One was "cigar-shaped" and appeared over the New Jersey Turnpike. Another looked like "a huge electric light bulb"; he saw it in Central Park. "If you look into the sky in the early morning you see them playing tag between the stars," he said.

2. **David Bowie:** David "The Man Who Fell To Earth" Bowie claimed to have seen many UFOs when he was growing up in England. In fact, he saw UFOs so frequently that he actually published a magazine about his sightings. "They came over so regularly," he once said in an interview, "we could time them." Bowie also reported, "sometimes they stood still, other times they moved so fast it was hard to keep a steady eye on them."

3. **Jimmy Carter:** Former President Carter claims to have seen a UFO on January 6, 1969. He was governor of Georgia at the time, Carter said it changed colors and was as big as the moon. There is conjecture today that

what he (and the others he was with) saw was actually the planet Venus. Although his description of the object sure as heck doesn't sound like a stationary planet.

4. **Jamie Farr:** Farr played Corporal Klinger on the hit TV series *M*A*S*H*, and claims to have once seen an erratically flying light in Yuma, Arizona. He says it stopped in midair above his car. No further information about this sighting ever came to light.

5. **Jackie Gleason:** The Great One was extremely interested in the paranormal and the occult and claimed to have seen several UFOs in London and Florida (as well as having seen retrieved alien craft and corpses). He possessed a massive library of books about UFOs and the supernatural and subscribed to many UFO journals. Gleason even named his home in Peekskill, New York, the Mothership.

6. **Dick Gregory:** According to activist Gregory, he saw three red and green lights dance in the sky for close to an hour one night.

7. **John Lennon:** The former Beatle told his UFO story to biographer Ray Coleman during an interview in Lennon's Dakota apartment. "Look, it's true," he told Coleman. "I was standing, naked, by this window leading on to that roof when an oval-shaped object started flying from left to right. After about twenty minutes it disappeared over the East River and behind the United Nations Building. I wonder if it had been carrying out some research here. They all think I'm potty," John continued, "but it's true. I shouted after it, 'Wait for

me, wait for me!'" John also told Coleman that he immediately called the police to report the sighting and was told that there had been other reports of flying saucers seen over New York that evening. "But I didn't tell them who was on the phone," he went on. "I didn't want newspaper headlines saying, 'Beatle Sees Flying Saucer.' I've got enough trouble with the immigration people already."

8. **Gordon MacRae:** Six months before he died, during an appearance on a TV talk show, actor Gordon MacRae (*Oklahoma, Carousel*) stated that he had been a security sergeant at Wright-Patterson Air Force Base in July, 1947. He then told the fantastic story of being ordered to stand watch over a large pallet covered with a tarpaulin that had been brought in under tight security. MacRae remembered being specifically ordered not to remove the tarp under any circumstances, but admitted that curiosity got the better of him and his fellow guards and they did, in fact, peek under the tarp MacRae said that they all saw four small humanoid creatures laid out on the pallet

9. **Richard Nixon:** Reportedly, President Nixon was fully aware of the crash and retrieval of alien spacecraft and alien bodies and was known to have visited the repository of these extraterrestrial artifacts at Homestead Air Force Base in Florida. Nixon even supposedly once arranged a 1973 tour of the facility (complete with a viewing of the alien bodies) for his good friend Jackie Gleason, who, according to his wife, returned home from the experience quite shaken.

10. Ronald Reagan: In 1974, when Ronald Reagan was governor of California, he, his pilot, and two security agents all saw a UFO while flying aboard a Cessna Citation near Bakersfield, California. Reagan's pilot, Bill Paynter, described the object as "a big light flying a bit behind [the] plane." He also reported that "It seemed to be several hundred yards away," and that it was "a fairly steady light until it began to accelerate, then it appeared to elongate." Paynter also said the object then "went up at a 45-degree angle," a behavior reported in many other UFO sightings. Ronald Reagan himself later described the incident to a reporter for the *Wall Street Journal,* saying, "We followed it for several minutes. All of a sudden, to our utter amazement it went straight up into the heavens. When I got off the plane I told Nancy about it. And we read up on the long history of UFOs…"

11. William Shatner: Known around the galaxy as Captain James T. Kirk of the Starship *Enterprise*—Shatner reported that a silver spacecraft flew over him in the Mojave Desert as he pushed his inoperative motorcycle. Shatner also claims to have received a telepathic message from the beings in the craft advising him which direction to walk.

From *The Big Book of UFO Facts, Figures & Truth* by Stephen Spignesi & William J. Byrnes, Skyhorse Publishing, © 2017. Used by permission.

Chapter 35

9 FRINGE MYTHS & BELIEFS

Weird beliefs, interests, and obsessions have been around since the first caveman saw a light in the northern sky and imagined a monster from *out there* coming to get him.

There are people who believe that the earth is flat. Or hollow. Or that they can channel spirits from another realm through their own bodies. Or that they have been abducted by aliens. Or that a piece of amethyst can heal their inflamed gallbladder. Or that the world will come to an end on Wednesday Whatever. Or that they have lived before as an Assyrian slave concubine named Oha.

And what's especially interesting about these enthusiasts of the odd is that they are as fervent about their convictions as any church-going, communion-taking, genuflecting and confessing Roman Catholic could ever be. It's just that their strange doctrines and dogmas are a little bit more unusual than the strange doctrines and dogmas many people are accustomed to accepting on faith. Their argument is, if you can believe that your God was born of a virgin, rose from the dead, and walked on water, why can't I believe that a million year old entity from the planet Venus speaks to me every Thursday morning in my vegetable garden? It is, of course, a Good Question.

This feature looks briefly at nine of the more intriguing fringe interests.

1. **Astral Projection:** Astral Projection is also known as an Out-of-Body Experience and involves leaving the physical body and traveling to a place outside of and away from where the body happens to be at the time.

   OBEs have been reported throughout history and they all share similar characteristics. In many cases, stress will trigger one, and occasionally, there are reports of people being able to initiate an Astral Projection at will. Evidence exists that these experiences are real, mainly because the "traveler" can describe a place he or she has never been to, or report on events that occurred at a distant location while they were physically someplace else.

2. **Channeling:** Jon Klimo, in his 1987 book on channeling called, appropriately, *Channeling*, defines the experience: "Channeling is the communication of information to or through a physically embodied human being from a source that is said to exist on some other level or dimension of reality than the physical as we know it, and that is not from the normal mind (or self) of the channel. Although the human mind might be considered nonphysical, I want to rule out by definition not only communication from one's own normal mind

as source, but communication from fellow physically embodied minds."

Apparently there is a realm where legions of spirits exist, many of whom have a lot to say and really like to talk, and whose preferred mode of communication with our world seems to be to inhabit one of us Earthlings and speak through his or her body.

There are advocates who are convinced that they have spoken to entities from another plane, channeled through someone they know. Some channelers claim to channel big names, like Jesus Christ, Mark Twain, and Albert Einstein. Others claim their sources are from other planets, including the mundane ones, like Mars and Venus, as well as planets we allegedly don't know about yet. There are numerous channelers who claim many paranormal sources, including Seth, Lazaris, Ramtha, and Ra.

3. **Crystal Healing:** Crystal healing is a practice that uses the positive "energy" in natural, mined quartz crystals to heal. According to its advocates, crystals are a type of natural therapeutic tool that can be utilized to cure all manner of ailments, both physical and emotional.

And it seems that crystals may be more than just rocks. This is from Gari Gold's 1987 book, *Crystal Energy*:

"Clearing your crystal and charging it can often be accomplished simultaneously. For example, exposure to the sun will both clear a crystal of old energy and recharge it with new. Sometimes, however, old energy won't be gotten rid of simply by exposure to new, positive energy; while the crystal is charged with new energy, it also retains the old. I usually do a salt-water cleansing before charging in the sun, but it is not always necessary. Do whatever you feel your crystal needs. If you desire a quick cleanse and charge, cleansing and charging with intent is particularly effective."

4. **Doomsday Mythologies:** Doomsdayers look to the Bible, to prophets, and occasionally to science (both mainstream and fringe) to predict with absolute certainty the day the world is going to end. (Or at least until the day they predict as doomsday comes and goes with nary a peep.)

The book of Revelation in the Bible is a big favorite for doomsayers, as are the writings of Nostradamus. Gullible, credulous people sometimes put all their faith into these "prophets."

Far Out magazine recently detailed one such travesty:

> Doomsday predictions are generally harmless, usually resulting in nothing worse than Christian best-sellers and bad television miniseries. But sometimes the consequences can be deadly. The most recent example is the Dami Mission, a Korean Christian sect that believed the world was coming to an end on October 28, 1992. Four of the mission's followers committed suicide in anticipation shortly before midnight of that day. Others sold their houses, had abortions and bequeathed their life savings to less fortunate pilgrims. Now they have nothing.

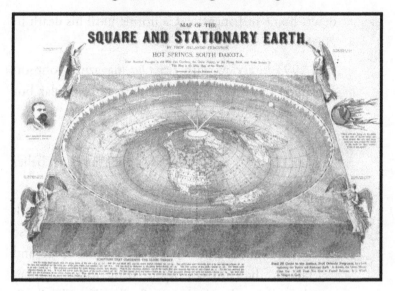

Flat Earth Theory

5. **Flat Earth Theory:** The people who propound the Flat Earth theory (their motto is "Restoring the World to Sanity") reject the notion that our planet is round, satellite photos notwithstanding. They believe that NASA imagery is nothing more than "entertainment for the masses."

The Flat Earth people believe that Gaia is an enormous flat disk floating in space. According to Flat Earthers, we are all in constant danger of falling off the edge into the great void. The father of the Flat Earth movement was a retired aircraft mechanic named Charles K. Johnson, who operated the Flat Earth Society and published the *Flat Earth News* for his 3,500 subscribers out of his desert home in Lancaster, California until his death in 2001.

In a 1993 interview with *Far Out* magazine, Johnson explained why he believes our globe is not globular, but is, instead, plainly a plane:

Far Out: What do you base your Flat Earth belief in?

Johnson: The Greeceball theory, or the Greek ball theory; Greeceball means "Greek ball." These Greeks sat around, sipped on a wine bottle and talked. The entire theory [that the earth is globe-shaped] just hatched out of talks. The Flat Earth Society, on the other hand, had nothing to do with talk; we went out, checked the world and found it was flat.

Far Out: You checked? How?

Johnson: Most of the world is water; you have to check the water, in lakes, canals or the ocean. To give you a good example: the Suez Canal, that's water and it joins two seas. It's 100 miles long. If the world were a globe, this thing would be humped in the center. But it's not. It's flat. All water that's been examined by using telescopes, markers and by airplane, it's just flat, that's all.

Far Out: Where exactly are the boundaries for the end of the Earth? Do people fall off there?

Johnson: There is a frozen ring of ice that surrounds the known world. That is the area where
the sun doesn't shine. It's all a frozen great wall of
ice, plain ice that can't be penetrated. You come to
it when you leave north, the farther you go south
you come to this ice ring. You could follow the ice
ring around the known world; it comes to around
64,000 miles. If the world were a globe they would
fall off; they'd certainly go over the edge! You'd get
to Australia and you'd have to sail over the edge. If
you had some magic glue, gravy or gravity holding
you, you'd still go over the edge and you'd hang
underneath the world. With a flat Earth you have
no danger of going over the edge, since water follows the laws of physics. Water seeks its own level
and lays flat.

The Flat Earth Society published a map of what they
call the "real world" that posits that "This Flat Earth
Does Not Spin or Whirl" and lays claim to the Earth
as the "Center of the Universe." In one of their news-
letters, they proudly included George Washington and
Christopher Columbus in the ranks of Flat Earthers.

6. **Hollow Earth Theory:** Hollow Earthers believe that
the world is a hollow sphere, entered by large holes at
either pole, or by secret entrances scattered around the
globe. Inside the Earth is a small sun, as well as a race
of advanced beings who are responsible for all the UFO
sightings throughout history. Photos exist that purport
to show the polar entrances.

7. **Past Lives & Reincarnation:** Reincarnation zealots believe that this life is just one of many that our eternal soul will live. They believe that we have all lived before and that our past lives are stored somewhere within us, deeply buried in our unconscious/subconscious, ready to be accessed by the proper technique. Many believers look to the concept of karma as the determining factor as to whether we move forward or backward on our eternal, celestial journey.

The theory goes that our soul is like an empty bank account when we are born into a certain life. The good we do during our life adds to the account; the bad we do deducts from our account. If there's a positive balance in the account at the time of our death, we move forward; if we're in the red, we move backwards. When we have developed our spiritual self to its highest level, we reach nirvana and enter into a oneness with the universe.

Nirvana releases us from the cycle of reincarnations and completely extinguishes the self, thereby allowing us to become part of the all. Most religions have a similar philosophy, although the language may be different. Entering heaven, becoming one with God, knowing God, and other terms are all used to describe this state of absolute blessedness.

A "Past Lives Counselor" is a person who can supposedly allow you to tap into your past lives at will and learn from what you were in the past. How much of these regression sessions are pure imagination is hard to say, although advocates claim to recall people and events that they could not be aware of unless they had lived during another period.

8. **Spontaneous Human Combustion:** In 1853, Charles Dickens killed off his character Krook in *Bleak House* by spontaneous combustion. According to an 1859 newspaper report, at the time, people cringed and doctors smiled: such a ridiculous death could never occur in the real world.

Now, almost 150 years after Dickens' bitter tale, incidences of spontaneous human combustion are still being reported worldwide.

Spontaneous human combustion is the term used to describe a person burning up from within. There is usually no external source of fire, and the fire is often contained to the immediate surroundings of the person, such as the chair or bed. Oftentimes, the person's clothing does not completely burn up, but the body does, although sometimes the extremities are left intact. A photo exists of a person who spontaneously combusted, and all that was left of him was his right calf and foot.

Medical science has no definitive explanation for SHC, although some have tried to find a link between excessive alcohol ingestion and bursting into flames. Students of the supernatural look to poltergeists and "fire-spooks" as the cause, but the truth is that SHC is one of the genuinely unexplainable phenomena on the paranormal landscape.

9. **Unidentified Flying Objects & Alien Abductions:**
UFO sightings are a ubiquitous element of human experience and a phenomena that has been reported since Biblical times.

What are UFOs? Where do they come from? The speculative answers to these questions have filled volumes of books. Carl Jung posited that UFOs might be some kind of subconscious hallucinatory manifestations of our collective unconscious. But then there are those clearly rational people (military people, law enforcement people, doctors, and lawyers, among others) who have seen UFOs and who purport to have real evidence of their experiences, such as photos, objects from alien crafts, and physical wounds from close encounters.

There are many people who claim to have been abducted by aliens and taken aboard extraterrestrial spacecraft, where they have been examined and/or assaulted. Most of these abductees cannot be shaken in their belief that they were kidnapped by aliens.

Most UFO sightings can be attributed to natural phenomena such as ball lightning, clouds, planets, and weird geographical anomalies. But no matter how many sightings are "written off," so to speak, there will always be that percentage of encounters that are genuinely unexplainable and that could possibly be of extraterrestrial origin.

Chapter 36

9 TYPES OF ANGELS

Catholics grow up believing that everyone has a Guardian Angel watching over them.

This is comforting, but also a little scary. According to the "rules," our angel is with us from the moment of birth until we breathe our last breath, and then even after we've died, as our angel sticks by us and accompanies us into Heaven.

As you can well imagine, this is pretty heady stuff for impressionable grammar school kids.

This feature lists the nine different types of angels that float around outside our earthly plane. This ranking is based on the writings of St. Paul and other theologians.

Interestingly, there is an actual rank called "Angel," and ironically, it is at the bottom of the "spiritual totem pole," so to speak.

There are eight angelic ranks superior to just plain old Angels. As to how these spiritual bodyguards get promoted...it just might be who you know, you know?

First Hierarchy

1. Seraphim
2. Cherubim
3. Thrones

Second Hierarchy

4. Dominions
5. Principalities
6. Powers

Third Hierarchy

7. Virtues
8. Archangels
9. Angels

Chapter 37

THE 6 TYPES OF DEVILS

In 1608, Friar Francesco-Maria Guazzo wrote a book called *Compendium Maleficarum* in which he attempted to document the six different types of devils that exist in our world.

Apparently, these six different kinds of devils all work to serve Lucifer (the head honcho) and his sixteen servants, from Beelzebub (the patron devil of pride) to Iuvart, a devil who is on hiatus, so to speak. (In 1612, Iuvart was trapped in the body of a nun at Louviers Convent.)

This feature provides a listing of these six devilish types and describes their main body of interest.

1. **Fire Devils:** These fiends are the upper management of devils. They reside in our upper atmosphere and supervise the nefarious doings of the other five demons.

2. **Aerial Devils:** These guys are everywhere: They live in the very air that surrounds us. These are considered the most dangerous and malefic type of demons because they are so ubiquitous.

3. **Terrestrial Devils:** These villains are your basic "back-to-nature" devils. They live in the forests and the rural areas of our world.

4. **Aqueous Devils:** These rogues are into water sports: They live in the lakes, oceans, and rivers of Mother Earth. They are said to be responsible for catastrophes at sea.

5. **Subterranean Devils:** As you might guess, these brutes are your cave-dweller types. They live beneath mountains and in caves.

6. **Heliophobic Devils:** Consider the vampire legends. One of a vampire's most recognizable characteristics was their fear and "allergy" to light. It is possible that vampires were (are?) a form of Heliophobic Devils since these chaps are the demons who appear only after sunset and who hate the light.

This painting, Rebel Angels, depicts the fall of angels
who then become devils.

Chapter 38

6 WAYS OF DYING ACCIDENTALLY ON A FARM

"Farm living is the life for me."
—Oliver Douglas, The *Green Acres* theme song

City-trapped Americans often dream about giving up the rat race and moving out to the country where they will live and work on a farm. They fantasize about the endless acres of rich soil and the beauty of sunrises and sunsets.

They think the peace and contentment they seek will be found there.

Perhaps.

But before you sell the co-op and buy three dozen flannel shirts and a bunch of overalls, read this feature on odd ways you can die on a farm. Okay, you might be killed in a hold-up or by a runaway cab in the big city. But at least you'll never have to worry about getting stuck in a corn picker or being stampeded to death (unless you're at a Who concert, that is) in the concrete jungle.

This feature looks at ways of dying on a farm.

1. **Being Crushed:** A painful way of dying on a farm is to be crushed to death when a tractor or another piece of heavy riding equipment rolls over on you.

2. **Being Fumigated:** Inhaling deadly fumes or gases in a silo is a mode of death on a farm.

3. **Being "Picked":** A nasty form of farm death is getting caught in the machine called the corn picker.

4. **Being Stampeded:** Death can occur when a farm hand is crushed by stampeding or running cattle. If a cowboy falls down in the midst of a covey of cows, it can be fatal.

5. **Buried Alive:** Farm personnel sometimes fall into corn bins, are buried, and then suffocate to death when they can't climb out.

6. **Strangled:** A loose piece of clothing can get caught in a piece of moving farm equipment and strangle the wearer to death.

Chapter 39

34 BIZARRO THINGS PEOPLE EAT, INCLUDING DISHES THAT USE INSECTS, SPERM, RATS, SHARK FINS, TESTICLES, FACES & BLOOD AS THEIR MAIN INGREDIENTS

*"Tell me what you eat and I will tell
you what you are."*
—Anthelme Brillat-Savarin, *Physiologie de gout*

1. **Baked Armadillo (*American*):** This tank-like mammal is stuffed with potatoes, cabbage, apple slices, carrots, and spices, and then baked until tender.

2. **Baked Bat (*Samoan*):** First the bat is torched to "de-hair" it. Then it is cleaned and baked or fried with salt, pepper, and onions.

3. **Barbecued Cow Heart (*Peruvian*):** The cow's heart is chopped up, basted with ground chili peppers, and broiled.

4. **Bear's Paw Stew (*Chinese*):** The paw is cut into chunks and simmered in a pot with ham, chicken, and sherry.

5. **Beef Blood Pudding (*Norwegian*):** Beef's blood is mixed with milk, sugar, ginger, and cloves.

6. **Beef Udder Pot Roast (*French*):** The cow's mammaries are simmered with vegetables in beef stock.

7. **Broiled Beetle Grubs (*Japanese*):** The larvae are marinated and then broiled.

8. **Broiled Puppy (*Hawaiian*):** The puppy is broiled flat over hot coals and served with sweet potatoes.

9. **Broiled Sparrows (*Japanese*):** The birds are split, marinated, and then grilled.

10. **Coconut-Cream-Marinated Dog (*Indonesian*):** Pieces of dog are marinated in a coconut cream and then broiled on skewers.

11. **Cow Brain Fritters (*French*):** The cow brains are mashed up, mixed with spinach, and fried.

12. **Cow Heels (*English*):** The cow's heels are cut up and simmered in a stew with beef stock and spices.

13. **Cow Lung Stew (*Jewish*):** The cow's lung is chopped into pieces and simmered with tomatoes, carrots, and potatoes.

14. **Cow Tongue Salad (*Danish*):** Julienned beef tongue is served with beets, apples, and hard-boiled eggs.

15. **Fish Sperm Crepes (*French*):** Fish sperm is baked in crepes with mushrooms, butter, and cheese.

16. **Fried Calf's Head (*Hungarian*):** The head is sliced, breaded, and fried.

17. **Fried Grasshoppers (*Chinese*):** The bugs are quick-fried in sesame oil and allowed to drain and cool. They crunch.

Fried grasshoppers

18. **Fried Turkey Testes (*American*):** The gonads are coated with bread crumbs and then fried in olive oil or butter.

19. **Golden Calf Testicles (*French*):** The testes are sliced and fried and then baked in a casserole.

20. Grilled Horsemeat (*Japanese*): The meat is sliced up, marinated, and then broiled on a hibachi.

21. Grilled Rat (*French*): Le rat is brushed with olive oil and shallots and then broiled.

22. Lamb Brain Tacos (*Mexican*): The lamb's brain is chopped up, fried with onions, tomatoes, and chilies, and then used as a taco stuffing.

23. Pig's Face and Cabbage (*Irish*): The blanched face is baked with seasonings and served with boiled cabbage.

24. Pig's Feet with Bananas (*Filipino*): The feet are simmered with bananas in a soup.

25. Pork Testicles in Cream (*French*): The testes are fried in butter and cream.

26. Roasted Caterpillars (*Laotian*): The insects are salted, roasted, and then eaten with white rice.

27. Sea Urchin Gonad Sauce (*French*): Fish testes or ovaries are mashed with olive oil and then mixed with either Hollandaise sauce or mayonnaise.

28. Shark's Fin Soup (*Chinese*): Pieces of shark fin are simmered in a chicken stock with flaked crabmeat.

29. Snake Soup (*Chinese*): Chunks of snake are simmered in a fish or chicken stock with scallions.

30. Stewed Cat (*Ghanaian*): Sliced cat is fried in peanut oil and butter and then simmered in a pot with red peppers.

31. Stuffed Calf's Eyes (*French*): The eyes are stuffed with mushrooms (after the corneas, lenses, and irises have been removed) and baked.

32. Stuffed Cow Spleen (*Jewish*): The cow's spleen is stuffed with bread crumbs and baked.

33. Sun-dried Maggots (*Chinese*): Fly larvae are dried in the sun and then eaten as a snack or as a side dish with a meal.

34. White Ant Pie (*Zanzibari*): White termites are mixed with sugar and banana flour and blended into a paste.

Chapter 40

THE ULTIMATE COLLECTION OF "PAUL IS DEAD" CLUES[1]

"However foolish its guise, the McCartney rumor clearly indicates that there is a potential for irrational belief and action—be it constructive or be it destructive to what or whose values—that is alive and well in the modern, industrialized, 'enlightened' world."

—Barbara Suzek[2]

Paul McCartney was killed in a car accident in 1966 and the Beatles decided to keep it a secret...but to plant clues in their recordings so that the attentive fan would eventually know the truth.

The result of the dissemination of this theory has been multifaceted: Believers think that Paul McCartney is dead and the Beatles told the world about the tragic car accident that killed him in a series of hidden clues in and on their records.

The skeptics, on the other hand, say that the "Paul is Dead" mystery was an elaborate hoax nurtured by the fact that many

---

1   Some of the material in this chapter appeared in a different form in the 1998 Kensington book, *The Weird 100*.
2   Urban Life and Culture, 1972.

alleged "clues" on the Beatles records actually could be interpreted to mean that Paul had died.

There is no denying that finding and analyzing all the "Paul is Dead" clues is an enormous amount of fun.

This is probably what prolonged the worldwide frenzy back in September, October, and November of 1969 when the rumor that Paul had died in a car crash first surfaced, thanks to an intentionally satirical review of *Abbey Road* in a college newspaper that alleged to find all kinds of secret messages and clues the surviving Beatles planted to tell the world that Mr. McCartney (he wasn't Sir Paul back then) was no longer with us.

The article that started it all was written by University of Michigan sophomore Fred LaBour. LaBour was inspired to write the review after Detroit's WKNR-FM disk jockey Russ Gibb received a call from a guy named Tom who claimed to have found secret messages on Beatles records revealing that McCartney was dead.

LaBour heard Gibb's conversation with the caller and decided to deliberately expand on the "Paul is Dead" thesis in his *Abbey Road* review for the University of Michigan's school newspaper, *The Michigan Daily*.

LaBour's article began:

> *Paul McCartney was killed in an automobile accident in early November, 1966 after leaving EMI recording studios tired, sad and dejected.*
> *The Beatles had been preparing their forthcoming album, tentatively entitled* Smile, *when progress bogged down in intragroup hassles and bickering.*
> *Paul climbed into his Aston-Martin, sped away*

> *into the rainy, chilly night, and was found four*
> *hours later pinned under his car in a culvert with*
> *the top of his head sheared off. He was deader*
> *than a doornail.*

LaBour's article discussed the most common "Paul is Dead" clues, including Paul's "O.P.D." ("Officially Pronounced Dead") jacket patch on the *Sgt. Pepper* album; the "I buried Paul" fadeout on "Strawberry Fields Forever"; all the appearances of hands above Paul's head in Beatles' photographs; the *Abbey Road* funeral procession; and the backwards message "Turn me on, dead man" in "Revolution 9" on what's come to be called the *White Album* (but was officially titled *The Beatles*.)

The myth immediately took hold and blossomed. It was learned that the surviving Beatles decided that they would not reveal this terrible tragedy to their fans but instead, replace Paul with a double, a musical doppelganger.

Paul's "replacement" was a guy by the name of William Campbell, a lucky bloke who just so happened to be the winner of a Paul McCartney Look-Alike Contest. Not only was Campbell the spitting image of the "cute" Beatle, he was also musically and vocally gifted enough to be able to duplicate Paul's writing, playing, and singing abilities. After a period of "training" by John, George, and Ringo, Campbell took Paul's place in The Beatles.

Even though The Beatles did not want to shock the world by revealing the truth about Paul's violent death, they had too much respect for their fans not to let them somehow know of his death. Thus, they began planting "clues" on Beatles albums that would alert the attentive fan to the terrible reality.

The rumors surrounding Paul's alleged death grew into a cottage industry. Special edition magazines and TV and radio programs were devoted to the rumors, and countless newspaper articles fueled the fervor. (I can remember trading clues with fellow Beatlefans when I was in my teens, aghast at the thought that the rumors might actually prove to be true. They weren't, as we now know, and it would be another decade before we actually would have to go through the real death of a Beatle.)

This chapter compiles all (or at least most) of the intriguing "hidden" clues. The focus is on primarily visual clues found on record albums and on aural clues heard in The Beatles' songs. There is little attention to song lyrics because they are open to a wide range of interpretation—almost anything can be read into a line from a song. Song lyrics that seem to be a deliberate attempt by The Beatles to address the whole "Paul is Dead" phenomenon (such as the "walrus was Paul" line in "Glass Onion.") are cited and discussed.

Yesterday and Today

- **The Two *Yesterday and Today* Album Covers:** *Yesterday and Today* was the first Beatles album released after Paul's rumored death and the two versions of the album's cover are supposed to contain the first of the hidden messages from The Fab Four.

  The first cover, the infamous recalled "butcher" cover, is supposed to contain the most blatant acknowledgment of Paul's death. (The "butcher" cover was originally shot for the "Paperback Writer" single and added to the album as an afterthought. This cover, which is now an extremely valuable collectible, shows the four Beatles in white butcher coats, covered with decapitated dolls and bloody meat.) The clues here are that the two headless dolls in the picture are resting on Paul's right and left shoulders and a doll's head sits in his lap. (George holds the other severed head.) This is supposed to be The Beatles' way of visually illustrating the bloody results of Paul's car crash. Also, there is a pair of false teeth on Paul's right arm, apparently indicating that his teeth were knocked out during the accident and they could not identify his body from dental records.

The second cover—the "trunk" cover—shows us Paul sitting in a trunk that is standing on its side with its cover open. This trunk is supposed to symbolize a coffin and indicate that Paul is buried somewhere. In the picture, none of The Beatles are smiling and John, George, and Ringo are all standing above the trunk supposedly looking down into Paul's casket.

Rubber Soul

- **The *Rubber Soul* Album Cover:** This cover is supposed to be a photograph taken from inside Paul's grave looking up. The four Beatles are all seen from below in sort of a fisheye view and it is their way of telling fans that Paul is dead. Also, the title *Rubber Soul* is their way of hinting at the bogus nature of the Paul replacement.

Revolver

- **The *Revolver* Cover:** This cover, designed by Beatlepal and fellow Brian Epstein artist Klaus Voorman, consists of a collage of line drawings and black-and-white photos of the four Beatles. The death clue? Paul's face is the only one shown in profile; all the others are seen full face. Why this means Paul is dead baffles the mind, but cluesters have considered this to be one of the hints.

"Strawberry Fields Forever" Single & Video

- **The "Strawberry Fields Forever"/"Penny Lane" Single Sleeve:** This sleeve has a framed photo of The Beatles on a stage. Four stage spotlights highlight the boys: one above John's head; one above Ringo's head; and one to the left of George. Paul's spotlight, however, emanates from a mirror directly in front of him, indicating, presumably, that he is on another plane, and that his "inner light" is in a mirror world somewhere. Quite clever if intended, wouldn't you say?

- **The "Strawberry Fields Forever" Video:** Paul is seen in a tree looking down on the other three, symbolically representing once again that he has risen above the survivors to another plane.

Sgt. Pepper's Lonely Hearts Club Band

- **The Sgt. Pepper's Lonely Hearts Club Band Album Front Cover Scene:** There are several visual clues on the cover of Sgt. Pepper that indicate that The Beatles are trying to tell the world that Paul is dead. The first and most obvious is that the cover photo depicts a funeral. Whose? Why, Paul's of course!

- **The Flower Guitar:** In the foreground is a bass guitar made of flowers that has only three strings. This is Paul's bass and the three strings symbolize the three remaining Beatles. Some people also claim that they can see "Paul?" spelled out in the flowers.

- **The Propped-Up Paul:** Paul is the only one facing front and the other three Beatles are all turned towards him as though they were holding him up. If he were dead, he would need to be held up, right? (Shades of *Weekend at Bernie's!*) Outtakes of the *Sgt. Pepper* photo shoot session show Paul in a variety of positions and locations on the set, including sitting down.

- **Paul's Black Instrument:** John, George, and Ringo are all holding brass instruments. Paul's is black, symbolizing, of course, his death.

- **The Doll and Her Car:** There is a doll to the left of The Beatles wearing a dress that reads "Welcome The Rolling Stones." On the doll's lap is a toy car that is supposed to be either on fire or filled with blood. This is the Aston-Martin that Paul was driving when he had his fateful accident on November 9, 1966. Also, there appears to be what looks like streaks of blood running down the doll's dress.

- **The Secret Message on the Bass Drum:** If you take a mirror and place it so that you split the words "Lonely" and "Hearts" horizontally, the resultant "words" spell out the secret message "ONE HE DIE." This is a stretch but this message can actually be seen if you're generous about interpreting certain symbols and curves as letters. The actual text that appears if you cover the bottom half of the letters so that the top halves are doubled and reversed is "1ONE1X HE|DIE."

- **The Hand Above Paul's Head:** There is an open palm above Paul's head. According to the "Paul is Dead" mythology, this is supposed to be an Eastern gesture that is made over someone about to be buried. No such symbology exists.

- **The Shiva Doll:** A four-armed Indian Shiva doll points his "death" hand (the left rear hand) at Paul.

- **George's Message:** On the back cover of the *Sgt. Pepper* album, George can be seen pointing directly at the lyric "Wednesday morning at five o'clock" in "She's Leaving Home." This was supposed to be the time and day of Paul's fatal accident.

- **Without Paul?:** Paul's head touches the words "Without You" from George's song, "Within You Without You," indicating that The Beatles—and the world— must, duh, now survive without the esteemed Mr. McCartney.

- **Paul's Back?:** On the back cover of the *Sgt. Pepper* album, Paul is the only one with his back to the camera. This means that he is dead. There are conflicting stories explaining why Paul is, indeed, seen only from behind. One explanation was that it wasn't even Paul in the picture. In the 1982 book, *The Long and Winding Road: A History of The Beatles on Record,* Neville Stannard wrote:

  Also on the back cover is a small picture of The Beatles, but one Beatle has his back turned. This is because it isn't a Beatle at all, and is, in fact, Mal Evans—Mal deputised for Paul, who was in America to be with Jane Asher on her twenty-first birthday...As the sleeve had to go into production by the end of April, before Paul was due to return, Mal donned Paul's *Sgt. Pepper* gear and stood in for him, but turned his back so that people would not suspect that Paul was absent.

And to further confuse matters, Paul himself has talked about his backwards pose on the cover. Paul claims that he is, in fact, the person seen in the photograph. In 1980, he told *Musician* magazine, "[I]t was just a goof when we were doing the photos. I turned my back and it was just a joke."

Also, in Mark Lewisohn's essential *The Beatles Recording Sessions,* there are several rare, full-color outtakes from the *Sgt. Pepper* photo shoot and Paul is in every one of them.

• **Paul's "O.P.D." Patch:** Inside the album, Paul is seen wearing a patch on his jacket that reads "O P D," initials which supposedly stand for "Officially Pronounced Dead," the British equivalent of the American phrase "Dead On Arrival." This was allegedly a very blatant way for The Beatles to tell us all that Paul was dead. The truth is that the patch actually reads "O. P. P.," which stands for "Ontario Provincial Police." The garment has a fold in it which makes the last "P" look like a "D" to some people. All of The Beatles received these patches as a gift during their 1965 North American tour. (The

Fab Four played the Toronto Maple Leaf Stadium on August 17, 1965.)

- **Paul's Medal of Valor:** In the inside photo, Paul is seen wearing what was said to be a British Medal of Valor. This was alleged to be the surviving Beatles' way of telling his fans that he died a heroic death. The only trouble with this clue is that the medal he (and George, for that matter) are wearing is not a British Medal of Valor. What does the medal he's wearing represent? Who knows?

- **The Bloody Sleeve:** Some fans have noted that the original inner sleeve of the *Sgt. Pepper* album is colored red at the bottom and gets progressively lighter as the color rises to the top of the sleeve. This is supposed to mean that the album was standing in blood and the red liquid seeped its way up through the paper. This means that Paul is dead.

- **Selected *Sgt. Pepper* Lyrics:** To many "Paul is Dead" cluesters, *Sgt. Pepper's* is the album that includes the most candid lyrical admissions that Paul died and was replaced by lookalike William Campbell. The first clue comes in the first song, "Sgt. Pepper's Lonely Heart's Club Band" in which "Paul" sings "So let me introduce to you the one and only Billy Shears." "Billy Shears" is supposed to actually be the words "Billy's here," revealing that Paul has been replaced by William "Billy" Campbell.

In "She's Leaving Home" is the aforementioned line "Wednesday morning at five o'clock" which is supposed to be the time of Paul's fatal car accident.

In "Lovely Rita," Paul tells us that he "caught a glimpse of Rita" and was so distracted that he "took her home" and "nearly made it." This leads us to the line telling us that he "didn't notice that the light had changed," from "A Day in the Life." We are also told in "A Day in the Life," that "he blew his mind out in a car."

In "Good Morning, Good Morning," we once again are told the time of Paul's accident: "People running 'round, it's five o'clock."

In "Within You Without You," we again are told that life goes on "without you [Paul]."

- **In the British Groove:** On the inner groove of side two of the British *Sgt. Pepper* disk, the words "Never could be any other way" are repeated over and over. This is supposed to be The Beatles' was of telling Paul's fans to accept his death.

- **Really?!:** On mono pressings of the album, during the reprise of the title cut, author Andru Reeve claims that a voice can be heard shouting, "Paul McCartney is dead, everybody! Really, really dead!"

- **Paul's Where?:** On European pressings of *Sgt. Pepper*, after "A Day in the Life," there are two seconds of chatter which allegedly can be interpreted as the phrase "Paul's found heaven."

Magical Mystery Tour

- **The *Magical Mystery Tour* Album Cover Phone Number:** The word "Beatles" is written in stars on the cover of the *Magical Mystery Tour* album and if you read the word upside down it reveals the phone number 537-1038, or the phone number 231-7438, depending on how you interpret certain "digits." According to the "Paul is Dead" mythology, if you called this number at a certain time (revealed in the lyrics of "She's Leaving Home") you would be connected with none other than Billy Shears himself (actually Paul's replacement William Campbell), who would then tell you the truth about Paul's death.

- **The Magical Beatles:** On the inside cover of the *Magical Mystery Tour* album, there is a drawing of the Fabs dressed as magicians. Paul's hat has black flowers on it which, of course, means that he is dead.

- **The Walrus was Paul?:** On the *Magical Mystery Tour* album cover, Paul is dressed as a black Walrus, supposedly a symbol of death in some Scandinavian cultures. This is totally inaccurate and there is no connection between the symbol of the walrus and the concept of death in any of the Scandinavian mythologies.

- **Paul Was?:** On page 3 of the souvenir booklet that came with the *Magical Mystery Tour* album, Paul is seen sitting behind a desk that has a sign on it that reads "I WAS." Some people see this sign as reading "I YOU WAS." Whatever. This sign means, of course, that Paul is dead.

- **John Buried Paul:** At the conclusion of "Strawberry Fields Forever," John can be heard saying, "I buried Paul." What he is actually saying is "cranberry sauce," which can be clearly heard on the alternate takes of the song on *Anthology*.

- **The Black Flower:** As mentioned in the intro to this chapter, in the "white tails" photograph in the *Magical Mystery Tour* photo booklet, John, George, and Ringo are all wearing red carnations and Paul is wearing a black one. This means that he is dead, even though he just happened to be the Beatle who got the black one after the florist ran out of red flowers. Can you imagine the confusion if one of the other Beatles had worn the black one for that picture? The "Paul is Dead" legend would have entered a whole new phase and befuddled fans who were certain they had already figured the whole shebang out!

- **Another Hand Over Paul's Head:** On page twenty-four of the booklet, a man in a bowler hat has his hand held above Paul's head. (See number 12.)

- **"Your Mother Should Know":** If this entire song (sheesh) is played backwards, it supposedly contains such lines as "Why doesn't she know me dead?" and "I shed the light."

The White Album

- **"Glass Onion" = casket handles?:** Russ Gibb claimed that the term "glass onion" was British slang for casket handles because that's what the old-style handles looked like. Another theory is that John was referring to a glass lens in the cover of some coffins that allowed people to see the face of the person inside. All of which meant that Paul was dead, of course.

- **"The Walrus Was Paul":** When John sang this line in "Glass Onion," fans considered it in light of the *Magical Mystery Tour* photo of a Beatle dressed as a walrus (the supposed symbol of death, remember?) and concluded that John was confirming that Paul was dead. He wasn't, and he wasn't.

- **The End of "I'm So Tired":** If you play backwards the mumbling at the conclusion of John's "I'm So Tired" on the *White Album* and listen carefully, you can hear, "Paul is dead, miss him, miss him." In Mark Lewisohn's chronicle of The Beatles in the studio, *The Beatles: The Recording Sessions*, he reveals that John actually muttered (in forward speech, of course), "Monsieur, monsieur, how about another one?"

- **George's Lament:** At the end of "While My Guitar Gently Weeps," George cries out, "Paul, Paul, Paul." This meant that Paul was dead. What George actually sings/moans is, "oh, oh, oh."

- **"Number 9. Number 9. Number 9. Number…":** This is a spooky one. When the "Number 9" mantra from "Revolution 9" on the *White Album* is played backwards, it really does sound like "Turn me on, dead man." John Lennon admitted that all the EMI recording engineers would say the take number onto the tape before beginning a recording and John just happened to like the sound of the guy saying, "Number 9." Andru Reeve, in his "Paul is Dead" book *Turn Me On, Dead*

Man, suggests that the phonetic reversal might have been intentional; that John played "Turn me on, dead man" backwards and decided it sounded enough like "Number 9" to ultimately work. John Lennon himself refutes this theory but, then again, maybe John's denial was part of the conspiracy, too! (Only kidding.)

Yellow Submarine

- **Yet Another Hand Over Paul's Head:** On the *Yellow Submarine* album cover, John is seen holding his hand over Paul's head. (See numbers 12 and 29.)

Abbey Road

- **The *Abbey Road* Funeral Procession:** The *Abbey Road* album cover was the visual confirmation of Paul's death that really pushed a lot of fans over the edge. The photo of The Beatles crossing Abbey Road supposedly contained scads of "How can it not be so!?" clues that drove "Paul is Dead" theorists crazy.

  First, The Beatles' attire tells the tale. John is dressed in all white. This meant that symbolically he was the priest at Paul's funeral. Ringo is dressed in a tailored black suit. This meant he was the funeral director. George is in denim, meaning he was the gravedigger. And Paul was dressed in a suit, but barefoot, with his eyes closed, and carrying an unlit cigarette in the wrong hand. This meant that he was the corpse. In addition to The Beatles themselves, other clues include the Volkswagen Beetle parked on the street. This vehicle has the license plate "LMW 28IF." The "LMW" was supposed to translate as "Linda McCartney Weeps" and the "28IF" meant that Paul would have been twenty-eight if he had lived.

All of these "clues" have been quite effectively debunked but the fact that fans were able to come up with such detailed interpretations from one photo illustrates the rabid interest the "Paul is Dead" theory provoked in Beatles watchers.

The clothes were just what each Beatle happened to decide to wear the day the picture was taken. (During a 1969 radio interview, John said, "We all decided individually what to wear that day for the photograph.") Paul being barefoot is coincidence: He showed up for the shoot in sandals and decided to take them off for one shot. There are five outtakes from this session in which Paul is seen crossing the street wearing the sandals in two of them.

The VW just happened to be parked there and couldn't be moved. (This car sold for $4,000 at auction in 1986.) The license plate was the car's actual plate.

- **We've Just Seen a Face?:** On the back of the *Abbey Road* album cover, a girl in a blue dress is seen passing in front of the wall on which "The Beatles" is written. If you look carefully, you can see Paul's face (actually his nose and mouth) in the girl's elbow. To be fair, there is something in the photo that can be interpreted as a face, but who the hell would have seen it if no one believed Paul was dead? Also on the back cover are a series of eight dots that form the number "3" when connected with a pen or marker. This was how the surviving Beatles told us that there were only three of them left. In reality, the number could also be seen as a "5" which would add whole new dimension to the rumor, wouldn't it?

- **One and One and One…:** This was blatant. In "Come Together," John sang the line, "One and one and one is three," which was interpreted as yet another "three" message about the loss of one Beatle.

- **Octopus's Garden:** Supposedly, the term "octopus's garden" is a slang British naval term for burial at sea, from either drowning or as an intentional internment. This was Ringo's way of telling us that Paul was dead.

In a 1996 interview, Ringo talked about writing "Octopus's Garden" and revealed that someone once told him that it was common for octopuses to collect shiny things from the ocean floor and neatly arrange them in their nest…almost like flowers in a garden. Upon hearing this Ringo thought it was the "happiest" thing he had ever heard and, thus, was inspired to write the song.

Chapter 41

38 BIZARRO TOURIST ATTRACTIONS

There's a funny moment in the Chevy Chase film, *National Lampoon's Vacation*, that perfectly encapsulates America's fascination with peculiar tourist attractions. In one scene, Chevy's character, the astonishingly inept yet undeniably awesome Clark Griswold, tells his family to hurry up so that they can get the Family Truckster back on the road. If they wait much longer, he frets, they won't have enough time to visit the World's Largest House Of Mud on their way to Wally World.

America has some very unusual tourist attractions and this is a visit to 38 of America's most peculiar and wonderful road stops.

(By the way, there is also a Museum of Celebrity Leftovers in Kingsand, England that is impossible not to mention, because it is exactly what it sounds like: a collection of half-eaten foods abandoned by British celebrities and collected and displayed. They have a piece of bread and butter pudding that Prince Charles didn't finish, and a piece of cheese and pesto toastie left behind by British musician Pete Doherty.)

1. **The Atomic Bomb Crater** (Mars Bluff, Florence, South Carolina): This one serves as a metaphor for all this is wonderful about tourist sites. In 1958, a B-47 pilot accidentally dropped a bomb on a guy's farm. It made a big hole that is now a tourist attraction. The farm's owner Walter Gregg later said, "Not too many people can say they've had a nuclear bomb dropped on them, not too many would want to."

2. **The Dan Blocker Memorial Head** (O'Donnell, Texas): It's a big granite head of Hoss in the O'Donnell (his hometown) town square.

3. **The Donner Party Museum** (Truckee, California): This is a museum commemorating the mountain excursion that culminated in members of the Donner Party eating each other (dead) in order to survive.

4. **The Five-Story-Tall Chicken** (Marietta, Georgia): This known as the Big Chicken, is made of sheet-metal, and is fifty-five feet tall. (It'd be worth a trip just to be able to stand there and say, "That's a big chicken.")

5. **Flintstone Bedrock City** (Vail, Arizona): Visit a replica of the town the modern Stone Age family calls home.

6. **Frederick's Bra Museum** (Hollywood, California): Bras, bras, and more bras!

7. **Leila's Hair Museum** (Independence, Missouri): Weird things made out of human hair. A look at the history of "hair art."

8. **The Hall of Mosses** (Port Angeles, Washington): The Hall of Mosses Trail is a hiking trail in Olympic Na-

tional Park. It is located in the Hoh Rain Forest on the Olympic Peninsula in the west of Washington state. It takes about an hour to walk the trail and there is no admission fee.

9. **Hobbiton, USA** (Phillipsville, California): This is a half-mile nature walk offering visits to cement tableaux from J. R. R. Tolkien's *Lord of the Rings* trilogy. Gandalf stands outside of Bilbo's round-doored home in the first diorama.

10. **The Hoegh Pet Casket Company** (Gladstone, Michigan): The tour includes the casket showroom and factory, as well as a look at a prototype pet cemetery.

11. **Holy Land, U.S.A.** (Waterbury, Connecticut): This now defunct attraction (it closed permanently in 1984) showcased religious shrines, Biblical dioramas, and statues galore.

12. **Jimi Hendrix Memorial** (Greenwood Memorial Park, Renton Cemetery): Dedicated in 2003, it features a granite dome supported by three pillars. Hendrix's remains were moved here from his original burial site.

13. **The Liberace Museum** (Las Vegas, Nevada): The Liberace Museum Collection is housed at Thriller Villa, the former Las Vegas home of Michael Jackson and can be experienced with a private guide, by a limited number of visitors daily.

14. **The Museum Of Questionable Medical Devices** (Minneapolis, Minnesota): They boast the "largest collection of medical chicanery and mayhem ever assembled under one roof."

15. **The Good Vibrations Antique Vibrator Museum** (San Francisco, California): The history of the dildo and the vibrator.

16. **The Nut Museum** (Old Lyme, Connecticut): It was run by the late Elizabeth Tashjian, who appeared on *Late Night with David Letterman* with a giant nut. Twice. Elizabeth loved nuts and has even composed a "Nut Anthem."

17. **Philip Morris Cigarette Tours** (Richmond, Virginia): They show you how they make 600 million cigarettes a day.

18. **The Campbell Collection of Soup Tureens** (Wilmington, Delaware): It's a museum dedicated to the noble soup tureen.

19. **The Spam Museum** (Austin, Minnesota): This 14,000 square foot museum features 9 SPAMtastic galleries with interactive games and photo opportunities. Admission is free.

20. **Spongeorama Sponge Factory Museum** (Tarpon Springs, Florida): Sponges, sponges, and more sponges! They have the world's largest selection of sea sponges.

21. **The Testicle Festival** (Clinton, Montana): This annual event is also known as the Testy Festy and includes bands, DJs, vendor booths and, yes, testicle eating competitions.

22. **Toilet Rock** (City of Rocks State Park, Farwood, New Mexico): It's a giant rock formation that looks like a flush toilet. *Roadside America* says Toilet Rock is "especially beautiful when silhouetted against a sunset."

23. **The Tupperware World HQ Museum** (Kissimmee, Florida): Admission is free to this very popular attraction and includes a tour of historical and contemporary Tupperware devices, the opportunity to buy a Tupperware key chain from a vending machine for a dollar, and, purportedly, a look at a Tupperware casket.

24. **The Urinal Used By JFK** (Salem, Ohio): It's in the men's room in Reilly Stadium. "C'mon in and take my picture standing next to it, honey. The guys won't mind."

25. **The World's Largest Artichoke** (Castroville, California): It's twenty feet tall, twelve feet wide, and made out of concrete. Castroville bills itself as the "Artichoke

Center of the World" and boasts an annual Artichoke Festival.

26. **The World's Largest Chest of Drawers** (High Point, North Carolina): It's thirty-eight feet tall and is the tallest free-standing chest of drawers in existence. There also exists an eighty-foot tall chest of drawers in High Point but it's attached to a furniture store.

27. **The World's Largest Crucifix** (Bardstown, Kentucky): It's sixty feet high and made of stainless steel rods.

28. **The World's Largest Chair** (Anniston, Alabama): It's thirty-one feet tall and belongs to Miller's Office Furniture. If you want to put your feet up while sitting in it, use the building across the street.

29. **The World's Largest Sycamore Stump** (Kokomo, Indiana): It's fifty-seven feet around, eighteen feet wide, and twelve feet high. (Not sure where the largest Pine Stump might reside.)

30. **The World's Largest Twine Ball** (Darwin, Minnesota): It is twelve feet around and weighs 21,140 pounds. The Twine Ball is on display 24/7 in an outside gazebo.

31. **The Kansas Barbed Wire Museum** (La Crosse Kansas): The history of the invention the proprietors state "tamed the Wild West."

32. **The House of Mugs** (Collettsville, North Carolina): A cabin covered completely in coffee mugs. Visitors are invited to nail in their own mug, if they can find a spot.

33. **The Billy Bass Adoption Center** (Little Rock, Arkansas): This collection resides in the Flying Fish Restau-

rant and consists of donated Billy Bass singing fish toys that have either died or outlived their appeal. Most of the donations come from women.

34. **The U.S. National Tick Collection** (Statesboro, Georgia): This collection is located on the campus of Georgia Southern University and is the world's largest curated tick collection.

35. **Barney Smith's Toilet Seat Art Museum** (San Antonio, Texas): This collection consists of decorated toilet seats. Almost 1,300 of them.

36. **The Mustard Museum** (Middleton, Wisconsin): This collection comprises more than 5,000 contemporary and antique mustards from around the world. Their gift shop offers hundreds of mustards and you can easily wile away an afternoon taste-testing every one of them.

37. **The Angel Museum** (Benoit, Wisconsin): Angel figurines, close to 14,000 of them from sixty countries around the world. The collection includes 600 black angels donated by Oprah Winfrey.

38. **The Lunch Box Museum** (Columbus, Georgia): More than 3,500 lunch boxes, some of which are valued at thousands of dollars.

Chapter 42

THE NUMEROLOGICAL MEANING OF THE NUMBERS 1 THROUGH 9

Numerology is a form of divination in which numbers are said to possess prognosticative powers.

Numerology zealots (who embrace as their "hero" the Greek philosopher and mathematician Pythagoras) point to the universal notion held by many that particular numbers are "lucky" as evidence of the assumed mystical power of numbers. They assert that our leaning towards (and away, in the case of "unlucky" numbers) a particular number is a subconscious acknowledgment of their sway over our life paths.

Bernard Gittelson, in his informative 1987 overview of psychic phenomena, *Intangible Evidence*, defined the subtext of numerology:

> *Numbers are the tool of choice for the numerologist. Much as an astrologer uses the position of the planets at the time of your birth as the basis for analysis of character and to*

forecast your future, numerologists use calculations based on the numerological values of your name and birth date. How can numbers have any predictive value? How can they reveal character? Numbers, say the adepts, have accumulated meanings in the collective unconscious to which we unknowingly respond. Our name, our birth date, is an intrinsic part of our makeup; we are under its influence. We also build personal associations to numbers throughout our lives, which add to the universal associations another layer of significance. Many adepts claim that numerology is not actually the study of numbers so much as it is the study of the symbols for the numbers and their cultural and psychological significance, both conscious and unconscious, symbolic and literal. [pp. 385-86]

Numerologists differ on assigning "carved in stone" meanings to specific numbers, but generally, the following traits and characteristics apply to the numbers 1 through 9.

1. Strength of will and individualism.
2. Reason and docility.
3. Happiness and energy.
4. Stability and organization.
5. Self-confidence and impatience.
6. Art and balance.
7. Thought and introspection.
8. Leadership and materialism.
9. Mental and spiritual wisdom.

There are several ways to determine your personal number and thus your personal numerological "reading." The most important personal number is your birth force number. This is arrived at by adding up the digits in the numbers of your birthday.

Another important and ostensibly revealing number is your name number which uses the letters in your name.

Other important numbers include the soul number, which is the numerical total of all the vowels in your name, and the personality number, which is the total of all the consonants in your name.

A professional numerologist will take many different calculations to arrive at a series of numbers which he will then interpret for a full-fledged reading.

Other important numbers in the annals of numerology include:

- **11:** This was the number of Christ's faithful disciples and thus stands for revelation and truth.

- **12:** This is a very significant number and some of its associations include the 12 Signs of the Zodiac, the 12 hours in the day and night, the 12 Gods of Olympus, the 12 Tribes of Israel, the 12 apostles, and the 12 days of Christmas. The number 12 thus stands for completeness.

- **13:** Traditionally considered an unlucky number that signifies doom and bad luck, 13's bad reputation is said to stem from the fact that Jesus and his 12 apostles totaled 13 men, and the 13th (Judas) was a traitor.

22: This number is said to be important because there are 22 letters in the Hebrew alphabet and because there are 22 cards in the "major arcana" of the Tarot deck. The number 22 also signifies completeness.

40: This number, like the number 12, has many associations in history and religion, including the 40 days and night of the great Flood, the 40 days Moses spent on Mt. Sinai, and the 40 days Jesus spent fasting in the desert. Once again, we have a number signifying completeness.

Numerology does have its followers, although it is always included in the basket of pseudosciences (some would call "phony" sciences) that contains astrology, palmistry, and the reading of tea leaves. Regardless of the veracity of its claims, though, if numerology is looked upon as a psychological tool that can possibly reveal truths about oneself, then it must be considered useful. For instance, if during a numerology reading a person is told that his or her number indicates stability and organization and yet he or she knows the opposite to be true, the person may then make a conscious effort to change negative traits into positive ones.

Hey, it's cheaper than ten years of psychotherapy, right?

Chapter 43

12 BIZARRO PSYCHIATRIC DISORDERS

Behold 12 strange psychological conditions.

1. **Abasia:** A person feels that he or she has lost the ability to walk.

2. **Achiria:** A person feels that one or both of his or her hands is missing.

3. **Astasia:** A person feels that he or she has lost the ability to stand.

4. **Cataphasia:** A person frequently repeats the same word or phrase over and over.

5. **Chionophobia:** A person has a phobic fear of snow.

6. **Coprophilia:** A person has an abnormal interest in feces.

7. **Echolalia:** A person compulsively repeats the last thing he or she heard.

8. **Erythrophobia:** A person has a phobic fear of blushing.

9. **Hebephrenia:** This is a form of schizophrenia distinguished by primitive, regressive behavior and a permanent silly grin.

10. **Logorrhea:** This is distinguished by nonstop irrational babbling.

11. **Pagophobia:** A person has an irrational fear of ice or frost.

12. **Theomania:** A person has the delusion that he or she (usually he) is Jesus Christ.

Chapter 44

7 TAMPERED-WITH PRODUCTS & THE POISONS USED TO TAMPER THEM

Are you afraid of what you put in your mouth?

Ever since the 1982 Tylenol tragedy, every consumer is safety conscious, some to the point of paranoia. Companies are acknowledging peoples' fears by cloaking everything in more safety seals than Carter's got pills. The typical bottle of pills today bears at least four safety features: the box is usually glued closed, there is a plastic seal around the cap, there is a glued safety seal covering the top of the bottle, and the bottle covers themselves all require either finger gymnastics or some form of cryptographic code-breaking ability to open.

The packaging for Extra-Strength Tylenol Liquid Pain Reliever is probably one of the more vivid examples of corporate concern. Realizing that liquids are likely to be the most easily tampered-with product, and recognizing what another Tylenol tamper scare would do to the company, Johnson & Johnson made absolutely sure that no one was getting into Tylenol Liquid, and if they did, you'd know about it.

First, the box is glued. The bottle of liquid inside the box is completely shrink-wrapped from top to bottom in tight plastic. The cap of the bottle proper is childproof, and then the liquid itself is protected by a glued foil seal.

Any one of these precautions would probably be enough. All four guarantees it. This feature looks at seven horrifying incidents of product tampering, although to this day, Perrier claims that the benzene that got into Perrier in 1990 was due to an error, not tampering.

1. **Extra-Strength Tylenol Capsules (1982):** Cyanide. Seven people in the Chicago area died after swallowing capsules of Extra-Strength Tylenol pain reliever that had been laced with cyanide. This is the tampering case that led to putting safety seals on everything from mouthwash to vitamins. This case also led to the development of the solid-core capsule and the caplet, both of which are impervious to tampering. No one was ever charged with the tampering and Tylenol's manufacturer, Johnson & Johnson, settled with the families of the deceased for an undisclosed amount. Johnson & Johnson's corporate response to this crisis is a textbook example of how a company can experience what appears to be an absolutely devastating catastrophe with one of its products and be able to reduce brand damages to a minimum with the effective implementation of crisis team action and smart and irreproachably correct public relations.

2. **Contac, Dietac, And Teldrin Capsules (1986):** Rat poison. These products were all contaminated by a man who was trying to manipulate the price of the company's stock was arrested and convicted of the tampering. No deaths were reported.

3. **Gerber Baby Food (1986):** Glass fragments. Glass was found in several varieties of Gerber baby food in different areas of the country. The Food & Drug Administration said that some of these cases were due to bottle breakage during shipping but also attributed some of the glass fragments to tampering. No deaths were reported.

4. **Extra-Strength Excedrin Capsules (1986):** Cyanide. Two people in Washington state died after ingesting Extra-Strength Excedrin that was contaminated with cyanide. The wife of one of the dead victims was arrested and convicted in the tampering.

5. **Perrier Mineral Water (1990):** Benzene. Bottles of Perrier that had been shipped to the United States, Canada, Denmark, and West Germany were found to contain traces of the chemical benzene, a clear, colorless, flammable liquid that is used to manufacture the DDT, detergents, motor fuels, and insecticides. Perrier officials claim that the benzene entered the water because of a dirty pipe filter at the underground spring "Source Perrier" at Vergeze in southern France.

6. **Sudafed Capsules (1991):** Cyanide. Two people—again in Washington state—died after taking cyanide-laced Sudafed capsules. A man who poisoned the cap-

sules in an attempt to murder his wife was arrested and convicted of the tampering.

The talk shows had a field day with this tampering incident in their monologues (they also went to town with the Perrier incident) and David Letterman even did an entire Top Ten list about Sudafed:

David Letterman's Top Ten Promotional Slogans for Tampered-With Sudafed

10. Sudafed: I dare you
9. Comes in regular nonfatal, and now new fatal!
8. Kills bugs on contact.
7. Sudafed—it rhymes with dead .
6. Claus von Bülow liked it so much he bought the company!
5. Take a dance lesson with Arthur Murray .
4. If Shirley MacLaine is right, you've got nothing to worry about .
3. Sudafed—take me away!
2. If you're not dead in thirty minutes—the Sudafed's free!
1. No more food, no more folks, no more fun!

Chapter 45

329 BIZARRO REAL NAMES

"With a name like yours, you might be any shape, almost."
—Lewis Carroll, *Through the Looking Glass*

Here are 329 actual names of people as determined from birth records and other sources over the past century or so.

These names are all real, and were actually assigned to children at birth by parents who may or may not have asked themselves later, "What was I thinking?"

When a single name is given, it is the first name of the person and it is included because of its oddness. (Like "Constipation.") Sometimes a first and middle name are given when the combined form is particularly interesting, like "Immaculate Conception." (I can hear the conversation now: "Uh, Fred, I'd like you to meet Immaculate Conception Malinowski.") When the complete name is given, it is usually because it is strange, funny, or both. (Like "Fuk Eyw.")

87 People Named For Body Parts, Diseases, Medications, Cosmetics, or Something Having To Do With Sex

1. A. Pimple	22. Dick Wacker
2. Abolena Sweat	23. Digesta
3. Ammonia	24. Diptheria
4. Angina Keys	25. Distemper
5. Appendicites	26. Doloris Puke
6. Aspirin	27. Douche
7. Autopsy	28. Duncas Hymen
8. Bernard Nicewanger	29. Edward Vagina
9. Blanch Kidney	30. Esophagus
10. Bobby Joe Gothard	31. Exczema
11. Castor Oil	32. Fallopian
12. Charlie Hymen	33. Flu
13. Chlorine	34. Fred Dilldoe
14. Chloroform	35. Fuk Eyw
15. Citronella	36. Gladys Pantzeroff
16. Constance Hiccup	37. Glycine
17. Constipation	38. Granuloma
18. Cornelia Tonsil	39. Halitosis
19. Depression	40. Hang Nails
20. Diaphragm	41. Hernia
21. Dichloramentine	42. Hyman Pleasure

43. I. P. Blood
44. Iodine
45. Iona Outhouse
46. Kotex
47. Larry Ovary
48. Latrina
49. Lee Lung
50. Lemaza Hotballs
51. Listerine
52. Maria Piles
53. Meconium
54. Meninges
55. Menses
56. Morphine
57. Mr. Balls
58. Mr. Fuck
59. Nancy Nipples
60. Nausaeous
61. Nausea
62. Ophelia Rotincrotch
63. Penis
64. Placenta
65. Placenta Previa
66. Poopie
67. Positive Wasserman
68. Pregmancy
69. Pyelitis
70. Rectum
71. Sal Hepatica
72. Saline
73. Saliva Brown
74. Smallpox Dingle
75. Steve Spleen
76. Syphillis
77. Thomas Headache
78. Thomas Measles
79. Thyroid
80. Toilet Preparations
81. Twila Anus
82. Urine
83. Uvula
84. Vagina
85. Valve
86. Vaseline
87. Vomita Willis

37 People with Names for Which, I'm Sure, There Are Good Explanations

1. Artificial Flowers
2. Auditorium
3. Beautiful Swindler
4. Bigamy
5. Charity Ward
6. Devotee War
7. Emancipation Proclamation Freedom
8. Fertilizer
9. Gasoline
10. Immaculate Conception
11. Kidnap
12. Larceny
13. Large Smash
14. Laundry
15. League of Nations
16. Let's Stay Here
17. Leverage
18. Libel
19. Limousine
20. Machine
21. Magazine
22. Miscellaneous
23. No Parking
24. Petty Larceny
25. Pictorial Review
26. Refund
27. Sparkplug
28. Sylvania
29. Thermal
30. Tomb
31. Try-em-and-See
32. Victrola
33. Weatherstrip
34. What
35. X.Y.Z.
36. Y.Z.
37. Z.

97 People Whose Names Were Probably a Source of Merciless Torment on the Playground

1. Amazon
2. Average
3. Boozer
4. Bright
5. Charles Smellybelly
6. Constance Stench
7. Critic
8. Crook
9. Cute
10. Darling
11. Delerious
12. Delight
13. Dimples
14. Dream-Child
15. Equal
16. Etta Roach
17. Evil
18. Extra
19. Fairest
20. Famous
21. Fatty
22. Favorite
23. Felony
24. Fertilizer
25. Filthy McNasty
26. Flake
27. Flunkey
28. Fool Head
29. Foreward March
30. Free Love
31. Gift of God
32. Hallowed
33. Handsome
34. Haphazard
35. Hasty
36. Hazard
37. Heathen
38. Himself
39. Honest
40. Hot
41. Hot Shot
42. Ima Goose
43. Ima Rose Bush
44. Ima Valentine

45. John Smellie
46. Jolly
47. Knowledge
48. Largie
49. Lassie
50. Lawless
51. Lawyer
52. Lonely
53. Looney
54. Looney Head
55. Lord
56. Love
57. Love Bird
58. Low
59. Lucifer
60. Lucky Blunder
61. Luscious
62. Margaret Black Butts
63. Midget
64. Modest
65. Normal
66. Old
67. Peculier
68. Perfect

69. Person
70. Pleasant
71. Poor Boy
72. Right
73. Rimmer
74. Roach
75. Rodent
76. Rudolph Goldshitter
77. Silent
78. Soggie
79. Special
80. Strange Odor Andrews
81. Suck
82. Sylvester Smells
83. Tiny Small
84. Too Late
85. Toy
86. Trouble
87. Truly White
88. Tweetie
89. Unexpected
90. Useless
91. Vice

92. Wealthy

93. Weary

94. Willibald Thumbfart

95. Wimpy

96. Wonderful

97. Zero

35 People Whose Names Nicely Fit Their Occupations

1. Albert Palm: Masseur

2. Arthur Blessit: Baptist evangelist

3. Brenda Love: author of *The Encyclopedia of Unusual Sex Practices*

4. Deloris Hearsum: Deaf typist for a deaf social agency

5. Denver Driver: Truck driver

6. Don Tree: Gardener

7. Donald Moos: Washington state official in charge of dairy reports

8. Dorothy Reading: Librarian

9. Filmore Graves: Mortician

10. Frank Deadman: Mortician

11. Gordon Marsh: Biologist

12. Hazel Wolf: Works for the Audubon Society

13. Jack Putz: Golf pro

14. James Bond: Detective

15. James Bugg: Exterminator

16. John Barber: Barber

17. Judge Judge: Judge

18. Ken Priest: Protestant minister

19. Lee Coffin: Mortician

20. Max Money: Tax collector

21. Michael Angelo: Artist

22. Michael Fox: Veterinarian

23. Milo B. High: Elvis's pilot

24. Mr. Brain: Teacher

25. Mr. Bury: Mortician

26. Mr. Sexsmith: Marriage counselor

27. Mrs. Bowman: Archery instructor

28. Mrs. Cook: Baking teacher

29. Muffin Fry: Baker

30. Ronald Drown: Lifeguard

31. Sam Wood: Lumber dealer

32. Storm Field: Weatherman

33. Sweep Hand: Watch repairman

34. Virgil Buryman: Mortician

35. Wake Doom: Mortician

21 Doctors Who Probably Have to Talk About Their Names A Lot

1. Dr. Bees: Veterinary assistant (to Dr. Lyons)
2. Dr. Blood: Hematologist
3. Dr. Brain: Neurologist
4. Dr. Cartledge: Podiatrist
5. Dr. Childs: Pediatrician
6. Dr. Cure: Doctor
7. Dr. Docter: Doctor
8. Dr. Dolphin: Veterinarian
9. Dr. Eather: Anesthesiologist
10. Dr. Head: Neurologist
11. Dr. Heard: Eye, Ear, Nose, and Throat Specialist
12. Dr. Hertz: Chiropractor
13. Dr. Jack Fealy: Gynecologist
14. Dr. Leak: Urologist
15. Dr. Lyons: Veterinarian
16. Dr. Organ: Doctor
17. Dr. Saw: Orthopedist
18. Dr. Sawbones: Doctor
19. Dr. Shrink: Psychiatrist
20. Dr. Will Diddle: Obstetrician/Gynecologist
21. Dr. William Rash: Dermatologist

3 Nurses Who Picked the Right Specialty

1. A. Nurse: Nurse

2. Ida Toomer: Oncology Nurse

3. Prue Cramp: OB/GYN Nurse

48 People Having Food Names or Names Having Something to Do with Food

1. Apple Cider
2. Baby Ruth
3. Bannana
4. Barbara Beans
5. Champagne
6. Cold Turkey
7. Dill Pickle
8. Gardenia Salad
9. Garlic
10. Hearty Meal
11. Herb Rice
12. Hershey Bar
13. Hominy
14. Ice Cream
15. Jelly Bean
16. Lemon Custer
17. Lemon Freeze
18. Lettuce Fields
19. Liza Cucumber
20. Loin
21. Lunch
22. Margarine
23. Mazola
24. Meat Grease
25. Meat Loaf
26. Oatmeal
27. Oleomargarine
28. Olive Green
29. Orange Jello
30. Orangeade
31. Piece O. Cake
32. Pork Chop
33. Sam Broccoli
34. Sam Omelette

35. Sasparilla
36. Sausage
37. Soda
38. Spicy Fudge
39. Strawberry Commode
40. Summer Butter
41. Turnip
42. Utensil
43. Vanilla
44. Watermellon Patch
45. Weldon Rumproast
46. Wheat Bread
47. Whisky
48. Wine

The World's Longest Last Name

The world's longest last name, according to nomenphiliac (name scholar) Elsdon C. Smith, is:

Wolfeschlegelsteinhausenbergerdorffvoralternawarengewissenhaftschaferswessenchafewarenwohlgepflegeundsorgfaltigkeitbeschutzenvonangreifendurchihrraubgierigfeingdewelchevoralternzwolftausendjahrevorandierscheinenvanderersteerdemenschderraumschiffgebrauchlichlichtalsseinursprungvonkraftgestartseinlangefahrthinzwischensternartigraumaufdersuchenachenachidesternwelchegehabtbtbewohnbarplaneetenkreisedrehensichundwohinderneurassevonversstandingmenschlichkeitkonntefortpfflanzenundsicherfreuenanlebenslanglichfreudeundruhemitnichteinfurchtvorangreifenvonanvonanderintelligentgeschopfsvonhinzwischensternartigraun, Senior

(608 letters)

The name means, "a descendant of Wolfschegelstein (one who prepared wool for manufacture on a stone, of the house of Bergerdorf mountain village." The gentleman's 26 first names are:

Adolph Blaine Charles David Earl Frederick Gerald Hubert Irvin John Kenneth Lloyd Martin Nero Oliver Paul Quincy Randolph Sherman Thomas Uncas Victor William Xerxes Yancy Zesus (51 letters).

The 1993 *Guinness Book of Records* lists a girl born in Beaumont, Texas in 1984 who has a first name with 1,019 letters, and a middle name with 36 letters.

Chapter 46

93 UNIQUE "GIRL NAME" SONGS

This chapter is a great source if you're looking for cool and unusual girl baby names.

These are all songs named after a girl. And it's limited to songs titled with a one- or two-word name only.

1. "Adelaide" (Anberlin, 2007)
2. "Adia" (Sarah MacLachlan, 1997)
3. "Anya" (Deep Purple, 1993)
4. "Ariel" (Ritchie Blackmore's Rainbow, 1995)
5. "Athena" (Don Cornell, 1954)
6. "Aubrey" (Bread, 1972)
7. "Aurora" (Therefore I Am, 2005)
8. "Avery" (Seth Glier, 2013)
9. "Brielle" (Sky Sailing, 2010)
10. "Bryn" (Vampire Weekend, 2008)

11. "Candida" (Dawn, 1970)

12. "Carolyna" (Melanie C, 2007)

13. "Celena" (The Pixies, 1990)

14. "Charlena" (The Sevilles, 1961)

15. "Cinderella" (Vince Gill, 1987)

16. "Cinnamon" (Derek, 1968)

17. "Colene" (Trent Summar and The New Row Mob, 2002)

18. "Cordelia" (Tragically Hip, 1991)

19. "Dakota" (A Rocket to the Moon, 2009)

20. "Dardanella" (Acker Nilk, 1919)

21. "Delaware" (Perry Como, 1959)

22. "Elena" (from Kean, 1961)

23. "Emaline" (Wayne King and His Orchestra, 1934)

24. "Emmaretta" (Deep Purple, 1969)

25. "Enid" (Barenaked Ladies, 1992)

26. "Estella" (Ace Troubleshooter, 2002)

27. "Ethyl" (Dan Morgan, 2016)

28. "Fancy" (Reba McEntire. 1990)

29. "Feleena" (Marty Robbins, 1959)

30. "Freya" (The Sword, 2010)

31. "Galadriel" (Barclay James Harvest, 1971)

32. "Gaye" (Clifford T. Ward, 1966)

33. "Gayla" (Richard Harris, 1968)

34. "Gee" (The Crows, 1953)

35. "Glendora" (Perry Como, 1956)

36. "Grizelda" (Vegas in Furs, 2013)

37. "Guenevere" (from Camelot, 1960)

38. "Guinevere" (Crosby, Stills, Nash, & Young, 1969)

39. "Harmony" (Elton John, 1973)

40. "Harper" (Driftwood Bones, 2013)

41. "Havalina" (The Pixies, 1998)

42. "Iesha" (Another Bad Creation, 1990)

43. "Isla" (Mike Pinera, 2011)

44. "Jaiden" (Emblem3, 2013)

45. "Jasey Rae" (All Time Low, 2010)

46. "Jesamine" (The Casuals, 1968)

47. "Jesse" (Roberta Flack, 1972)

48. "Jet" (Paul McCartney and Wings, 1974)

49. "Kayla" (Carrie Lennard, 2005)

50. "Kaylee" (Exhale Desire, 2015)

51. "Lalena" (Donovan, 1968)

52. "Lolene" (Marty Robbins, 1962)

53. "Lorena" (John Hartford, 1978)

54. "Lua" (Bright Eyes, 2004)

55. "Lyla" (Oasis, 2005)

56. "Lysendre" (Christopher Owens, 2013)

57. "Mabelle" (Ruth, 2010)

58. "Maisie" (Guataka, 2006)

59. "Makayla" (Andy Macintyre, 2009)

60. "Marja" (George Baker Selection, 1977)

61. "Marliese" (Fischer-Z, 1981)

62. "Minerva" (The Deftones, 2003)

63. "Mira" (from Carnival, 1961)

64. "Moana" (The Deftones, 2011)

65. "Molina" (Creedence Clearwater Revival, 1970)

66. "Nikita" (Elton John, 1986)

67. "Nola" (Vincent Lopez and His Orchestra, 1916)

68. "Odessa" (Caribou, 2010)

69. "Olena" (Don Nix, 1971)

70. "Pollyanna" (Northstar, 2005)

71. "Raina" (Nick Waterhouse, 2012)

72. "Rapunzel" (Emilie Autumn, 2007)

73. "Rhiannon" (Fleetwood Mac, 1976)

74. "Rio" (Duran Duran, 1982)

75. "Rolene" (Moon Martin, 1979)

76. "Rosalenna" (Conway Twitty, 1959)

77. "Rosealia" (Better Than Ezra, 1995)

78. "Saro Jane" (Kingston Trio, 1958)

79. "Shilo" (Neil Diamond, 1967)

80. "Spooky" (Classics IV, 1967)

81. "Starla" (Smashing Pumpkins, 1991)

82. "Stormy" (Classics IV, 1968)

83. "Sugaree" (Grateful Dead, 1972)

84. "Sunny" (Bobby Hebb, 1966)

85. "Tangerine" (Led Zeppelin, 1970)

86. "Tela" (Phish, 1987)

87. "Thumbelina" (Danny Kaye, 1952)

88. "Tristessa" (Smashing Pumpkins, 1990)

89. "Velouria" (The Pixies, 1990)

90. "Vidalia" (Sammy Kershaw, 1996)

91. "Xena" (Daniel Caine Orchestra, 1995)

92. "Zerlene" (Gene and Billy, 1955)

Chapter 47

7 BIZARRO SEXUAL PHOBIAS

Brenda Love, in her book *Encyclopedia of Unusual Sex Practices* had this to say about sex phobias: A sex oriented phobia may be caused by societal guilt, a negative experience with intimacy, a lack of experience in coping with fear, temporary stress, or by separation, overprotection, or rejection by parents when young.

Phobias come in many shapes and forms: Most of us are familiar with "dirt" phobias, often manifested by compulsive hand-washing and other "cleanliness" behavior; and with agoraphobia, the fear of open spaces: This is the phobia that keeps people confined to their houses for years at a time.

But sexual phobias aren't often talked about. And yet they can be as equally crippling as any of the other more "social" terrors.

A phobia becomes a problem when it becomes all-consuming. A fear of pregnancy is a good thing when you're a single teenager. But when you're a married woman and you're so terrified of pregnancy that you steadfastly avoid sex with your husband—even when you're using birth control pills, a condom, and a diaphragm, and want children—then you're into the realm of phobic behavior.

The following is just a sampling of some of the things many people fear.

1. **Coitophobia:** This is a repugnance for and fear of sexual intercourse.

2. **Gamophobia:** This a complete obsessive aversion to marriage. A simple unwillingness to give up a carefree bachelor/bachelorette life is a lifestyle choice. When the single person does find Mr. or Miss Right, though, and even then is terrified of wedding this person, then it's a phobia.

3. **Gymnophobia:** No, this is not an aversion to taking gym class. Gymnophobia is a problem with being naked. (Come to think of it, maybe this is a gym class phobia after all?!) Gymnophobes are afraid to be unclothed in front of someone else, and as you can imagine, this type of phobia can have a somewhat dampening effect on a lover's libido. (We've all heard of people who get undressed in the closet year after year and who will only have sex with the lights off.)

4. **Harmataphobia:** This is a paralyzing fear of sexual inadequacy, either in the size department (penis length for men, breast size/butt size/et al for women) or in the performance department. There are some who contend that online porn has contributed to a flare-up of this particular phobia. In professional (as compared to amateur) porn, the men all have huge penises, some over ten inches when erect, and the women are all sexual dynamos, always ready and will-

ing for a romp. There are some people, the argument goes, who cannot help but compare themselves and their own performance to these sexual superstars, and since such an assessment is clearly a no-win situation, phobic fears can easily rear their incapacitating heads.

5. **Pathophobia:** A fear of sexually-transmitted diseases.

6. **Scopophobia:** This is an obsessive fear of being looked at, but only when it comes to a sexual situation. Most people with this phobia have no problem getting through their day and having people look at them. It's when it comes to sex that they have a problem. This would seem to be an offshoot of Gymnophobia, although I suppose there are instance when people with this fear even have a problem with being looked at during necking and clothed foreplay.

7. **Spermatophobia:** This is a crippling fear of semen loss. In some Eastern religions, semen loss is considered deadly—a serious drain of the man's vital life force. To circumvent this and yet still be able to enjoy orgasm, some men have developed a technique whereby they press on their "Jen Mo" spot at the moment of orgasm. This spot is between the scrotum and the anus and it supposedly re-routes the ejaculation into the bladder. This supposedly preserves the life-giving properties of the sperm for the man's body and does not deplete the life force. Sounds like it would hurt to me.

CASE HISTORY: A young man became ensorcelled with the sexology of Tao philosophy for a while and actually attempted to detour his ejaculation by pressing on his Jen Mo spot during intercourse. He encountered a problem: How does one reach beneath one's scrotum, during intercourse, to apply pressure to one's "spot" at the precise moment of orgasm without causing your partner to wonder just what the hell you're doing down there, and without interrupting the "rhythm" of the moment? The young experimenter also attempted to re-route his ejaculation during masturbation. He thought it might be easier to learn it that way first. After a few weeks of trying, though, he had carpal tunnel syndrome in his left wrist from bending it repeatedly into a somewhat "unusual" position; he had somehow made his hemorrhoids bleed, and he was still ejaculating out of the head of his penis and "wasting" all his life essence. True story.

Chapter 48

62 EUPHEMISMS FOR ALCOHOL

"A man who exposes himself when he is intoxicated
has not the art of getting drunk."
—Samuel Johnson

Alcohol is one of the world's legal drugs. It is quite popular. There are many ways of describing that certain chemical compound which makes us slur our words, lose our inhibitions, and try to take our pants off over our head

Here are 62 of them.

1. Belly Vengeance
2. Belly Wash
3. Bitch's Wine
4. Booze
5. Bubbly
6. Bug Juice
7. Caper Juice
8. Catgut
9. Charley Frisky
10. Choke Dog
11. Coffin Varnish
12. Cold Coffee
13. Colorado Coolaid
14. Drudge

15. Dutch Courage
16. Embalming Fluid
17. Eyewash
18. Family Disturbance
19. Firewater
20. Flash of Lightning
21. Gay and Frisky
22. Greek Fire
23. Highland Frisky
24. Hooch
25. John Barleycorn
26. Juice
27. Jungle Juice
28. Liquid Fire
29. Lubrication
30. Mexican Milk
31. Moonshine
32. Mountain Dew
33. Nanny Goat Sweat
34. Panther Piss
35. Pig Sweat
36. Piss Maker
37. Potato Soup
38. Prairie Dew
39. Prune Juice
40. Queer Beer
41. Red Eye
42. Rotgut
43. Sauce
44. Screech
45. Shampoo
46. Sky
47. Snake Juice
48. Snake Medicine
49. Snake Poison
50. Snake
51. Snakebite Medicine
52. Squaw Piss
53. Strip Me Naked
54. Tangle Leg
55. Tarantula Juice
56. Tiger Sweat
57. Tonsil Bath
58. Whishkola
59. White Coffee
60. White Lightning
61. Witch Piss
62. Woozle Water

Chapter 49

25 PROSTITUTION SERVICES OFFERED ON A TYPICAL "MENU" AT LEGAL BORDELLOS

*"I enjoy sex. It's fun. I don't have an orgasm every time,
but I do sometimes, and if that's what you want to hear,
let me know. If you want me to act like your wife in bed,
make a lot of noise, and say that 'You're the best ever,'
I'll be happy to do it. Just tell me what you want. I enjoy
having a nice time and making the guy feel good."*

—Cissy, one of the ladies at The New Sagebrush Ranch

Scene from a 19th century bordello

Prostitution has long been known as the oldest profession for a reason. It dates back thousands and thousands of years, and has never been regulated, legislated, taxed, or preached out of existence.

Today there exists respectable, clean, and unquestionably safe legal brothels where any and all manner of sexual delights can be had for a price.

There are nineteen (as of 2013) licensed brothels (or "cat-houses" as they are known) in Nevada.

All of these establishments offer one thing: sex. The ladies at these houses will usually do anything a gentleman wants, including anal sex, oral sex, golden showers, and bondage and discipline.

Men frequent these places for many reasons. Loneliness, physical problems, being away from home, and what is probably the most important reason of all: the girls in these houses will do the things that many men say their wives or girlfriends won't.

Owners of a popular club put together a "Menu" of erotic specialties for their clientele, samples from which are reprinted below. (For your edification, the items with a superscript number refers to footnotes that explain the terminology.)

MENU

A wide selection of delectable treats for the discriminating gentleman

Appetizers...[3]

1. Massage
2. Breast Massage
3. X-Rated Movies
4. Hot Tub Party
5. Champagne Bath
6. Bubble Bath
7. Lingerie Show
8. Body Paint

---

3   These are all fairly self-explanatory.

Entrees...

9. Straight Party
10. Half & Half[4]
11. 69 Party
12. 69 Party Lay
13. Double Party Show
14. Double Party French
15. Double Party Lay
16. Drag Party
17. Dominating Woman
18. Vibrator Party
19. Friends & Lovers
20. All Night Date[5]
21. Out Date[6]

Desserts...

22. Hot & Cold French[7]
23. Creme De Menthe French[8]
24. Binaca Blast French[9]
25. Flavored Pussy Party[10]

If you don't see your personal preference listed, do not hesitate to ask.

---

4   Half oral sex, half straight intercourse.
5   From 2:00 A.M. to 7:00 A.M.
6   A house call.
7   Oral sex alternating hot and cold, often using coffee and ice cubes.
8   Oral sex with Creme De Menthe liquor in the girl's mouth.
9   Oral sex with Binaca breath freshener in the girl's mouth.
10   Cunnilingus with various flavorings added to the vagina.

Chapter 50

THE PERSONALITY CHARACTERISTICS OF THE 12 ASTROLOGICAL SIGNS

"The stars do not compel; but rather impel."
—John White

Astrological Signs
(in calendar order)

1. **Capricorn** (The Goat); December 22-January 19
   Positive Trait: Ambition.
   Negative Trait: Rigidity.

2. **Aquarius** (The Water Bearer); January 20-February 18
   Positive Trait: Wisdom.
   Negative Trait: Perversity.

3. **Pisces** (The Fishes); February 19-March 20
   Positive Trait: Compassion.
   Negative Trait: Weakness.

4. **Aries** (The Ram); March 21-April 19
   Positive Trait: Leadership.
   Negative Trait: Selfishness.

5. **Taurus** (The Bull); April 20-May 20
   Positive Trait: Stability.
   Negative Trait: Stubbornness.

6. **Gemini** (The Twins); May 21-June 21
   Positive Trait: Intelligence.
   Negative Trait: Triteness.

7. **Cancer** (The Crab); June 22-July 22
   Positive Trait: Creativity.
   Negative Trait: Self-Pity.

8. **Leo** (The Lion); July 23-August 22
   Positive Trait: Generosity.
   Negative Trait: Intolerance.

9. **Virgo** (The Virgin); August 23-September 22
   Positive Trait: Organization.
   Negative Trait: Obsessive/Compulsive Tendencies.

10. **Libra** (The Balance); September 23-October 23
    Positive Trait: Judgment.
    Negative Trait: Indecisiveness.

11. Scorpio (The Scorpion); October 24-November 21
Positive Trait: Passion.
Negative Trait: Covertness.

12. Sagittarius (The Archer); November 22-December 21
Positive Trait: Optimism.
Negative Trait: Irresponsibility

Chapter 51

THE ULTIMATE LINCOLN/
KENNEDY
COINCIDENCES LIST

"Coincidences are spiritual puns."
—G. K. Chesterton

There are many seemingly amazing coincidences between the lives and assassinations of Presidents Abraham Lincoln and John F. Kennedy.

Believers say that there are too many coincidences to be merely coincidences. There must be some kind of paranormal connection between John F. Kennedy and Abraham Lincoln. Subsequently, there must also be some type of profound meaning for the United States (and possibly the world) in their lives and how they were killed.

Skeptics, on the other hand, believe that the coincidences between Kennedy and Lincoln are just that: coincidences. All of the seemingly bizarre similarities in their histories can be attributed to nothing but chance. Anyone attempting to find a meaning in these weird occurrences is on a futile mission. There simply is no connection between the two men and their assassinations other than the fact that they were both Presidents of the United States. That, skeptics proclaim, we will concede.

You've likely heard many of these before. There is a core group of Lincoln/Kennedy coincidences that has been circulating for years. Lately, more research has been done and even more commonalities in the lives and deaths of the two Presidents has been uncovered.[11]

Here we look at 70 of these eerie similarities, including some of the newer ones. Some are not the least bit surprising; some are undeniably stunning in their synchronous connections.

- Both Presidents liked rocking chairs.

- The name of Lincoln's assassin, "John Wilkes Booth," contains fifteen letters. The name of Kennedy's assassin, "Lee Harvey Oswald," contains fifteen letters.

- The name of Lincoln's successor, "Andrew Johnson," contains thirteen letters. The name of Kennedy's successor, "Lyndon Johnson," contains thirteen letters.

- "Lincoln" and "Kennedy" each consist of seven letters.

- Both presidents were named after their grandfathers.

- Both Presidents were second children.

- Both Presidents experienced the death of a sister die before they became President.

---

11 Special acknowledgment must go to Lu Ann Paletta and Fred L. Worth's *World Almanac of Presidential Facts*, a valuable resource in the compiling of this list.

- Both Presidents did not marry until they were in their thirties: Lincoln was 33; Kennedy was 36.

- Both Presidents married socially prominent, 24-year-old brunettes who were fluent in French, known for their fashion sense, and both of whom had been previously engaged.

- Both First Ladies oversaw major renovations of the White House.

- Each President experienced the death of a son while president.

- The Lincoln and Kennedy children rode ponies on the White House lawn.

- Lincoln's son Tad's funeral was held on July 16, 1871. John F. Kennedy Jr. died on July 16, 1999. Mary Todd Lincoln died on July 16, 1882.

- Two of Lincoln's sons were named Robert and Edward; two of Kennedy's brothers were named Robert and Edward.

- Both Presidents were related to United States Senators.

- After Lincoln was assassinated, his family moved into a house at 3014 N Street, N.W, in Georgetown. After Kennedy was assassinated, his family moved into a house at 3017 N Street, N.W, in Georgetown.

- Both Presidents were related to Democratic United States Attorney Generals who were graduates of Harvard University.

- Both Presidents were related to ambassadors to the Court of St. James in Great Britain.

- Both Presidents were friends with an Adlai E. Stevenson. Lincoln's friend would become Grover Cleveland's second Vice President. Kennedy's friend would twice be the Democratic Presidential nominee.

- Both Presidents knew a Dr. Charles Taft. Lincoln was treated by Dr. Charles Sabin Taft; Kennedy knew Dr. Charles Phelps Taft (the son of President Taft).

- Both Presidents were advised by a Billy Graham: Lincoln's friend was a New Salem, Illinois schoolteacher; Kennedy's was the Reverend Billy Graham.

- Kennedy had a secretary named Evelyn Lincoln.[12] Her husband's nickname was Abe.

- Lincoln was first elected to the U.S. House of Representatives in 1846; Kennedy was first elected to the U.S. House of Representatives in 1946.

- Lincoln was runner-up for his party's Vice Presidential nomination in 1856; Kennedy was runner-up for his party's Vice Presidential nomination in 1956.

- Lincoln was elected President in 1860; Kennedy was elected President in 1960.

- Both Presidents were involved in seminal political debates: Lincoln participated in the Lincoln-Douglas debates in 1858; Kennedy participated in the Kennedy-Nixon debates in 1960.

---

12   Also, one glaring error in earlier lists has been corrected. One of the coincidences that regularly made the rounds was: "Lincoln's secretary was named Kennedy; Kennedy's secretary was named Lincoln." Not so. Apparently, Lincoln never had a secretary named Kennedy.

- Both Presidents were concerned about African-Americans. Lincoln wrote the Emancipation Proclamation; Kennedy submitted a report on civil rights to Congress.

- Both Presidents were writers and were well-read; both Presidents were versed in Shakespeare and the Bible.

- Both had genetic diseases: Kennedy had Addison's disease; Lincoln (it is suspected) had Marfan's disease.

- Both Presidents were in the military.

- Both Presidents had been skippers of a boat: Lincoln had been captain of the *Talisman*; Kennedy had captained the *PT 109*.

- Both Presidents did not worry about their personal safety, much to the consternation of their Secret Service protection.

- In the year of his death, Abraham Lincoln received 80 death threats in the mail. In the year of his death, John F. Kennedy received 800 death threats in the mail.

- Both Presidents were shot in the back of the head.

- Both Presidents were shot on a Friday before a holiday: Lincoln, Easter; Kennedy, Thanksgiving (the national holiday Lincoln made official, incidentally, in 1863).

- Both Presidents were sitting next to their wives when they were shot.

- Neither of the First Ladies were injured in the shootings.

- Both Presidents were with another couple when they were shot: Kennedy was with Governor and Mrs. John

Connally; Lincoln was with Major Henry Rathbone and his fiancée, Clara Harris.

- Both of the men with the Presidents, Major Rathbone and Governor Connally, were injured but not killed.

- Lincoln was shot at Ford's Theater; Kennedy was shot in a Ford motor vehicle (a Lincoln).

- Lincoln was shot in Box 7 at the theater; Kennedy was shot in car 7 of his motorcade.

- Both Presidents received closed chest massage after the shooting; in both cases, it was ineffective.

- Both Presidents died in a place with the initials "P.H.": Lincoln died in the Peterson House; Kennedy died in Parkland Hospital.

- Both Presidents were buried in mahogany caskets.

- The coffins of both Lincoln and JFK were displayed in the Capitol Rotunda and the same black-draped catafalque was used for both men.

- Both assassins were known by three names: John Wilkes Booth and Lee Harvey Oswald.

- Both assassins were in their mid-twenties when they shot the President.

- Both assassins had brothers with successful careers that they envied: Booth's brothers were acclaimed actors; Oswald's brothers had successful military careers.

- Both assassins never went past the rank of private in the military.

- Both assassins were born in the South.

- Both assassins ideologically supported enemies of the United States: Booth supported the Confederacy; Oswald endorsed Marxism.

- Both assassins kept a journal or diary.

- Booth shot Lincoln in a theater (Ford's Theater) and was cornered in a warehouse; Oswald shot Kennedy from a warehouse and was cornered in a theater (the Texas Theater).

- The concession stand operator at Ford's Theater was named Burroughs. The concession stand operator at the Texas Theater was named Burroughs.

- Booth was aided in his escape by a man named Paine. Oswald got his job at the School Book Depository with the help of a woman named Paine.

- Booth was trapped on Garrett's farm by a contingent of soldiers led by an office named Baker. Oswald was questioned on the second floor of the School Book Depository by a cop named Baker.

- Both assassins were killed by a single shot from a Colt revolver.

- Both assassins were murdered before they could be questioned about their crimes.

- Oswald and Booth were both shot by religious zealots: Booth by Boston Corbett; Oswald by Jack Ruby.

- Both Presidents were succeeded in office by Southern Democrats named Johnson: Lincoln, by Andrew Johnson; Kennedy by Lyndon Johnson.

- Both Vice President Johnsons became President in their fifties: Andrew Johnson was 56; Lyndon Johnson was 55.

- Andrew Johnson's father once worked as a janitor; Lyndon Johnson's father once worked as a janitor.

- Andrew Johnson was born in 1808; Lyndon Johnson was born in 1908.

- "Andrew" and "Lyndon" both have six letters.

- Both President Johnsons had two daughters.

- Both President Johnsons served in the military.

- Both President Johnsons had previously been Senators from a southern state.

- Both President Johnsons suffered from kidney stones. They were the only two Presidents ever to experience this malady.

- The reelection opponents of both President Johnsons were men whose name began with G: Andrew Johnson against Ulysses S. Grant; Lyndon Johnson against Barry Goldwater.

- Andrew Johnson chose not to run for reelection in 1868. Lyndon Johnson chose not to run for reelection in 1968.

Chapter 52

22 THINGS INVENTED BY LEONARDO DA VINCI HUNDREDS OF YEARS BEFORE THEY WERE INVENTED

Leonardo da Vinci lived from 1452 to 1519, when he died at the age of sixty-seven.

During his life, he conceived and designed dozens of "devices" we recognize today as the forerunners of many of our modern necessities, including the airplane, eyeglasses, and the life preserver.

This list comprises only 22 of his most remarkable brainstorms, all of which were conceptualized hundreds of years before their modern versions came into being. Actual sketches of these inventions are available in the many published editions of Da Vinci's notebooks.

1. The Revolving Stage
2. The Flying Machine
3. The Parachute

4. The Air Conditioner
5. The Oil Lamp
6. The Alarm Clock
7. The Printing Press
8. The Odometer
9. The Pedometer
10. The Magnetic Compass
11. A Clock with Minute and Hour Hands
12. Eyeglasses
13. The Telescope
14. The Differential Transmission
15. The Water Turbine
16. The Horseless Wagon
17. The Machine Gun
18. The Shrapnel Explosive
19. The Tank
20. The Double-Hull Ship
21. An Underwater Diving Suit
22. The Life Preserver

Chapter 53

14 BIZARRO US SEX LAWS

Government will legislate against anything, it seems, and nowhere is this more evident than in the battery of laws against any and all kinds of sexual behavior. Some of these may have been abrogated by now, but they were all on the books at one time or another in our nation.

1. **In Harrisburg, Pennsylvania, There's a Law Against:** Having sex with a truck driver in a toll booth.

2. **In Nevada, There's A Law Against:** Having sex without a condom.

3. **In Willowdale, Oregon, There's A Law Against:** A husband talking dirty in his wife's ears during sex.

4. **In Clinton, Oklahoma, There's A Law Against:** Masturbating while watching two people have sex in a car.

5. **In the state of Washington, There's A Law Against:** Having sex with a virgin under any circumstances, including the wedding night. (Think about it.)

6. **In Tremonton, Utah, There's A Law Against:** Having sex in an ambulance.

7. **In Newcastle, Wyoming, There's A Law Against:** Having sex in a butcher shop's meat freezer.

8. **In Alexandria, Minnesota, There's A Law Against:** A man having sex with his wife with the stink of onions, sardines, or garlic on his breath.

9. **In Every State in the Union, There's A Law Against:** Having sex with a corpse.

10. **In Ames, Iowa, There's A Law Against:** Drinking more than three slugs of beer while lying in bed with a woman.

11. **In Fairbanks, Alaska, There's A Law Against:** Two moose having sex on the city sidewalks.

12. **In Kingsville, Texas, There's A Law Against:** Two pigs having sex on Kingsville airport property.

13. **In Ventura County, California, There's A Law Against:** Cats and dogs having sex without a permit.

14. **In Washington, D.C., There's A Law Against:** Having sex in any position other than face-to-face.

Source: *Loony Laws That You Never Knew You Were Breaking* by Robert Wayne Pelton

Chapter 54

THE 22 STEPS OF A MEDICAL-LEGAL AUTOPSY

"Sing, my tongue, of the mysteries of the glorious Body."
—Thomas Aquinas

"A [medical-legal autopsy is a] specialized type of autopsy authorized or ordered by the proper legal authorities (usually the medical examiner) in cases of suspicious deaths, including suicide, homicide, and unattended or unexpected deaths in order to assure justice for the purpose of determining the cause of death. If a person dies without having been attended by a doctor in the past fourteen days, or under suspicious circumstances, or during a surgical operation, the coroner may rule that an autopsy is required. A medical-legal autopsy is required in all homicide cases."
—Dr. Keith Wilson, *Cause of Death*

Here is what happens, step-by-step during a medical-legal autopsy.

1. The dead body arrives at the morgue.
2. The body's identity is confirmed, assigned an identification number, and given a toe-tag, which is a card-

board ticket with all of the corpse's pertinent information written on it. This tag is tied to a big toe.

3. The body is photographed from head to toe, front and back, in the clothing it was wearing when it arrived at the morgue.

4. The body is photographed naked, from head to toe, and front to back.

5. The body is weighed on a scale, and the weight is recorded. The body is also measured for length, and completely x-rayed.

6. The fingerprints of the corpse are taken. In instances in which hands and/or fingers are missing, prints are taken of what remains of the extremities, and missing parts are duly noted.

7. The clothing the deceased was wearing upon arrival at the morgue is carefully and methodically examined. Fiber samples from the garments are taken for later study, and stains on the clothing are noted and examined.

8. Any and all moles, wounds, tattoos, scars (including surgical scars), and other physical body anomalies are noted and examined.

9. The corpse's fingernails, toenails, skin, and hair are examined. The skin of the arms and legs are carefully checked for syringe marks.

10. During a medical-legal autopsy of a female, a rigorous examination of the external genitalia (labia, pubic hair, etc.) is performed to determine whether or not

there was a rape or sexual assault committed against the woman prior to (and/or after) her death.

11. Bodily fluids (blood, urine, etc.) are withdrawn from the body and subjected to comprehensive toxicology tests.

12. The coroner makes a huge, full-body-length "Y" incision that opens up the entire front of the body. The incision starts at each shoulder, proceeds on an angle down to the mid-chest, and then joins into a straight line that extends all the way to the pubis. This is the most dramatic element of a medical-legal autopsy and many people who have never seen one performed are startled by the visceral way the body is spread wide by this incision. Many people have, at one time or another, witnessed some sort of surgical procedure performed. (The plethora of "emergency room"-type show of late have contributed to this reality.) Incisions, even for major abdominal surgery, are commonly thin, neat, and relatively "clean." An autopsy incision need not be neat, nor concerned with excessive bleeding. Thus, the corpse is split wide open by a deep cut that is a very effective reminder that the person being autopsied is, in fact, quite dead.

13. First, the organs of the upper abdominal cavity—the lungs, heart, esophagus, and trachea—are removed. The coroner then takes out the lower abdominal organs, which include the liver, spleen, kidneys, adrenals, stomach, and intestines. Slices of each organ are taken and tested.

14. The internal genitals of both males and females are examined. In the case of females, the uterus and vagina are carefully studied for signs of pregnancy, rape, or some form of sexual assault.

15. The organs of the pelvic region, including the bladder, the uterus, and the ovaries, are removed. Samples of each organ are taken and analyzed.

16. When the cause of death is either drowning or a suspected poisoning or drug overdose, the contents of the stomach are removed, examined, and carefully analyzed. All findings are recorded.

17. Any and all bullet wounds are recorded. The number of wounds is noted, as well as the perceived direction(s) of the bullet(s). An estimate, based on the configuration of the bullet entrance wounds, is made as to what distance the gun was from the victim when it was fired. All bullets are removed from the body and placed in plastic bags. The bullets are then examined by a ballistics lab and findings are recorded as evidence.

18. First, a deep incision is made in the skin of the scalp. The cut, which is called intermastoid, begins behind one ear, travels over the top of the head, and ends behind the opposite ear. The scalp is then grasped firmly and pulled forward over the face, baring the bony skull. Using an electric saw, a wedge-shaped portion of the skull is cut out and removed, exposing the brain. The brain is then removed in its entirety, weighed, and examined.

19. Since the coroner is now through with them, he or she returns all of the removed internal organs to the body cavities.

20. The autopsy findings, complete with a final opinion as to cause of death, as well as all reports and photographs, are turned over to legal authorities. This "package" becomes part of the *corpus delecti*, and is used as evidence in a court of law when necessary. The folder containing all of this detailed information is known as the case file.

21. A final determination is made as to the cause of death and a death certificate is filled out and signed by the medical examiner.

22. The body is turned over to the funeral director selected by the family. The body is then prepared for burial, cremation, or donation.

See the next chapter for more on post-death undertakings...

Chapter 55

THE 11 STEPS OF EMBALMING A BODY & PREPARING IT FOR OPEN-CASKET VIEWING

"I look where he lies white-faced and still in the coffin—I draw near-death
Bend down and touch lightly with my lips the white face in the coffin."
—Walt Whitman, "Reconciliation"

The shepherding of the dead to their final resting place is at once a scary and awe-inspiring duty.

Morticians or undertakers (who now prefer to be called funeral directors) are responsible for the last vision a family will ever have of their loved one.

It is their job to make the dead person look good, comfort the family in their time of bewildering grief, and handle all of the bureaucratic requirements needed to write a beloved citizen "off the books," so to speak.

This section looks at what happens from the moment the body arrives at the funeral home and the embalming begins. (Sometimes bodies are stored in refrigerators until the morti-

cian is ready to begin the embalming.) Many of these procedures overlap one another and many morticians have their own
ways (and order) of working, but this is the general routine
necessary to prepare a dead body for viewing.

1. The body is completely undressed.

2. The limbs are gently stretched and massaged to lessen
   the effect of the relentless rigor mortis.

3. The body is washed.

4. An artery and vein in either the neck, armpit, or groin
   are cut open and all the corpse's blood is drained out.
   This is commonly done on a table with gutters or a
   drain hole that drains the fluid to a receptacle of some
   sort.

5. The veins are filled with embalming fluid. This is a
   formaldehyde-based liquid that, ironically, looks like
   blood. (This is coincidental, not aesthetically intentional.)

6. A large syringe is inserted into the navel and the contents of the stomach and abdomen are pumped out.

7. The abdomen is filled with between 8 and 10 pints of
   embalming fluid.

8. Cups or pads are placed over the eyeballs to prevent a
   sunken look and the eyelids are often sewn shut. The
   mouth and cheeks are stuffed with cotton to prevent
   a hollow look, and the lips are sewn shut if necessary.
   Any necessary reconstructive work is performed.

9. The body is attended to cosmetically. The hair is washed and set on women; the beard is shaved on normally clean-shaven men. The beard is tended to on men who wore one in life. Makeup is applied to both the face and neck, as well as the hands. There is an accepted fiction in the facial representation of the deceased. Glasses are left on. Although many people will comment "She looks like she's sleeping," (which is a hoped-for goal) no one wears glasses while they sleep. They are left on for the sake of a realistic appearance, i.e., the look of the person when they were alive.

10. The body is dressed. Usually, the family provides something for the deceased to wear and, of course, be buried in. However, if necessary, the funeral home will provide clothing from a wide selection.

11. The body is placed in the coffin and arranged for viewing. The hands are manipulated so as to have a natural fall, and religious items like rosaries are sometimes placed in the hands. If it is to be an open-casket wake, the upper half of the cover is left open until the final disposition and trip to the cemetery, with the lower half, covering the legs and feet kept open. (There are caskets in which the entire top comes off, to put the entire body on display—this is often done when a religious leader is to be on view in a house of worship. If it is to be a closed-casket wake, the coffin is sealed after the family has its final private viewing.)

Chapter 56

THE 7 STAGES OF THE SOUL'S ASCENT TO GOD

According to ancient mystic wisdom, the soul must travel through seven stages in order to ultimately know and experience true Divinity.

Upon attainment of the seventh stage, God enters the person's soul and the traveler becomes one with God. These seven stages are also known as the Castle of the Interior Man, which is an expressively poetic and metaphorical way of describing this inner journey.

1. **The State of Prayer:** During this stage, the traveler concentrates on God, using meditation and prayer as tools.

2. **The State of Mental Prayer:** Here, one attempts a deeper understanding of all things, with emphasis on the mystical and spiritual significance of existence and of the self as it relates to all things.

3. **The Obscure Night:** This stage is said to be especially difficult to achieve because it demands the total and complete surrender of the Self.

4. **The Prayer of Quietism:** Once the Obscure Night is achieved and the Self is renounced, the fourth stage requires that the traveler willingly him- or herself over to the will of God, whatever it might be.

5. **The State of Union:** The will of God becomes evident and the traveler begins to understand how that will relates to the will of is own soul.

6. **The State of Ecstatic Prayer:** This is a transcendent state in which awareness of a higher state of consciousness is present and the soul is flooded with joy and love.

7. **The State of Ravishment:** A mystical marriage between God and man is attained and God and the state of eternal bliss called Heaven enter into the soul.

Chapter 57

THE 26 STAGES OF DETERIORATION A CORPSE GOES THROUGH FROM THE MOMENT OF DEATH ON

"And so, from hour to hour, we ripe and ripe,
And then from hour to hour, we rot and rot
And thereby hangs a tale."
—William Shakespeare, *As You Like It*

Morticians understand the "need for speed" in their chosen profession. Here is what happens to us physically when we shuffle off this mortal coil.

The Moment of Death

1. The heart stops.

2. The skin tightens and turns ashen in color.

3. All the muscles relax.

4. The bladder and bowels empty.

5. The body temperature begins to drop 1½ ° Fahrenheit per hour.

After 30 minutes

6. The skin turns purple and waxy.

7. The lips, fingernails, and toenails fade to a pale color.

8. Blood pools at the bottom of the body.

9. The hands and feet turn blue.

10. The eyes sink into the skull.

After 4 hours

11. Rigor mortis has set in.

12. The purpling of the skin and the pooling of the blood continue.

13. Rigor continues to tighten muscles for another twenty-four hours or so.

After 12 hours

14. The body is in full rigor mortis.

After 24 hours

15. The body is now the temperature of the surrounding environment.

16. In males, the semen dies.

17. The head and neck are now a greenish-blue color.

18. The greenish-blue color spreads to the rest of the body.

19. There is a pervasive smell of rotting meat.

20. The face of the person is essentially no longer recognizable.

After 3 days

21. The gas in the body tissues forms large blisters on the skin.

22. The whole body begins to bloat and swell grotesquely.

23. Fluids leak from the mouth, nose, vagina, and rectum.

After 3 weeks

24. The skin, hair, and nails are so loose they can easily be pulled off the corpse.

25. The skin bursts open in many places on the body.

26. Decomposition will continue until the body is nothing but skeletal remains, a process that can take a month or so in hot climates, and two months or more in cold climates.

Chapter 58

10 "DAY-IN-THE-LIFE" QUOTES BY MOZART

All quotes are from *The Letters of Wolfgang Amadeus Mozart, Vol. 1*, translated by Lady Wallace.

1. **Mozart Plays Games**
   "Salzburg, 1769

   "Cuperem scire, de qua causa, a quam plurimis adolescentibus ottium usque adeo oestimetur, ut ipsi se nec verbis, nec verberibus ad hoc sinant abduci."

   Mozart wrote this in a letter to "My Dear Young Lady" and intentionally did not provide the translation. He insisted that she translate it herself and reply to him via letter by messenger.

   The translation is "I should like to know the reason why indolence is so highly prized by very many young men, that neither by words nor blows will they suffer themselves to be roused from it."

2. **Mozart Reviews the Performance of an Opera**

"Milan, Jan. 26, 1770.

- The opera at Mantua was very good. They gave *Demetrio*.

- The *prima donna* sings well, but is inanimate, and if you did not see her acting, but only singing, you might suppose she was not singing at all, for she can't open her mouth, and whines out everything; but this is nothing new to us.

- The *seconda donna* looks like a grenadier, and has a very powerful voice; she really does not sing badly, considering that this is her first appearance.

- *Il primo uomo, il musico*, sings beautifully, but his voice is uneven; his name is Caselli.

- *Il secondo uomo* is quite old, and does not at all please me.

- The tenor's name is Ottini; he does not sing unpleasingly, but with effort, like all Italian tenors. We know him very well.

- The name of the second I don't know; he is still young, but nothing at all remarkable.

- *Primo ballerino* good; *prima ballerina* good, and people say pretty, but I have not seen her near.

- There is a *grotesco* who jumps cleverly, but cannot write as I do—just as pigs grunt.

- The orchestra is tolerable."

3. **Mozart Reviews the Performance of Another Opera**
   "Milan, Jan. 26, 1770.

   - In Cremona, the orchestra is good, and Spagnoletta is the name of the first violinist there.

   - *Prima donna* very passable—rather ancient, I fancy, and as ugly as sin. She does not sing as well as she acts, and is the wife of a violin-player at the opera. Her name is Masci.

   - The opera was the *Clemenza di Tito. Seconda donna* not ugly on the stage, young, but nothing superior.

   - *Primo uomo, un musico,* Cicognani, a fine voice, and a beautiful cantabile.

   - The other two *musici* young and passable.

   - The tenor's name is non lo so [I don't know what]. He has a pleasing exterior, and resembles *Le Roi* at Vienna.

   - *Ballerino primo* good, but an ugly dog.

   - There was a *ballerina* who danced far from badly, and, what is a *capo d'opera*, she is anything but plain, either on the stage or off it.

   - The rest were the usual average."

4. **To Monkey Face**
   "Milan, Feb. 17, 1770.

   I kiss mamma's hands a thousand times, and send you a thousand kisses and salutes on your queer monkey face."

5. Kissing St. Peter's Foot

"Rome, April 14, 1770.

I am thankful to say that my stupid pen and I are all right, so we send a thousand kisses to you both. I wish that my sister were in Rome, for this city would assuredly delight her, because St. Peter's is symmetrical, and many other things in Rome are also symmetrical. Papa has just told me that the loveliest flowers are being carried past at this moment. That I am no wiseacre is pretty well known.

Oh! I have one annoyance—there is only a single bed in our lodgings, so mamma may easily imagine that I get no rest beside papa. I rejoice at the thoughts of a new lodging. I have just finished sketching St. Peter with his keys, St. Paul with his sword, and St. Luke with—my sister, &c., &c. I had the honor of kissing St. Peter's foot at San Pietro, and as I have the misfortune to be so short, your good old Wolfgang Mozart was lifted up!"

6. **Dining with a Hypocritical Dominican**
"Bologna, August 21, 1770.

I am not only still alive, but in capital spirits. To-day I took
a fancy to ride a donkey, for such is the custom in Italy, so
I thought that I too must give it a trial. We have the honor
to associate with a certain Dominican who is considered a
very pious ascetic. I somehow don't quite think so, for he

constantly takes a cup of chocolate for breakfast, and immediately afterwards a large glass of strong Spanish wine; and I have myself had the privilege of dining with this holy man, when he drank a lot of wine at dinner and a full glass of very strong wine afterwards, two large slices of melons, some peaches and pears for dessert, five cups of coffee, a whole plateful of nuts, and two dishes of milk and lemons. This he may perhaps do out of bravado, but I don't think so—at all events, it is far too much; and he eats a great deal also at his afternoon collation."

7. Mozart Doesn't Play the Lottery

"Milan, Oct. 26, 1771.

My work being now completed, I have more time to write, but have nothing to say, as papa has written you all I could have said. I am well, thank God! but have no news, except that in the lottery the numbers 35, 59, 60, 61, and 62 have turned up prizes, so if we had selected these we should have won; but as we did not put in at all we neither won nor lost, but only laughed at those who did the latter."

8. Mozart Sees a Hanging

"Milan, Nov. 30, 1771.

That you may not suppose I am ill, I write you a few lines. I saw four fellows hanged in the Dom Platz. They hang here just as they do in Lyons."

9. **Dear Sister**
"Milan, Dec. 18, 1772.

I hope, dear sister, that you are well, dear sister. When this letter reaches you, dear sister, my opera will be in scena, dear sister. Think of me, dear sister, and try, dear sister, to imagine with all your might that my dear sister sees and hears it also."

10. **The Good Son**
"Mannheim, Dec. 20, 1777.

I wish you, dearest papa, a very happy new-year, and that your health, so precious in my eyes, may daily improve, for the benefit and happiness of your wife and children, the satisfaction of your true friends, and for the annoyance and vexation of your enemies. I hope also that in the coming year you will love me with the same fatherly tenderness you have hitherto shown me. I on my part will strive, and honestly strive, to deserve still more the love of such an admirable father."

Chapter 59

17 SUPERHEROES & THEIR SUPERPOWERS

"My strength is as the strength of ten,
Because my heart is pure."
—Alfred, Lord Tennyson, *Sir Galahad*

"Look! Up in the sky! It's a bird! It's a plane!"

It was none of the above, of course. It was Superman.

Who didn't watch *The Adventures of Superman* growing up? Clark Kent was terminally laid-back in his double-breasted suits and black horn-rimmed glasses, and no one—not Jimmy Olsen, not Lois Lane—saw the resemblance between Clark and Superman. Those glasses were quite the disguise.

Superheroes have always been very appealing.

They can do all the things we can't and thus, by reading about them, or watching them in movies or on TV, we can vicariously leave our own limitations behind and imagine what it's like to be able to fly, or freeze a lake with our breath, or stretch ourselves so super-thin that we can slide through keyholes. Enviable powers, indeed.

1. **Aquaman:** He is essentially a "superfish." He has the powers of a fish, magnified many times. He can swim incredibly fast, execute really high dives (like off cliffs), and he has amazing breath control. But unlike fish (it is assumed?) Aquaman can also exert control over other people's minds, albeit in a limited manner. The arena of his super abilities, however, is also the source of his vulnerability: His powers begin to diminish and wane after he is out of water for about an hour.

2. **Batman:** He is one of the most-loved superheroes of all time, due in part to the "Dark Knight" Batman graphic novels of the 1980s that were aimed at an older audience, and the *Batman* series of movies that acknowledged the icon's dark side and did not play his character for laughs the way the *Batman* TV series of the '60s did. Batman is not a supernatural being but rather just a wounded man who witnessed the murder of his parents and who has dedicated his life to fighting crime. He is smart, wealthy, and in great physical condition. He is also one of the coolest superheroes who has ever lived and nowhere is this more evident than in the scene in the first *Batman* movie when Michael Keaton glares at a crook and tells him, "I'm Batman."

   Batman has at his disposal an enormous variety of tools, gadgets, weapons, and vehicles.

   His vehicle inventory includes, of course, the Bat-Mobile, as well as the BatBoat, BatCopter, BatCycle, BatPlane, BatRocket, BatWings, Bat Jetpack, and the Whirly-Bat.

Batman also wears a Utility Belt that contains any number of amazing devices and paraphernalia. The belt contains an infrared flashlight, a two-way radio, a gas mask, a "Bat-a-rang" boomerang, a Bat Rope, tear gas pellets, smoke grenades, a laser torch, and a camera.

Batman works out of stately Wayne Manor (Bruce Wayne, Batman's alter ego is a millionaire entrepreneur) and in the Manor's basement is a complete crime lab and a state-of-the-art computer. Bruce Wayne's longtime butler Alfred knows that his employer is Batman. The elderly gentleman is well-versed in the Dark Knight's legend as well as in the logistics of Batman's crime-fighting endeavors.

3. **Captain America:** He was injected with an experimental Super-Soldier Serum during World War II, which provided him with strength, endurance, agility, speed, reflexes, durability, and healing at the peak of natural human potential. He was frozen and was unthawed from suspended animation in our modern times.

4. **Doctor Strange:** He is a practicing magician who draws powers from mystical entities, which enable him to fly, ward off evil spells, practice clairvoyance, and conjure weapons. He also is highly trained in martial arts.

5. **The Flash:** He is capable of physical movement at super speeds. This speed allows him to actually travel invisibly because he can move faster than the eye can follow. This also permits him to travel through time, since he can move faster than the speed of light.

6. **The Green Hornet:** He has a sleeping-gas gun and a souped-up, gadget-laden car. That's about it.

7. **The Green Lantern:** There is something really weird and mystical about that power-charging green lantern and that awesome power ring. Said ring lets the Lantern do anything he wants to do. By invoking the ring's power he can fly, become invulnerable and invisible, and call upon any super power he needs at the moment. Unlike other superheroes' powers, with their specific limitations and vulnerabilities, The Green Lantern's powers are limitless.

8. **The Hulk:** He has astounding super human strength when he metamorphoses into His Hulkness. The price is high though: In order to use his powers he has to change into a being that looks like a green midget version of Arnold Schwarzenegger cloned with a water buffalo.

9. **The Human Torch:** "Flame on!" is The Human Torch's battle cry and what it does is turn him into a human torch and give him flying power. He literally becomes a flaming, flying crime fighter. It's always a bizarre, surrealistic treat to see the Torch's face hidden in flames after he flames on.

10. **Mighty Mouse:** Everyone grew up with Mighty Mouse and he is probably America's favorite rodent, after Mickey, of course.

His powers include flight, super strength, super speed, and invulnerability. He also has magical hypnotic powers, X-ray vision, super, long-distance sight, and super, long-distance hearing. (In one episode he actually heard something happening on Pluto.)

11. **Mr. Fantastic:** He is a member of The Fantastic Four and his one and only superpower is stretchability. He can stretch himself to super thinness, thus making himself invulnerable to bullets, knives, and all manner of destruction.

12. **Popeye the Sailor:** He manifests incredible super strength when he eats spinach. He can pick up buildings, run across water, juggle battleships, and do all manner of amazing feats. But he can be overcome if not under the influence of spinach.

13. **Luke Skywalker:** As a Jedi Knight, he possesses many powers and abilities far beyond mortal man (and that includes Wookies and Droids, too). Luke is adept at the use of a Light Saber, which is a laser-like sword that can cut through metal and sever limbs in an eye-blink. Luke can also access The Force, an invisible power that surges through all living things in the universe. With The Force at his command, Luke manifests astonishing super strength. Using The Force, Luke is also telekinetic (he can move huge objects (even enormous spacecraft) with his mind) precognitive (he can see the future), and he can miraculously heal with his hands and mind.

14. **Spiderman:** Spidey has the powers of a spider, including spider sense, super climbing abilities, and proportionate super spider strength. He also has a "web shooter" on his wrist that exudes a super strong filament-

type "web" that Spiderman uses to climb with, and to tie up bad guys.

15. **Superman**: Superman, who came to Earth as a child from Planet Krypton, quickly discovered (much to the surprise of Ma and Pa Kent, the kindly folks who found and adopted him) that living on Earth invested him with an extraordinary array of superpowers and abilities.

Superman's talents include super-strength and invulnerability (bullets bounce off him); the ability to fly (although early on he only leaped enormous distances); enhanced sensory powers, including super-hearing, and microscopic, telescopic, heat, and X-ray vision; a super brain with 100% total recall; time-traveling ability via his speed-of-light travel powers; and freezing super-breath. He can also hypnotize at will, speak every language on Earth (and elsewhere), solve any math problem instantly, and write with both hands at once.

Superman is vulnerable to three of the seven different kinds of Kryptonite. When exposed, his superpowers are negated.

Superman is probably the coolest of all superheroes and he is the legend that many kids emulated when growing up. (Admit it: At some point in your adolescence, you walked around with a cape hidden beneath your shirt, right?)

The character of Superman represents the ultimate metaphorical "super man" and in 1883, decades before Clark Kent was born, Friedrich Nietzsche acknowledged this in his prologue to Also Sprach Zarathustra when he wrote, "I teach you the superman. Man is something to be surpassed."

And the cape is awesome.

16. **Underdog**: He is kind of like Superman as a dog, only Underdog needs special Energy Pills to access his superpowers, which includes flying, super-strength, and X-ray vision.

17. **Wonder Woman**: She was the first feminist superhero. She taps into the "feminine goddess" archetype for her "image" and her bullet-blocking bracelets are actually made of "Feminium." A daughter of the Gods, she has an invisible robot plane that can fly at 300 miles per hour, she possesses some magical powers, and she wields a golden lasso that extracts the truth from anyone she ties up in it.

Chapter 60

40 REPUGNANT BAND NAMES

Rock on.

1. Accidental Goat Sodomy

2. Angry Amputees

3. Biff Hitler and the Violent Mood Swings

4. Bingo Hand Job

5. Bloated Scrotum

6. Bloody Stools

7. Bumgravy

8. Cannibal Corpse

9. Catherine Wheel

10. Cherry Coke Enema

11. Club Foot Orchestra

12. Defecation

13. Dickless

14. Drew Barrymore's Dealer

15. Electric Vomit

16. The Elvis Diet

17. The Fat Chick from Wilson Phillips Band

18. Foetus

19. The Glands of External Secretion

20. Gregg Turner and the Blood Drained Cows

21. Halo of Flies

22. Iron Prostate

23. The Luminous Toilet Bowls

24. Lung Mustard

25. My Uncle's Asshole

26. Nearly Died Laughing While Shaving My Butt

27. Nurse With Wound

28. Painful Discharge

29. Public Enema Number One

30. Pungent Stench

31. Rats of Unusual Size

32. Revolting Cocks

33. Sandy Duncan's Eye

34. Ted Bundy's Volkswagen

35. Throbbing Gristle

36. Vic Morrow's Head

37. Violent Anal Death
38. Vomit Launch
39. Voodoo Meat Bucket
40. Women of the SS

Chapter 60

176 FORMS OF SEXUAL AROUSAL

It does seem that almost anything, in a given situation, can be a sexual turn-on.

1. Acting like an adolescent.
2. Admitting to sins.
3. Amputees and stumps.
4. Ants.
5. Anuses.
6. Armpit hair.
7. Armpits.
8. Arranging a disaster.
9. Baby paraphernalia.
10. Being a fugitive.
11. Being at a great height or high altitude.
12. Being buried alive.

13. Being cold.

14. Being dirty.

15. Being fondled in a crowd.

16. Being hit with a pie.

17. Being raped.

18. Being robbed.

19. Being stared at.

20. Being tied up.

21. Being whipped.

22. Birds.

23. Biting.

24. Blindfolds.

25. Bloodletting.

26. Bloody sanitary pads.

27. Bodily fluids of any kind.

28. Breasts.

29. Buttocks.

30. Cannibalism.

31. Catheters.

32. Change.

33. Clothed partners.

34. Cold weather.

35. Computer sex games.

36. Consuming blood.

37. Cross-dresing.

38. Crowds.

39. Dancing.

40. Darkness.

41. Defecation.

42. Discussing sex.

43. Dolls.

44. Electrical stimulation.

45. Enemas.

46. Exposing one's body to a doctor.

47. Exposing one's genitals.

48. Eyes.

49. Faking an illness.

50. Fantasizing about someone else during sex.

51. Fear.

52. Feces.

53. Feet.

54. Female corpses.

55. Females dressed like men.

56. Fire.

57. Flatulence.

58. Food.

59. Fur.

60. Genital odor.

61. Giving a sermon.

62. Hair.

63. Hate.

64. Having one's hair shampooed.

65. Having sex in public.

66. Having sex with one's own brother.

67. Having sex with one's own father.

68. Having sex with one's own mother.

69. Having sex with one's own sister.

70. Hearing a sermon.

71. Heat.

72. High heels.

73. Horses.

74. Hot weather.

75. Humiliation.

76. Inserting one's penis into one's own anus.

77. Items of women's clothing.

78. Jealousy.

79. Kissing.

80. Lack of oxygen.

81. Lactating women.

82. Large genitals.

83. Leather.

84. Legs.

85. Licking a partner's eyeball.

86. Listening to others have sex.

87. Long penises.

88. Lotions.

89. Making obscene phone calls.

90. Male corpses.

91. Males dressed like women.

92. Mannequins.

93. Massage.

94. Masturbating while someone watches.

95. Menstruating women.

96. Music.

97. Mutilating corpses.

98. Mutilation.

99. Noses.

100. Nude photographs.

101. Nudity.

102. Nursing.

103. Obesity.

104. Obscene language.

105. Oil.

106. Older females.

107. Older males.

108. Pain.

109. A partner's terminal illness.

110. Partners from a different age group.

111. The passage of time.

112. People pretending to be asleep.

113. Perspiration odor.

114. Pinching others.

115. Pregnant women.

116. Pubic hair.

117. Racially-different partners.

118. Rape.

119. Receiving obscene phone calls.

120. Ripping off someone's clothes.

121. Robots.

122. Sacred objects.

123. Sausages.

124. Sex with many partners.

125. Sexual incompetence, naivete, or mistakes.

126. Shaved or hairless genitals.

127. Shaving a partner.

128. Shaving oneself.

129. Short people.

130. Shorter partners.

131. Silk.

132. Sinning.

133. Slapping a partner.

134. Smelling flowers.

135. Smells.

136. Snakes.

137. Soiled clothing.

138. Someone else's spouse.

139. Sounds.

140. Spiders.

141. Statues.

142. Stealing.

143. Stomachs.

144. Strangers.

145. Strength.

146. Struggle.

147. Sucking someone's nose.

148. Sunlight.

149. Talking about penises.

150. Taller partners.

151. Tattoos.

152. Teasing.

153. Teeth.

154. Telling sex jokes.

155. Terror.

156. Testicles.

157. Tickling.

158. Toes.

159. Tooth extractions.

160. Trains.

161. Trauma.

162. Traveling.

163. Urine.

164. Using needles.

165. Virgins.

166. Vomit.

167. Voyeurism.

168. Watching others freeze.

169. Watching others have sex.

170. Watching others smoke.

171. Water.

172. Weakness.

173. Wealth.

174. Witchcraft rituals.

175. Wounds.

176. Writing love letters.

Chapter 62

8 NOVELS OF A MILLION WORDS OR MORE

Some people really like to write.

1. *Men of Goodwill* (1933)
   Words: 2,070,000 words, English
   Author: Jules Romains
   Edition: 8,000 pages, twenty-seven volumes

2. *Artamène ou le Grand Cyrus [Artamène, or the Grand Cyprus]* (1649-1653)
   Words: 1,954,300 words, French
   Authors: Georges and/or Madeleine de Scudéry
   Edition: 13,095 pages, ten volumes

3. *Het Bureau [The Desk]* (1996-2000)
   Words: 1,590,000 words, Dutch
   Author: J. J. Voskuil
   Edition: 5,058 pages, seven volumes

4. *Gordana* **(2007)**
   Words: 1,400,000 (est.), Croatian
   Author: Marija Jurić Zagorka
   Edition: 8,768 pages, twelve volumes

5. *À la recherche du temps perdu [Remembrance of Things Past]* **(1913)**
   Words: 1,267,069, French
   Author: Marcel Proust
   Edition: 3,031 pages, seven volumes

6. *English Couplets in VI Volumes* **(2005-2016)**
   Words: 1,168,687, English
   Author: Mulki Radhakrishna Shetty
   Edition: 5,094 pages, six volumes

7. *Zettels Traum* **[Bottom's Dream] (1970)**
   Words: 1,100,000 (est.), German
   Author: Arno Schmidt
   Edition: 1,536 pages

8. *Min Kamp* **[My Struggle] (2209-2011)**
   Words: 1,000,000, Norwegian
   Author: Karl Ove Knausgård
   Edition: 3,600 pages, six volumes

Chapter 63

30 INTERESTING FACTS ABOUT *TITANIC*

1. *Titanic*'s trip from England to New York was nothing extraordinary, nor was it even out of the ordinary. Her sister ship, the *Olympic*, had made the voyage successfully

many times prior to *Titanic*'s launch. *Titanic* sinking on her maiden voyage is what made her the most famous shipwreck in history.

2. *Titanic* was the middle ship of White Star Line's "three biggest ships ever built" project: The *Olympic*, the *Titanic*, and the *Britannic*.

3. Some archival documents show that *Britannic*'s original name was *Gigantic*, but after *Titanic*'s sinking they changed it to *Britannic*. If this is true, they probably didn't think it was a good idea to continue to call attention to the size of the ships.

4. *Titanic* almost collided with the tender ship New York before setting sail while in Southampton harbor. Only quick thinking and the correct orders from the two ships' captains prevented a collision.

5. *Titanic*'s total capacity of passengers and crew was around 3,500. On her maiden voyage, there were approximately 2,200 souls aboard: around 1,300 passengers and 900 crew members.

6. *Titanic* carried enough food and beverages to feed 2,200 people three times a day. Her "cupboard" included forty tons of potatoes, thirty-eight tons of meat, 20,000 bottles of beer, 40,000 eggs and tons more of anything a passenger could possibly desire on board.

7. Third Class passengers on *Titanic* enjoyed accommodations comparable to Second Class on other ships.

8. Fourteen years before *Titanic* set sail, Morgan Robertson wrote a novella that many consider prophetic. It was called

Futility and was about the *Titan*, the biggest ship in the world. The *Titan* sank on her maiden voyage and her details uncannily mirrored those of the *Titanic*. After *Titanic* sank, they re-released the novella, retitled as *Wreck of the Titan*.

9. *Titanic*'s maiden voyage was meant to be Captain Smith's final voyage as a steamship captain. He planned on retiring upon his return to England at the conclusion of *Titanic*'s first transatlantic voyage.

10. *Titanic*'s fourth funnel was only used to vent cooking smoke from the kitchen.

11. The most-hated *Titanic* survivor was undoubtedly White Star Line's Managing Director J. Bruce Ismay. It was believed he saved himself by taking a lifeboat seat that should have gone to a passenger.

12. A longstanding myth about *Titanic* was that she was a victim of the "champagne curse": she sank because the champagne bottle used to christen her didn't break. The truth is that there was no champagne curse because there was no champagne bottle. The White Star Line never christened their ships.

13. If the walls of *Titanic*'s watertight compartments had gone all the way up to A Deck instead of stopping at E, she probably wouldn't have sunk, even with her first five compartments breached.

14. The sinking of the *Titanic* spurred the creation of the International Ice Patrol. Since then, in close to a century of Atlantic seafaring, not a single ship that heeded the IIP's warnings has struck an iceberg.

15. Even though Dr. Robert Ballard's 1985 discovery of the wreck confirmed that the ship had broken in two, a surviving *Titanic* crew member testified in 1912 that he had seen the ship break in half and his account was published in his hometown newspaper, the *Witney Gazette*. His report was, for the most part, ignored.

16. Another myth about the *Titanic* was that a worker had been trapped in the hull during construction and never recovered. The truth is slightly different. Newer hires were given the job of hammering in rivets in *Titanic*'s hull. The old-timers had to tap every rivet at the end of the day to make sure they were seated properly. They would taunt the newcomers by telling them that they would sometimes hear tapping back. Every one of the 3,000 men who built Titanic was accounted for. There was no worker trapped in the hull.

17. James Cameron depicted First Officer William Murdoch committing suicide on *Titanic*. His family said it wasn't true. In 1998, Twentieth Century Fox issued the family an apology.

18. *Titanic*'s triple-toned steam whistle was a (very loud) C hote.

19. A Third Class ticket on *Titanic* cost between $15 and $40 in 1912 currency. This would be equal to between $350 and $900 today. For many emigrating passengers, this was their life savings.

20. The April 15, 1912 edition of the *New York Evening Sun* reported: "All Saved From *Titanic* After Collision…Liner Is Being Towed to Halifax."

21. In 1907, none other than Bram Stoker, author of the 1897 Gothic horror novel *Dracula*, visited the Belfast site where the *Olympic* and the *Titanic* were being built.

22. *Titanic*'s E deck ran the entire length of the ship. It had cabins for second- and third-class passengers; cabins for the crew; and "Scotland Road," a corridor that stretched the length of the ship.

23. The *Titanic* offered its first-class passengers a heated salt-water swimming pool. The *Titanic*'s swimming pool was only the second swimming pool built into an ocean liner. The first was built on the *Olympic*, the *Titanic*'s sister ship.

24. Dr. Robert Ballard, who discovered the *Titanic* wreck in 1985, is adamantly against artifact salvaging. Regarding salvaging *Titanic*, he has said, "It'll get stripped until all the jewels have been taken off the old lady's body."

25. *Saved from the Titanic* was the first *Titanic* movie, and it's also the only one starring a survivor of the catastrophe. The movie starred Dorothy Gibson, who made this ten-minute silent film almost immediately after her rescue. It debuted on May 14, 1912, only twenty-nine days after the *Titanic* sank. In the movie, Gibson wore the same dress that she wore on the *Titanic*.

26. The film *A Night To Remember* has two major errors: The ship is christened and the ship sinks in one piece.

27. The largest *Titanic* artifact is the "Big Piece," which is the wall of two C Deck cabins, C79 and C81. It took two years to retrieve and is now on display at the permanent *Titanic* Artifact Exhibition at the Luxor Hotel in Las Vegas.

28. The first word said when *Titanic*'s wreck was discovered was "Wreckage."

29. In April 2012, James Cameron and Twentieth Century Fox re-released *Titanic* in 3-D. The conversion process took James Cameron a year and cost $18 million.

30. *Titanic*'s passengers and crew had a 32% survival rate. Two-thirds of those onboard perished, but 98% of First Class women survived.

Source: *The Titanic for Dummies* by Stephen Spignesi

Chapter 64

1 BIZARRO FACT ABOUT EACH OF AMERICA'S PRESIDENTS

1. George Washington
Term: 1789-1797
Birth: February 22, 1732
Death: December 14, 1799
George Washington never had wooden teeth. His dentures were made from hippopotamus ivory, they had gold hinges, and the teeth used were from dead soldiers.

2. John Adams
Term: 1797-1801
Birth: October 30, 1735
Death: July 4, 1826
Adams' last words were "Thomas Jefferson still survives." In one of American history's most astonishing coincidences, John Adams and Thomas Jefferson—the two signers of the Declaration of Independence to become president—both died on the same day, July 4, 1826, the fiftieth anniversary of the signing of the Declaration of Independence. When Adams uttered his final words, he

did not know that Thomas Jefferson had died five hours earlier.

3. Thomas Jefferson

Term: 1801-1809
Birth: April 13, 1743
Death: July 4, 1826

Thomas Jefferson rewrote the *New Testament*. In his version, known as *The Life and Morals of Jesus of Nazareth*, he removed all of the paranormal or supernatural elements. It not published until seventy-five years after his death. In his revision, Jesus was a mortal man blessed with great wisdom.

4. James Madison

Term: 1809-1817
Birth: March 16, 1751
Death: June 28, 1836

James Madison was the first president to wear pants. Prior to Madison the men in the Colonies wore knee breeches and stockings.

5. James Monroe

Term: 1817-1825
Birth: April 28, 1758
Death: July 4, 1831

When James Monroe left the White House after his presidency, his political debts were so high he was forced to sell off all his slaves and all his property to fend off bankruptcy.

6. **John Quincy Adams**
   Term: 1825-1829
   Birth: July 11, 1767
   Death: February 23, 1848
   John Quincy Adams apparently believed in the Hollow
   Earth Theory. He approved an expedition to the entrance
   to the earth's interior that was rumored to be at the North
   Pole. The expedition was later cancelled by his successor,
   Andrew Jackson.

7. **Andrew Jackson**
   Term: 1829-1837
   Birth: March 15, 1767
   Death: June 8, 1845
   To protect his twenty-six slaves from illegal seizure by
   authorities while on a journey away from his plantation,
   Jackson removed their chains, armed them with axes and
   clubs, and marched them past a checkpoint that been seen
   set up as an excuse to confiscate slaves on the premise that
   they were runaways. After passing the checkpoint, Jackson
   took back the weapons and put his slaves back in chains.

8. **Martin Van Buren**
   Term: 1837-1841
   Birth: December 5, 1782
   Death: July 24, 1862
   During dinner at the White House one evening, a waiter
   bent over and whispered to Van Buren that the kitchen
   was on fire. The president calmly excused himself and
   went to put out the fire by organizing a bucket brigade.

Reportedly, that was the only time he ever set foot in the White House kitchen.

9. William Henry Harrison

Term: 1841
Birth: February 9, 1773
Death: April 4, 1841

William Henry Harrison's family was attacked during the Revolutionary War by a regiment led by none other than Benedict Arnold. Everyone survived the attack, but Arnold's soldiers plundered the Harrison farm.

10. John Tyler

Term: 1841-1845
Birth: March 29, 1790
Death: January 18, 1862

John Tyler who officially supported slavery and who was buried with his coffin draped in the Confederate Flag, once became physically ill upon witnessing a slave auction.

11. James Polk

Term: 1845-1849
Birth: November 2, 1795
Death: June 15, 1849

James Polk liked to carry his money around with him in a suitcase. His wife Sarah tried to persuade him to put it in a bank, but she couldn't convince him.

12. Zachary Taylor

Term: 1849-1850
Birth: November 24, 1784

Death: July 9, 1850

Zachary Taylor did not learn of his June 1848 nomination as the Whig candidate for the presidency until a month later because the letter informing him of the decision arrived at his home with ten cents postage due and he wouldn't pay it.

13. Millard Fillmore

Term: 1850-1853
Birth: January 7, 1800
Death: March 8, 1874

In 1858, widower Millard Fillmore signed a prenup before marrying Caroline McIntosh. She was thirteen years younger than him, and the wealthy widow of a railroad magnate.

14. Franklin Pierce

Term: 1853-1857
Birth: November 23, 1804
Death: October 8, 1869

Even though Franklin Pierce was the first president to have a full-time bodyguard, he was still attacked when he was in office. A deranged man threw a hard-boiled egg at him. When caught, the eggsassin tried to kill himself with a pocketknife. He later died in a mental institution. Pierce didn't press charges.

15. James Buchanan

Term: 1857-1861
Birth: April 23, 1791
Death: June 1, 1868

James Buchanan, the only never-married president, had

a twenty-three-year friendship with William Rufus King, the only never-married vice president (under Franklin Pierce). Buchanan and King were referred to in the press as "Miss Fancy and Aunt Fancy."

16. Abraham Lincoln

Term: 1861-1865
Birth: February 12, 1809
Death: April 15, 1865

In 1863, fans of President Lincoln sent him a turkey for the Lincoln Thanksgiving table. Lincoln's young son Tad immediately embraced the bird as a pet and named it Jack. However, since it was supposed to be dinner, the White House cook took Jack away from Tad with the intent of killing it and cooking it. Tad burst into a Cabinet meeting crying. Lincoln immediately stopped the meeting and took the time to write an official reprieve, thus sparing Jack the fate of being Thanksgiving dinner. This is believed to be the first official pardoning of a turkey by the U.S. president. (What a dad, eh?)

17. Andrew Johnson

Term: 1865-1869
Birth: December 29, 1808
Death: July 31, 1875

Andrew Johnson was an avowed racist, slave owner, and confirmed white supremacist. After his elevation to the presidency following Lincoln's assassination, Johnson said, "This is a country for white men, and by God, as long as I am president, it shall be a government for white men."

18. Ulysses S. Grant

Term: 1869-1877

Birth: April 27, 1822

Death: July 23, 1885

Ulysses S. Grant never let anyone see him naked, except maybe his wife. On the battlefield, soldiers bathed by stripping down and having their similarly stripped comrades-in-arms pour water over them. Not Grant, however. He hid in a sealed tent so no one could glimpse him in the buff.

19. Rutherford B. Hayes

Term: 1877-1881

Birth: October 4, 1822

Death: January 17, 1893

The first phone in the White House was installed during Rutherford B. Hayes' term. The installer was one Alexander Graham Bell.

20. James Garfield

Term: 1881

Birth: November 19, 1831

Death: September 19, 1881

One of the earliest air conditioning "units" was built to make the suffering James Garfield more comfortable after he was shot. As the president lay in bed in the sweltering Washington, D.C. heat with a bullet in him, Navy engineers came up with a plan. They brought in six tons of ice and placed it in a container in the basement of the White House. They then rigged up a series of ducts and fans that blew cold air from the ice up into the president's bedroom. Amazingly, this contraption lowered the temperature of the room by twenty degrees.

21. Chester A. Arthur
Term: 1881-1885
Birth: October 5, 1829
Death: November 18, 1886
When Chester A. Arthur was president, he had eighty pairs of pants. He changed clothes throughout the day.

22. Grover Cleveland
Term: 1885-1889
Birth: March 18, 1837
Death: June 24, 1908
Prior to becoming president, Grover Cleveland was a hangman. As Sheriff of Erie County, New York, he took upon himself the duty of placing the hangman's noose around the necks of two criminals who had been sentenced to death.

23. Benjamin Harrison
Term: 1889-1893
Birth: August 20, 1833
Death: March 13, 1901
During Benjamin Harrison's time in the White House, electric lights were installed for the first time. Harrison was terrified of the light switches and thought that he would be zapped with electric shocks if he touched them. Thus, he left all the lights in the White House on all night long rather than turn them off and risk electrocution.

24. Grover Cleveland

Term: 1893-1897

Birth: March 18, 1837

Death: June 24, 1908

In 1893, Grover Cleveland, a heavy smoker, was
diagnosed as having a malignant tumor of the mouth.
Fearing a financial panic that would make the current
U.S. Depression (known as the Panic of 1893) worse,
Cleveland's condition was not revealed to the public.
Cleveland was secretly operated on aboard the yacht
Oneida on the East River in New York on July 1, 1893, by
five doctors and a dentist. They removed his left upper jaw
and a large tumor while he was strapped to a mast. The
president was fitted with a rubber jaw and spent months
learning how to speak naturally again. Cleveland's surgery
was not revealed to the American public until 1917,
twenty-four years after his operation.

25. William McKinley

Term: 1897-1901

Birth: January 29, 1843

Death: September 14, 1901

Supposedly, William McKinley was Frank Baum's
inspiration and model for the character of the Wizard of
Oz.

26. Theodore Roosevelt

Term: 1901-1909

Birth: October 27, 1858

Death: January 6, 1919

When Teddy Roosevelt traveled, he always carried a bottle of morphine with him. Roosevelt believed in euthanasia and said that if he contracted something away from home and became incapacitated, he would end his own life with the morphine, rather than linger on in agony.

27. William Howard Taft

Term: 1909-1913
Birth: September 15, 1857
Death: March 8, 1930

William Howard Taft weighed as much as 355 pounds when he was president. One of his favorite self-deprecating jokes was, "I got off a streetcar and gave my seat to three ladies."

28. Woodrow Wilson

Term: 1913-1921
Birth: December 28, 1856
Death: February 3, 1924

This isn't a bizarro fact, but it's worth including because it is, frankly, brilliant advice for public speakers and writers. Woodrow Wilson said, "If I am to speak for ten minutes, I need a week for preparations; if fifteen minutes, three days; if half an hour, two days; if an hour, I am ready now."

29. Warren G. Harding

Term: 1921-1923
Birth: November 2, 1865
Death: August 2, 1923

Warren Harding, who was inducted into the Ku Klux Klan in a White House ceremony in 1922, spent time in a psychiatric institution when he was in his twenties after a series of nervous breakdowns.

30. Calvin Coolidge
Term: 1923-1929
Birth: July 4, 1872
Death: January 5, 1933
Calvin Coolidge liked to have his head rubbed with Vaseline while he ate his favorite breakfast, boiled raw wheat and rye.

Calvin Coolidge's Sense of Humor

Calvin Coolidge and the First Lady visited a farm one day where Grace Coolidge was told that a rooster would have sex several times a day. "Tell that to Mr. Coolidge," the First Lady said, probably with a smirk. So the farmer did exactly that, to which the president responded, "With the same hen?" The farmer said no. Coolidge (likewise smirking, we hope) said, "Tell that to Mrs. Coolidge."

31. Herbert Hoover
Term: 1929-1933
Birth: August 10, 1874
Death: October 20, 1964
Herbert Hoover and his wife, Lou, spoke in Mandarin

Chinese when they were discussing private matters and did not want to be overheard talking. (Likewise, Calvin Coolidge and his wife spoke in sign language when they did not want to be overheard.)

32. Franklin D. Roosevelt

Term: 1933-1945
Birth: January 30, 1882
Death: April 12, 1945

FDR never used hand gestures when he spoke in front of a group because he had to hold onto the podium with both hands to prevent himself from falling down. He had contracted polio as a child and, because, of the resultant paralysis, he used heavy metal leg braces so he could stand in one place when speaking. The American public never knew. (There are 125,000 photos of FDR in his Presidential Library. Exactly two show him in a wheelchair.)

33. Harry S. Truman

Term: 1945-1953
Birth: May 8, 1884
Death: December 26, 1972

Harry Truman was a believer in the superiority of women. He once said, "I've always thought that the best man in the world is hardly good enough for any woman."

34. Dwight D. Eisenhower

Term: 1953-1961
Birth: October 14, 1890
Death: March 28, 1969

On October 7, 1957, Ghana finance minister Komla

Agbeli Gbedemah was kicked out of a Dover, Delaware diner because they refused to serve "colored people." When President Eisenhower heard about what happened, he remedied the racist insult three days later by having Gbedemah to the White House for breakfast.

35. John F. Kennedy
Term: 1961-1963
Birth: May 29, 1917
Death: November 22, 1963
The first doctor to attend to JFK after he was shot had delivered Lee Harvey Oswald's daughter Audrey a month earlier.

36. Lyndon B. Johnson
Term: 1963-1969
Birth: August 27, 1908
Death: January 22, 1973
Lyndon Johnson had a large johnson and he called it Jumbo. He was not averse to showing it off, oftentimes to unsuspecting female reporters. A story is told that when a reporter asked him "Why are we in Vietnam?" he pulled his penis out and slapped it on the desk. That was his answer. (As always, though, there are often two sides to every story. After Johnson left office, according to one source, a senior staff member who had seen Jumbo told a reporter he didn't think it was oversized, and that it may have only been average or even a little smaller.)

37. Richard Nixon
Term: 1969-1974
Birth: January 9, 1913

Death: April 22, 1994

When Elvis Presley visited Richard Nixon at the White House on December 21, 1970, he brought the president a World War II Colt .45 pistol mounted in a display case. The gun was confiscated by the Secret Service before the King was ushered into the Oval Office. However, Elvis was later allowed to present the president with the gun during his visit.

38. Gerald Ford

Term: 1974-1977

Birth: July 14, 1913

Death: December 26, 2006

Gerald Ford was a public "wind breaker." And whenever he let one fly, he would always look at a nearby Secret Service agent and say something like, "Was that you? Show some class!"

39. Jimmy Carter

Term: 1977-1981

Birth: October 1, 1924

Jimmy Carter was intent on portraying the image of a common, ordinary man. He would carry his own suit bag so the photographers could snap a picture of him being down-to-earth, but what only the Secret Service knew was that the bag was empty.

40. Ronald Reagan

Term: 1981-1989

Birth: February 6, 1911

Death: June 5, 2004

During presidential trips, Secret Service agents routinely

sweep hotel rooms the president will be staying in for electronic bugs. Sometimes they find listening devices intended for the previous guest. Once, when sweeping a room before Reagan's visit, the Secret Service did, indeed, find a bug that been placed to eavesdrop on the room's prior occupant. The previous guest? Elton John.

41. George H. W. Bush

Term: 1989-1993
Birth: June 12, 1924
George H. W. Bush vomited on the Prime Minister of Japan in 1992 during a banquet. Today, if you vomit in Japan, you are said to have *Bushu-suru*, which means "done the Bush thing."

42. Bill Clinton

Term: 1993-2001
Birth: August 19, 1946
Bill Clinton played saxophone in a jazz trio when he was in high school. They called themselves Three Blind Mice and their trademark was wearing sunglasses on stage.

43. George W. Bush

Term: 2001-2009
Birth: July 6, 1946
In high school, George Bush was a head cheerleader.

44. Barack Obama

Term: 2009-2017
Birth: August 4, 1961
Barack Obama and Brad Pitt are 9th cousins.

45. Donald Trump
Term: 2017-
Birth: June 14, 1946
Both Donald Trump and Ringo Starr once starred in
"Good Will Haunting," the Season 3, Episode 6, October
30, 1998 *Sabrina the Teenage Witch* episode. Ringo played
a Mummy and Trump played Daniel Ray McLeech.
Trump was uncredited.

Chapter 65

THE TOP 20 CAUSES OF DEATH IN AMERICA FROM 1999-2015

In America, 42,170,818 people died between the years 1999 and 2015. The big three causes? Heart Disease, Cancer, and Stroke. This is a look at the top 20 causes of death in the United states over a sixteen-year period.

CAUSE	NUMBER OF DEATHS	PERCENTAGE OF DEATHS
Heart Disease	10,939,923	25.9%
Cancer (Malignant Neoplasms)	9,646,497	22.9%
Stroke (Cerebrovascular Disease)	2,437,998	5.8%
Chronic Lower Respiratory Disease	2,280,130	5.4%
Alzheimer's Disease	1,257,309	3.0%
Diabetes	1,236,321	2.9%
Influenza & Pneumonia	987,432	2.3%
Nephritis (Kidney Disease)	757,934	1.8%

Traffic Accidents	664,177	1.6%
Septicemia (Blood Poisoning)	594,484	1.4%
Poisoning	579,252	1.4%
Firearms	523,344	1.2%
Liver Disease	521,837	1.2%
Hypertension	420,559	1.0%
Falls	396,874	0.9%
Parkinson's Disease	348,259	0.8%
Pneumonitis	294,900	0.7%
Suffocation	253,575	0.6%
Benign Neoplasms (Nonmalignant Tumors)	244,520	0.6%
Perinatal Period (SIDS)	227,475	0.5%

Source: CDC, ProCon.org

Chapter 66

5 CATHOLIC MARTYRS WHO DIED TERRIBLE DEATHS

1. **St. Lawrence (258 AD):** He was broiled alive.

2. **St. Hippolytus (235 AD):** He was pulled apart by horses.

3. **St. Ignatius (c. 110 AD):** He was killed and eaten by two lions in the Roman Colosseum.

4. **Pope St. Clement (101 AD):** He was tied to an anchor and thrown into the sea.

5. **St. Bartholomew (c. 100 AD):** He was skinned and then crucified upside down.

ACKNOWLEDGMENTS

I would like to thank my editor Mike Lewis; my literary agent John White; my main squeeze Valerie; my sister Janet; Anthony Ziccardi, Michael Wilson, Maddie Sturgeon, and all the fine folks at Post Hill Press; my friend and colleague Mark McFadden; all my friends at Aniello's Restaurant for keeping me fueled while working on this book; my best friend Chloe; my mom Lee; and of course, Dr. Bizarro for his strange and pioneering work seeking out and chronicling the weird and bizarre.

WORKS CONSULTED

- Andrews, William. *Old Time Punishments* (1890 edition). New York: Dorset Press, 1991.
- Augarde, Tony. *The Oxford Dictionary of Modern Quotations*. New York: Oxford University Press, 1991.
- Bernard, André, ed. *Rotten Rejections: A Literary Companion*. Wainscott, NY: Pushcart Press, 1990.
- Bernard, Jami. *First Films: Illustrious, Obscure and Embarrassing Movie Debuts*. New York: Citadel Press, 1993.
- Berra, Tim M. *Evolution and the Myth of Creationism: A Basic Guide to the Facts in the Evolution Debate*. Stanford, CA: Stanford University Press, 1990.
- Bord, Janet, and Colin Bord. *Unexplained Mysteries of the 20th Century*. Chicago, IL: Contemporary Books, 1989.
- Brooks, Tim, and Earl Marsh. *The Complete Directory to Prime Time Network TV Shows 1946-Present*. New York: Ballantine Books, 1988.
- Campbell, Colin, and Allan Murphy. *Things We Said Today: The Complete Lyrics and a Concordance to The Beatles' Songs*, 1962-1970. Ann Arbor, MI: Pierian Press, 1980.
- Cavendish, Richard, ed. *Encyclopedia of the Unexplained: Magic, Occultism and Parapsychology*. New York: Penguin/Arkana, 1989.
- Cheetham, Erika, translator and ed. *The Prophecies of Nostradamus*. New York: Berkley Books, 1981.

- Chilnick, Lawrence D., ed. *The Pill Book*. New York: Bantam Books, 1992.
- Cooper, Margaret. *The Inventions of Leonardo Da Vinci*. New York: Macmillan, 1965.
- Corliss, William R. *Ancient Man: A Handbook of Puzzling Artifacts*. Glen Arm, MD: The Sourcebook Project, 1980.
- *Incredible Life: A Handbook of Biological Mysteries*. Glen Arm, MD: The Sourcebook Project, 1981.
- *Mysterious Universe: A Handbook of Astronomical Anomalies*. Glen Arm, MD: The Sourcebook Project, 1979.
- *Unknown Earth: A Handbook of Geological Enigmas*. Glen Arm, MD: The Sourcebook Project, 1980.
- De Thuin, Richard. *The Official Identification and Price Guide to Movie Memorabilia*. New York: House of Collectibles, 1990.
- Delacoste, Frédérique, and Priscilla Alexander, eds. *Sex Work: Writings by Women* in the Sex Industry. Pittsburgh, PA: Cleis Press, 1987.
- Delaney, John J. *Pocket Dictionary of Saints*. New York: Doubleday, 1983. ^
- Drimmer, Frederick. *Until You Are Dead...The Book of Executions in America*. New York: Pinnacle Books, 1992.
- Ebert, Roger. Roger Ebert's *Movie Home Companion* 1993 Edition. Kansas City, MO: Andrews and McMeel, 1993.
- Ellis, Bret Easton. *American Psycho*. New York: Vintage Books, 1991.
- Ellis, James Anthony. *Preparing For the Best: A Guide to Earth Changes For 1993 and Beyond*. San Diego, CA: JAE Publishing, 1993.

- Fargis, Paul, and Sheree Bykofsky, editorial directors. *The New York Public Library Desk Reference.* New York: Stonesong Press, 1989.
- Fedler, Fred. *Media Hoaxes.* Ames, IA: Iowa State University Press, 1989.
- Ferm, Vergilius. *Lightning Never Strikes Twice (If You Own a Feather Bed) and 1904 Other American Superstitions from the Ordinary to the Eccentric.* New York: Gramercy Publishing Company, 1989.
- Fletcher, Barbara. *Don't Blame the Stork!: The Cyclopedia of Unusual Names.* Seattle, WA: Rainbow Publications, 1981.
- Fletcher, Lynne Yamaguchi, and Adrien Saks. *Lavender Lists: New Lists About Lesbian and Gay Culture, History, and Personalities.* Boston, MA: Alyson Publications, 1990.
- Flexner, Stuart, with Doris Flexner. The Pessimist's Guide to History. New York: Avon Books, 1992.
- Fodor, Nandor. *Encyclopædia of Psychic Science.* New Hyde Park, NY: University Books, 1966.
- Fricke, John, Jay Scarfone, and William Stillman. *The Wizard of Oz: The Official 50th Anniversary Pictorial History.* New York: Warner Books, 1989.
- Fowler, Simon. *Workhouse: The People, The Places, The Life Behind Doors.* Kew. Richmond, Surrey, U.K., The National Archives, 2007.
- Galvin, Anthony. *Old Sparky: The Electric Chair and the History of the Death Penalty.* New York: Skyhorse Publishing, 2015.
- Gatten, Jeffrey N., compiler. *The Rolling Stone Index: Twenty-Five Years of Popular Culture 1967-1991.* Ann Arbor, MI: Popular Culture, Ink., 1993.

- Gipe, George. *The Last Time When*. New York: World Almanac Publications, 1981.
- Gittelson, Bernard, and Laura Torbett. *Intangible Evidence*. New York: Simon & Schuster, 1987.
- Givens, Bill. *Film Flubs, the Sequel: Even More Memorable Movie Mistakes*. New York: Citadel Press, 1992.
  —*Film Flubs: Memorable Movie Mistakes*. New York: Citadel Press, 1990.
  —*Son of Film Flubs: More Memorable Movie Mistakes*. New York: Citadel Press, 1991.
- Gold, Gari. *Crystal Energy: Put the Power in the Palm of Your Hand*. Chicago, IL: Contemporary Books, 1987.
- Goodman, Ruth. *How To Be a Victorian: A Dawn-to-Dusk Guide to Victorian Life*. New York: W. W. Norton, 2014.
- Gomez, Dr. Joan. *A Dictionary of Symptoms*. New York: Bantam Books, 1967.
- Graves, Kersey. *The World's Sixteen Crucified Saviors*. New York: The Truth Seeker Company, 1875.
- Hale, Mark. *Headbangers: The Worldwide MegaBook of Heavy Metal Bands*. Ann Arbor, MI: Popular Culture, Ink., 1993.
- Hammond, Allen, ed. *The 1993 Information Please Environmental Almanac*. New York: Houghton Mifflin Company, 1993.
- Harmetz, Aljean. *The Making of The Wizard of Oz*. New York: Dell Publishing/Delta, 1977.
- Hockinson, Michael J. *Nothing is Beatleproof: Advanced Beatles Trivia for Fab Four Fanciers*. Ann Arbor, MI: Popular Culture, Ink., 1990.
- Hoffman, Mark S. *The World Almanac and Book of Facts 1993*. New York: Pharos Books, 1993.

- Hosoda, Craig. *The Bare Facts Video Guide*. Santa Clara, CA: The Bare Facts, 1992.
- Jacobs, Dick. *Who Wrote That Song?* New York: Betterway Publications, 1988.
- Jones, Judy, and William Wilson. *An Incomplete Education*. New York: Ballantine Books, 1987.
- Key, Wilson Bryan. *Media Sexploitation*. New York: New American Library/Signet, 1976.
- Klimo, Jon. *Channeling: Investigations on Receiving Information from Paranormal Sources*. Los Angeles, CA: Jeremy P. Tarcher, 1987.
- Krantz, Les. *The Best and Worst of Everything*. New York: Prentice Hall, 1991.
- Lavigne, Yves. *Hell's Angels: Taking Care of Business*. New York: Ballantine Books, 1989.
- Lewisohn, Mark. *The Beatles Recording Sessions*. New York: Harmony Books, 1988.
- Love, Brenda. *The Encyclopedia of Unusual Sex Practices*. Fort Lee, NJ: Barricade Books, 1992.
- Lucaire, Ed. *The Celebrity Almanac*. New York: Prentice Hall, 1991.
- MacEachern, Sally, ed. *Illustrator's Reference Manual: Nudes*. Secaucus, NJ: Chartwell Books, 1989.
- Madonna. *Sex*. New York: Warner Books, 1992.
- Maltin, Leonard, ed. *Leonard Matlin's Movie and Video Guide 1993 Edition*. New York: New American Library/Signet, 1993.
- Mannix, Daniel P. *Freaks: We Who Are Not As Others*. San Francisco, CA: Re/Search Publications, 1990.

- Margulies, Edward, and Stephen Rebello. *Bad Movies We Love*. New York: Plume, 1993.
- Martin, Elizabeth A., ed. *The Bantam Medical Dictionary*. New York: Bantam Books, 1982.
- Martin, Mick, and Marsha Porter. *Video Movie Guide 1993*. New York: Ballantine Books, 1993.
- Matthews, Peter, ed. *The Guinness Book of Records 1993*. New York: Bantam Books, 1993.
- McArdle, Phil and Karen. *Fatal Fascination: Where Fact Meets Fiction in Police Work*. Boston, MA: Houghton Mifflin, 1988.
- McNeil, Alex. *Total Television: A Comprehensive Guide to Programming from 1948 to 1980*. New York: Penguin Books, 1980.
- Mitchell, Margaret. *Gone with the Wind*. New York: Macmillan, 1936.
- Monestier, Martin. *Human Oddities: A Book of Nature's Anomalies*. New York: Citadel Press, 1987.
- Moore, Jonathan J. *Dreadful Diseases and Terrible Treatments: The Story of Medicine Through the Ages*. New York: Metro Books, 2017.
- Morse, L. A. *Video Trash & Treasures*. Toronto: HarperCollins, 1989.
  —*Video Trash & Treasures II*. Toronto: HarperCollins, 1990.
- Nash, Bruce, and Allan Zullo. *The Misfortune 500*. New York: Pocket Books, 1988.
- Neiss, Charles P., ed. *The Beatles Reader: A Selection of Contemporary Views, News & Reviews of The Beatles In Their Heyday*. Ann Arbor, MI: Pierian Press, 1984.

- New York State Commission on Capital Punishment. *Report of the Commission to Investigate and Report the Most Humane and Practical Method of Carrying into Effect the Sentence of Death in Capital Cases*, Transmitted to the Legislature, January 17, 1888. Ithaca, NY: Cornell University Library, 1993.
- Oglesby, Carl. *The JFK Assassination: The Facts and the Theories*. New York: New American Library/Signet, 1992.
- *The Oxford Dictionary of Quotations*, Third Edition. New York: Oxford University Press, 1979.
- Paglia, Camille. *Sexual Personae: Art and Decadence from Nefertiti to Emily Dickinson*. New York: Vintage Books, 1990.
- Panati, Charles. *Panati's Extraordinary Endings of Practically Everything and Everybody*. New York: Harper & Row, 1989.
- Parker, Tom. *Rules of Thumb 2*. Boston, MA: Houghton Mifflin Company, 1987.
- Peary, Danny. *Cult Movie Stars*. New York: Simon & Schuster/Fireside, 1991.
- Pelosi, Michael. *A Date to Remember*. New York: deLuxx Editions, 1982.
- Pelton, Robert Wayne. *Loony Sex Laws That You Never Knew You Were Breaking*. New York: Walker and Company, 1992.
- The Phantom of the Movies. *The Phantom's Ultimate Video Guide*. New York: Dell Publishing, 1989.
- Pinckney, Cathy, and Edward R. Pinckney. *The Patient's Guide to Medical Tests*. New York: Facts on File, 1982.

- Poundstone, William. *Big Secrets: The Uncensored Truth About All Sorts of Stuff You Are Never Supposed to Know.* New York: William Morrow and Company, 1983.

  —*Bigger Secrets: More Than 125 Things They Prayed You'd Never Find Out.* Boston, MA: Houghton Mifflin Company, 1986.

- Price, Bill. *The Greatest Mysteries...Ever!: History's Biggest Puzzles and the People Who Made Them.* New York: Metro Books, 2017.

- Puckett, Newbell Niles, compiler. *Black Names in America: Origins and Usage.* Boston, MA: G. K. Hall & Co., 1975.

- Purvis, Kenneth, M.D., Ph.D. *The Male Sexual Machine: An Owner's Manual.* New York: St. Martin's Press, 1992.

- Rayborn, Tim. *Beethoven's Skull: Dark, Strange, and Fascinating Tales from the World of Classical Music and Beyond.* New York: Skyhorse Publishing, 2016.

- Rosenfeld, Isadore, *M.D. Symptoms.* New York: Bantam Books, 1989.

- Rovin, Jeff. *The Encyclopedia of Superheroes.* New York: Facts on File Publications, 1985.

  —*Laws of Order: A Book of Hierarchies, Rankings, Infrastructures, Measurements, and Sizes.* New York: Ballantine Books, 1992.

- Schaffner, Nicholas. *The Beatles Forever.* New York: McGraw-Hill, 1977.

- Schultheiss, Tom. *The Beatles: A Day in the Life: The Day-by-Day Diary 1960-1970.* Ann Arbor, MI: Pierian Press, 1981.

- Schwabe, Calvin W. *Unmentionable Cuisine.* Charlottesville, VA: University Press of Virginia, 1979.

- Schwartz, J. R. *The Official Guide to the Best Cat Houses in Nevada*. Boise, ID: J. R. Schwartz, 1993.
- Shepherd, Chuck, John J. Kohut, and Roland Sweet. *News of the Weird*. New York: Plume, 1989.
- Spears, Richard A. *Slang and Euphemism: A Dictionary of Oaths, Curses, Insults, Sexual Slang and Metaphor, Racial Slurs, Drug Talk, Homosexual Lingo, and Related Matters*. New York: New American Library/Signet, 1991s.
- Spence, Lewis. *An Encyclopaedia of Occultism: A Compendium of Information on the Occult Sciences, Occult Personalities, Psychic Science, Magic, Demonology, Spiritism, Mysticism and Metaphysics*. New Hyde Park, NY: University Books, 1960.
- Spignesi, Stephen J. *The Complete Stephen King Encyclopedia*. Chicago, IL: Contemporary Books, 1992.
  —*Mayberry, My Hometown: The Ultimate Guidebook To America's Favorite TV Small Town*. Ann Arbor, MI: Popular Culture, Ink., 1987.
  —*The Official Gone With the Wind Companion*. New York: Plume, 1993.
  —*The Woody Allen Companion*. Kansas City, MO: Andrews and McMeel, 1992.
- Stannard, Neville. *The Beatles' The Long & Winding Road: A History of the Beatles on Record*. New York: Avon Books, 1982.
- Steiger Brad and Sherry Steiger. *Conspiracies and Secret Societies: The Complete Dossier*. Canton, MI: Visible Ink Press, 2006.
- Stern, Jack I., M.D., and David L. Carroll. *The Home Medical Handbook*. New York: William Morrow and Company, 1987.

- Stern, Jane and Michael. *The Encyclopedia of Bad Taste*. New York: Harper Collins, 1990.

  —*Jane and Michael Stern's Encyclopedia of Pop Culture: An A to Z Guide of Who's Who and What's What, from Aerobics and Bubble Gum to Valley of the Dolls and Moon Unit Zappa*. New York: HarperPerennial, 1992.

- Stevens, Mark. *Life in the Victorian Asylum: The World of Nineteenth Century Mental Health Care*. Barnsley, South Yorkshire, England: Pen & Sword Books Ltd., 2014.

- Stevens, Serita Deborah, with Anne Klarner. *Deadly Doses: A Writer's Guide to Poisons*. Cincinatti, OH: Writer's Digest Books, 1990.

- Trager, James, ed. *The People's Chronology: A Year-by-Year Record of Human Events from Prehistory to the Present*. New York: Holt, Rinehart and Winston, 1979.

- Treffert, Darold A. *Extraordinary People: Understanding "Idiot Savants."* New York: Harper & Row, 1989.

- Walters, Mark Jerome. *Courtship in the Animal Kingdom*. New York: Doubleday, 1988.

- White, John. *A Practical Guide to Death and Dying*. Wheaton, IL: The Theosophical Publishing House, 1980.

  —*Pole Shift: Scientific Predictions and Prophecies of the Ultimate Natural Disaster*. Virginia Beach, VA: A.R.E. Press, 1980.

- Wiener, Tom. *The Book of Video Lists*. Kansas City, MO: Andrews and McMeel, 1992.

- Wilkins, Mike, and Ken Smith, and Doug Kirby. *The New Roadside America*. New York: Simon & Schuster, 1992.

- Wilson, Keith D. *Cause of Death: A Writer's Guide to Death, Murder and Forensic Medicine*. Cincinatti, OH: Writer's Digest Books, 1992.

- Woodward, Kenneth L. *Making Saints: How the Catholic Church Determines Who Becomes a Saint, Who Doesn't, and Why*. New York: Simon and Schuster, 1990.

- Wurman, Richard Saul. *Medical Access*. Los Angeles, CA: AccessPress, 1985.

- Zimdars-Swartz, Sandra L. *Encountering Mary: Visions of Mary from La Salette to Medjugorje*. New York: Avon Books, 1992.

- Zuramski, Paul, ed. *The New Age Catalogue*. New York: Doubleday, 1988.

Magazines Consulted

The Atlantic Monthly
Celebrity Sleuth
Circus
Cosmopolitan
Crime Beat
Details
Discover
Entertainment Weekly
Esquire
Far Out
Field & Stream
Film Threat
Gauntlet
Glamour

Harper's
Hustler
Inner Light
Leg Show
Life
MacUser
Macworld
Movieline
Musician
The National Lampoon
New Woman
New York
The New York Review of Books
The New York Times Book Review
The New Yorker
Newsweek
Omni
Option
Penthouse
People Weekly
Playboy
Premiere
Prevue
Publisher's Weekly
Pulse!
Rolling Stone
Science Digest
Soldier of Fortune
Spy
Time

True News
TV Guide
U.S. News World Report
UFO Review
US
The Utne Reader
Whole Earth Review
Yankee

Newspapers Consulted

The Advocate
The Boston Globe
The Boston Herald
The Boston Phoenix
The Connecticut Post
The Hartford Courant
The National Enquirer
The Los Angeles Times
The New Haven Advocate
The New Haven Register
The New York Daily News
The New York Post
The New York Times
The Star
USA Today
The Village Voice
The Washington Post
The Weekly World News

ABOUT THE AUTHOR

S tephen Spignesi is a writer, retired university professor, and author of more than seventy books on popular culture, TV, film, American and world history, the paranormal, and the American Presidents and Founding Fathers. He is considered an authority on the work of Stephen King (five books), The Beatles (three books), and the *Titanic* (two books).

Spignesi was christened "the world's leading authority on Stephen King" by *Entertainment Weekly* magazine and has worked with Stephen King, Turner Entertainment, the Margaret Mitchell Estate, Ron Howard, Andy Griffith, the Smithsonian Institution, George Washington's Mount Vernon, ITV, Viacom, and other personalities and entities on a wide range of projects.

Spignesi has also contributed short stories, essays, chapters, articles, and introductions to a wide range of books, his most recent being the short story "Lovely Rita" for the *Night of the Living Dead*-themed anthology *Rise of the Dead*.

He is the author of four of the acclaimed "For Dummies" nonfiction reference books. He is also a novelist whose thriller *Dialogues* was hailed upon release as "reinventing the psychological thriller," and which he has adapted into a screenplay.

Spignesi has appeared on CNN, MSNBC, the Fox News Channel, and many other TV and radio outlets. He also appeared in the 1998 E! Documentary *The Kennedys: Power, Seduction, and Hollywood,* the A & E *Biography of Stephen King* that aired in January 2000, and the 2015 documentary *Autopsy: The Last Hours of Robin Williams.*

Spignesi's 1997 book *JFK Jr.* was a *New York Times* bestseller. Spignesi's *Complete Stephen King Encyclopedia* was a 1991 Bram Stoker Award nominee. Spignesi is a retired Practitioner in Residence from the University of New Haven in West Haven, Connecticut where he was nominated for an Excellence in Teaching Award and taught English Composition and Literature and other literature courses, several of which were based on his books.

He lives in New Haven, Connecticut. His website is stephenspignesi.com.